Paradise Lost

A PRIMER

Paradise Lost

A PRIMER

Michael Cavanagh   Edited by Scott Newstok

THE CATHOLIC UNIVERSITY OF AMERICA PRESS
WASHINGTON, D.C.

Cover image: William Blake, "Satan Watching the Caresses
of Adam and Eve" (Illustration to Milton's *Paradise Lost*),
1808. Pen and watercolor on paper. Accession number 90.96.
Reproduced with permission. Photograph © 2019 Museum of
Fine Arts, Boston.

"Aristotle" from *Picnic, Lightning* by Billy Collins, © 1998.
Reprinted by permission of the University of Pittsburgh Press.

Radi os by Ronald Johnson, © 2013. Used with permission of
Peter O'Leary, the Ronald Johnson Estate.

"At the Fishhouses" from *The Complete Poems, 1927–1979* by
Elizabeth Bishop. © 1979, 1983 by Alice Helen Methfessel.
Used with permission of Victoria Fox at Farrar, Straus and
Giroux.

The paper used in this publication meets the minimum
requirements of American National Standards for Information
Science—Permanence of Paper for Printed Library Materials,
ANSI Z39.48-1984.
∞

Design and composition by Kachergis Book Design

Cataloging-in-Publication Data available from the
Library of Congress
ISBN 978-0-8132-3246-1

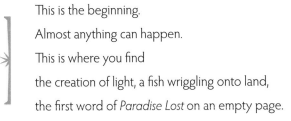

This is the beginning.
Almost anything can happen.
This is where you find
the creation of light, a fish wriggling onto land,
the first word of *Paradise Lost* on an empty page.

Billy Collins, "Aristotle"

CONTENTS

EDITOR'S FOREWORD

> A good book is the precious lifeblood of
> a master spirit, embalmed and treasured up
> on purpose to a life beyond life.

John Milton, *Areopagitica*

I was studying off campus when Michael Cavanagh offered his *Paradise Lost* seminar. When I returned to Grinnell, I envied my classmates, who regaled me with accounts of his contagious joy at the marvels of this poem. Given the laughter and insight I'd gained from his other courses, I lamented that I had missed my only opportunity to hear him revivify Milton.

He gave me a second chance. Some fifteen years later, paralyzed at the prospect of teaching my own first Milton seminar ("thou ... dost make us marble"),[1] I begged him for advice, strategies, assignments, shameless shortcuts. His gently prodding emails that summer's day persisted throughout the semester, bolstering my confidence. I would have drowned without him. (I even assigned his article on Books 11 and 12; to my students' elated shock, he graciously responded to each of their essays—comments from a real Milton scholar, in Wordsworth's words, "living at this hour"!)

The timing was fortuitous. Having completed *Professing Poetry*, his study of Heaney's prose, Cavanagh was drafting this book. Milton was

---

1. Milton, "On Shakespeare," in *The Complete Poetry and Essential Prose of John Milton*, ed. William Kerrigan, John Rumrich, and Stephen M. Fallon (New York: The Modern Library, 2007), 34. Unless otherwise noted, all quotations of Milton's works will come from this edition, hereafter abbreviated *CPEP*.

on his mind. Over the next decade, he continued to share chapters with me. While he never explained why he elected to call it a "Primer," I believe he modestly intended it to be not the last word on Milton, but rather something to "say first" (1.27)—to prime you for reading, just as we prime a pump, or apply a primer before painting. In Milton's era, primers were manuals for literacy or prayers, designed to be clear, concise, companionable. The instruction and delight that characterized his classroom similarly suffuse these pages. He shared the conviction that "to know the poetry of Milton is to have a liberal education."[2]

Following an abrupt series of strokes, Michael Cavanagh passed away in 2017, leaving this *Primer* under review at CUA Press. As I was eager to help his family make this needful *vade mecum* reach fellow lovers of verse, I offered to edit the manuscript, which I'd long admired for its practicing poet's sense of *craft*. In response to sympathetic suggestions from two anonymous readers, I've distilled the first chapter to concentrate on illustrative poems, rather than offer an overview of Milton's career, something much more comprehensively provided by biographers. Cavanagh had contemplated weaving the final chapter (on "style") into the body of the book, but I couldn't undertake this absent his guidance. Instead, I have sought to clarify the prose, amend minor errors, and supply references. As Alastair Fowler wrote of completing C. S. Lewis's book on *The Faerie Queene*, "My aim throughout has been to make a readable book."[3]

One solace from Cavanagh's sudden demise was the inducement to reconnect with former classmates (Emiliano Battista, Zander Cannon, Allison Carruth, James Crane, Julie Gard, Justus Nieland, Scott Samuelson, John Wenck), as well as exchange memories with his students whom I had never met but who held him in common as a generous mentor (Mike Borns, Matthew Brennan, Edward Hirsch, Erika Krouse, Heather Leith, Molly McArdle, Sam Tanenhaus, Lucinda

2. Marjorie Hope Nicholson, *John Milton: A Reader's Guide to His Poetry* (New York: Farrar, Straus and Giroux, 1963), vii.

3. Alastair Fowler, preface to *Spenser's Images of Life*, by C. S. Lewis, ed. Alastair Fowler (Cambridge: Cambridge University Press, 1967), viii.

Woodward). I am further grateful for Timothy Blackburn, Tom Day, Elizabeth Dobbs, John Guillory, Devin Johnston, Danny Kraft, Barbara Lewalski, Michael Leslie, Ellen Mease, Sarah, Ruth, Axel, and Pearl Newstok, Diane and John Newstrom, Peter O'Leary, Rabbi Abe Schacter-Gampel, Erik Simpson, Don Smith, Jim and Taryn Spake, Joseph Viscomi, Caki Wilkinson, and my own former Milton students. Trevor Lipscombe, Brian Roach, Libby Vivian, and Theresa Walker are to be commended for taking on this posthumous volume; Anne Needham, for her nuanced copyediting of an absent author. Above all, I thank Lynn, Pete, and Sean Cavanagh for entrusting me with the "Sad task and hard" (5.564) of bringing this *Primer* to print.

Mike once wrote to me, quoting *Lycidas*:

"Where the great vision of the guarded mount / Looks towards Namancos and Bayona's hold…" These lines I carry with me always, recite them many times a day. So have, I am sure, many, many others.

Memphis, Tennessee, 2019

PREFACE

"Paradise Lost": A Primer is the fruit of three decades of teaching Milton to college students. It is a record of my lifelong love affair with the beauty, wit, and profundity of *Paradise Lost*, an affair that is recharged every time I pick up the poem. This *Primer* returns again and again to Milton's un-doctrinal, complex, and therefore deeply satisfying perception of the human condition, both fallen and unfallen. It probes his "answerable style" (9.20), inseparable from that perception.

I begin by examining some choice early works, which establish Milton's recurrent struggle as a poetic reconciler of conflicting ideals. The heart of the book then undertakes a reading of *Paradise Lost*. Finally, I review key features of Milton's "various style" (5.146), and why we should treasure that style, protecting it from paraphrase. Intent as it is on the poetry, the *Primer* does not—with a few exceptions—treat Milton's prose, a venture that would require twice as much space. Instead, it constantly revisits, as if it can't help itself, Milton the singer and maker, and the artistic problems he faced in writing this almost impossible poem.

Though not remedial, this *Primer* is emphatically for first-time readers of Milton, with little or no prior exposure but with ambition to encounter challenging poetry. These are readers who tell you they "have always been meaning to read *Paradise Lost*," who seek to enjoy the epic without being overwhelmed by its daunting learning and expansive frame of reference. Just as emphatically, this book is not a commentary on allusions, historical events, echoings of earlier poets, and the like. These are, I believe, best taken up after an initial reading (and better provided by the editions of Alastair Fowler, David Kastan, or even Milton's first annotator, Patrick Hume). While the last chapter is sometimes technical, the book avoids the necessarily specialized focus of most Milton scholarship. It aspires to deal forthrightly with several issues that recur across generations of readers. Chiefly, it considers the ongoing, centuries-long controversy as to whether Milton is a fully consistent poet and thinker—and, if he is not, whether it matters.

Milton's poetry has given birth to a large body of brilliant, sometimes rancorous, commentary. No consideration of his poetry can afford to overlook this. One task I have set for myself is to distill that commentary to some essential critiques: those that have commanded assent, or, conversely, invited strong dissent. I have sought to be as broad-minded in the treatment of these critical documents as possible, trying not to pass judgment to excess, but not holding back my own opinions when they are impossible to resist. Without seeking to be a "Who's Who" of Milton criticism, the *Primer* gathers selected voices—from scholars and poets alike—from 1674 through the present. My citations are not lengthy; my goal is to harvest a succinct collection of prompts, which can become jumping-off points to further exploration. Nevertheless, I have made especially generous use of C. S. Lewis's *A Preface to "Paradise Lost"* (1942), Joseph Summers's *The Muse's Method* (1962), Christopher Ricks's *Milton's Grand Style* (1963), and John Leonard's magisterial *Faithful Labourers: A Reception History of "Paradise Lost," 1667–1970* (2013).

I have endeavored to write a jargon-free book, one that people will want to read as well as consult. It is my utmost desire to make *Paradise Lost* accessible and fresh. As for my book's relative brevity in light of the vast and boundless areas of knowledge taken in by Milton's poem, I concede that no single volume could ever be exhaustive. Yet I hope that this *Primer* offers a credible beginning to what is a great intellectual and aesthetic adventure.

Finally, I have taken the liberty of treating some books in *Paradise Lost* more extensively than others, because I find them more artistically accomplished, haunting our imaginations longer. This may displease some. I can only say in my defense that this is a book in which poetic taste figures prominently. In my estimate, Milton is the supreme non-dramatic poet in English, but he is not uniformly wonderful—how could he be? He usually commands our attention; occasionally, he does not. As we all know, from time to time even Homer nodded.

ACKNOWLEDGMENTS

In writing this book, I have been assisted, and in some cases inspired, by several people. One is the late Brewster Rogerson. When I heard him read aloud—

> Him the Almighty Power
> Hurled headlong flaming from th' ethereal sky
> With hideous ruin and combustion down
> To bottomless perdition (1.44–47)

—I became Milton's captive. Rogerson was a great Miltonist and a great teacher. I still read with his sensibility hovering over me. Scott Newstok was helpful in reading my manuscript and in alerting me to relevant scholarship. Younger than I am, he was my big brother. Angela Winburn's preparation of the manuscript was invaluable. Whenever I made any missteps, she was there to catch me. I could rely always on her good sense, not to mention good humor. Julia Broeker was a student assistant I could count on. Her sense of stylistic decorum is beyond her years, as revealed in some important corrections she made to the manuscript. I benefitted greatly from the services at the British Library, the Huntington Library, and the Robert J. Wickenheiser Collection of John Milton at University of South Carolina Libraries. Grinnell College provided me with grants and office space, for which I am very grateful. My wife, Lynn, without whom this book could not have been written, regarded my Milton obsession with tolerant amusement, which, for a writer who worries excessively about what he has written, was welcome and refreshing.

Grinnell, Iowa, 2017

Paradise Lost

A PRIMER

1

"Both Them I Serve"

MILTON'S RECONCILIATIONS

Readers of Milton's poetry sense the presence not merely of a writer, but of a powerful, shaping force, crying out to be fathomed. "Milton himself is in every line of the *Paradise Lost*," asserted Samuel Taylor Coleridge.[1] Ralph Waldo Emerson similarly insisted: "The man is paramount to the poet."[2] Stephen Greenblatt, among contemporary critics, affirms the same: like Shakespeare, Milton "infuses every character with the intense savor of [himself]."[3] Collin Burrow holds that Milton's poems constitute an "interior dialogue."[4] Milton himself set the bar high in when he asserted that a poet "ought himself to be a true poem,"[5] a sentiment echoed three centuries later by Gregory Corso: "The times demand that the poet … be as true as a poem."[6]

1. Samuel Taylor Coleridge, *Table Talk*, 1835, reprinted in *The Collected Works of Samuel Taylor* Coleridge, vol. 14, ed. Carl Woodring (London: Routledge, 1990), 125.

2. Ralph Waldo Emerson, "Milton," 1838, reprinted in *The Conduct of Life: Nature and Other Essays* (London: J. M. Dent, 1908), 89.

3. Stephen Greenblatt, "The Lonely Gods," *New York Review of Books* 58, no. 11 (June 23, 2011): 8.

4. Colin Burrow, "Shall I Go On?," *London Review of Books* 35, no. 5 (March 7, 2013): 3.

5. *Apology for Smectymnuus, CPEP,* 850.

6. Gregory Corso, "Some of My Beginning.… and What I Feel Right Now," in *Poets on Poetry,* ed. Howard Nemerov (New York: Basic Books, 1966), 176.

Yet Milton did not just write but *arrived* at *Paradise Lost*. Because his earlier poems track this unfolding journey, some of them deserve a brief notice here. They help us recognize in Milton a developing identity—what a writer does over and over, what he or she can't stop doing. Some of Milton's first poems already attempt the epic style; others try to "justify the ways of God to men" (1.26). Many of these poems seek to reconcile opposing ways of life by creating an everyday of Paradise out of the materials of this world, just as *Paradise Lost* forges the ultimate "reconcilement" (see 1.122, 3.264, 4.98, 10.924, 11.39).

Born in London on December 9, 1608, and tutored in Hebrew, Latin, and Greek, Milton started composing poetry early. His first literary attempts were paraphrases of biblical Psalms that celebrate (as he would do throughout his career) the power, majesty, and righteousness of God, qualities he aspired to himself. Some of the Psalms depart widely from the originals. Here is the 15-year-old Milton translating Psalm 114: "That glassy floods from rugged rocks can crush / And make soft rills from fiery flint-stones gush" (17–18).[7] We notice the force that comes from the heft of the passage. Donald Davie characterized Milton as a "kinetic" poet—a poet who translates his meaning into sensation, and we find that trait early in his work.[8] While the original describes Israel escaping Egyptian bondage, Milton's version pointedly speaks of the Israelites winning "After long toil their liberty" (2). The connection of sounds in the line is precocious: the *l-t* ("long toil") joined with *l-t* ("liberty"); the double stress "LONG TOIL" opposing the tripping "LIB-er-ty." Moreover, there is something here of the adult Milton insisting that true liberty is the result of *exertion*, not relaxation. The line in Psalm 136, "Let us blaze his name abroad" (5), answers to nothing in the original. Like the "warm" sun in *Paradise Lost* that "smotes" the bower of Adam and Eve (4.244), it is an ingenious addition, grounded on no antecedent. The evocative

7. Cf. the King James Version: "Which turned the rock into a standing water, the flint into a fountain of waters" (Ps 114:8).

8. Donald Davie, "Syntax and Music in *Paradise Lost*," in *The Living Milton: Essays by Various Hands*, ed. Frank Kermode (London: Routledge & Kegan Paul, 1960), 71.

place names ("Erythraean," "Amorean" [Psalm 136, lines 46, 66]) will become his trademark in later works; note also Milton's emerging aesthetics of sublimity in lines such as "That his mansion hath on high / Above the reach of mortal eye" (93–94). He habitually reaches above, and beyond.

While a student at Cambridge he wrote a poem, "At a Vacation Exercise" (c. 1628), in which he sets out a poetic program for himself that will involve choosing

> some graver subject …
> Such where the deep transported mind may soar
> Above the wheeling poles, and at Heav'n's door
> Look in, and see each blissful deity
> How he before the thunderous throne doth lie (30, 33–36)

Already yearning for the epic, Milton seeks grand stylistic "robes" to fit that "graver subject" (30, 20–21). Thirty years later, this ambition to "soar / Above" will be repeated in the first invocation of *Paradise Lost* (1.13–14), praised by Andrew Marvell: "And above human flight dost soar aloft."[9] One manifestation of "soar"ing is the way Milton strategically runs his syntax over line endings, enjambing them without pause.

In *Elegy 6*, a Latin poem, Milton divides poets into two kinds: the poet of wine and feasting (for whom a licentious life is appropriate), and the poet whose theme is wars and

> heaven under the rule of Jove in his maturity, and reverent heroes and semi-divine leaders, and sings now of the sacred deliberations of the supreme gods, now of the deep realm where the fierce dog barks (55–58)

This second type of poet must be abstemious, Milton says. His song is priestly. No one could deny that Milton in this period is heading in the direction of a "high," spiritual poetry. However, Milton does not take sides in *Elegy 6*. And later, in "Ad Patrem," he insists to his father that poets are not merely singers, but priests as well. We can see that he

9. Andrew Marvell, "On Mr. Milton's *Paradise Lost*," 1674, repr. in *The Poems of Andrew Marvell*, rev. ed., ed. Nigel Smith (London: Pearson Education, 2007), p. 183, line 37.

is connecting, not separating, the secular and spiritual life—an "ardor for religion and art considered as one," as Marianne Moore admired.[10]

One of his earliest sonnets, written in a *faux-naïf* style, speaks volumes about its author's anxieties:

> O Nightingale, that on yon bloomy spray
>   Warblest at eve, when all the woods are still,
>   Thou with fresh hope the lover's heart dost fill,
>   While the jolly Hours lead on propitious May;
> Thy liquid notes that close the eye of day,
>   First heard before the shallow cuckoo's bill
>   Portend success in love; O if Jove's will
>   Have linked that amorous power to thy soft lay,
> Now timely sing, ere the rude bird of hate
>   Foretell my hopeless doom in some grove nigh:
>   As thou from year to year hast sung too late
> For my relief, yet hadst no reason why:
>   Whether the Muse or Love call thee his mate,
>   Both them I serve, and of their train am I.[11]

The poet hasn't yet heard the nightingale's song (a conventional omen of love), and laments his lack of "success." In effect, "I do not love and perhaps I can't love"—which is close to Milton's own experience, by all accounts. The conflict is between a life of poetry and a life of love. This is what C. S. Lewis calls Milton's typical "hesitation": "the coexistence, in a lively and sensitive tension, of apparent opposites."[12] Milton strives for this coexistence for the rest of his career, even though he can't always achieve it. In a rather juvenile fashion, he dismisses his problem by bluff fiat. He serves the Muse *and* Love: *Both them I serve.* It would not be the last time we see Milton attempting to solve a problem that can't so easily be solved. And yet he tries, and that effort may explain why "Nightingale" has such seductive language, as if Milton

10. Marianne Moore, Review of Denis Saurat's *Blake and Milton*, 1925, reprinted in *The Complete Prose of Marianne Moore*, ed. Patricia Willis (New York: Viking, 1986), 233.
11. "O Nightingale," *CPEP*, 139.
12. C. S. Lewis, *A Preface to Paradise Lost* (New York: Oxford University Press, 1942), 7.

were trying to win us (and himself) over. He laps us in pleasing sound. L's run through the poem like a sibilant stream: *gale, bloomy, warblest, all, still, lover's, fill, while, jolly, lead, liquid, close, shallow, bill, love, will, linked, lay, timely, foretell, hopeless, late, relief, love, call.* The poem also smoothly modulates from the first eight lines (the octave) to the final six (the sestet) by making the "Now timely sing," which begins the sestet, push off the octave's "if Jove's will."

Milton received a B.A. from Cambridge in 1629 at age 20. The greatest product of that final school year was his Christmas ode, "On the Morning of Christ's Nativity," the most "Miltonic" of his early poems, according to Helen Vendler,[13] and reportedly a favorite of Dylan Thomas.[14] The poem manifests an awakening on his part, as it describes the drama and excitement of the spirit of God descending on nature. Louis Martz is right: the title of this poem, to which Milton added the date of its composition, 1629, marks out the youth of the poet as one of the poem's subjects.[15] *Paradise Lost* will likewise emphasize Milton himself as one of the subjects of his poem. Moreover, the "Nativity Ode," as it has come to be known, asserts Christ's redemptive power yet also eulogizes the pagan deities, now defeated and retreating. Indeed, the last part of the poem, devoted to this retreat, divulges the poet's sympathy for the other side. Lines such as "The Lars and Lemures moan with midnight plaint" (191) or "the yellow-skirted fays / Fly after the Night-steeds, leaving their moon-loved maze" (235–36) are lovely. (Compare *Elegy 5*'s sad wish that the pagan deities might stay year round.) Has Milton thwarted himself by showing sympathy for the old pagan order? William Blake certainly thought so: "The reason Milton wrote in fetters when he wrote of Angels & God, and at liberty when of Devils & Hell, is, because he was a true poet and

13. Helen Vendler, *Coming of Age as a Poet: Milton, Keats, Eliot, Plath* (Cambridge, Mass.: Harvard University Press, 2003), 13.

14. Kathleen Raine, "Dylan Thomas," *New Statesman and Nation* 50, no. 6 (November 14, 1953): 594.

15. Louis Martz, "The Rising Poet, 1645," in *The Lyric and Dramatic Milton: Selected Papers from the English Institute*, ed. Joseph H. Summers (New York: Columbia University Press, 1965), 21–22.

of the Devil's party without knowing it."[16] (Alicia Ostriker felt this "the best single thing anybody has ever said about *Paradise Lost*.")[17] Does he show such sympathy here? In presenting these deities in such an attractive way, Milton tempts the reader; hence his sympathy is a strategy of sorts. Yet the poem "paganize"s the Christian experience, a complication that is most evident in the fifth stanza:

> But peaceful was the night
> Wherein the Prince of Light
> His reign of peace upon the earth began:
> The Winds with wonder whist,
> Smoothly the waters kissed,
> Whispering new joys to the mild Ocean,
> Who now hath quite forgot to rave,
> While birds of calm sit brooding on the charmèd wave. (61–68)

"[N]ew joys" is the crucial phrase. The religion of Christ will not destroy, but *replace* the old with new pleasures. God sends "the meek-eyed Peace," which comes "softly sliding / Down through the turning sphere … With turtle wing the amorous clouds dividing" (46–50). When the angelic choir sings, the enraptured poet calls out for the music of the spheres. Even the lowly shepherds are taken in "blissful rapture" (98). Nature isn't renounced, as it appeared to be at the beginning of the poem, but folded into the new order. The infant Jesus sounds as if he were the baby Hercules: "Our babe to show his Godhead true, / Can in his swaddling bands control the damnèd crew" (227–28). This paganism doesn't deny so much as it enhances Christianity.

The "can" in line 228 speaks for a fundamental principle in Milton, one well-articulated by Stanley Fish. The poem moves us forward, then frustrates the completion of that action. The "Babe" *can* control the devils, but that does not mean that he *will* do so right away. Christ

16. William Blake, *The Marriage of Heaven and Hell*, in *The Poems of William Blake*, ed. W. H. Stevenson (London: Longman, 1971), 107.

17. Alicia Ostriker, "Dancing at the Devil's Party: Some Notes on Politics and Poetry," *Critical Inquiry* 13, no. 3 (Spring 1987): 579.

will redeem, but not now: "But wisest Fate says no, / This must not yet be so" (149–50). The true action in a poem by Milton, Fish says, "is not an event but a mode of being."[18] Accordingly, the angels surrounding the infant Jesus are not doing anything, but are "serviceable" (244). The idea isn't to *do* something for God (perhaps bring a gift?), but to *wait* on God: obedience over deeds. This helps explain the shifts back and forth between the present and past tenses: the event happened— *and* is always happening. The pagan deities are leaving—but never go away. When we read *Paradise Lost*, we shall likewise be invited (not required) to see that the action is happening "now" as well as "then."

Milton graduated from Cambridge in 1632 with a master's degree. So far, he hadn't yet chosen a career. Then he did something extraordinary that defined him for the rest of his life: he retired to the London countryside with his mother and father, where he wrote poems, read everything, but "did" nothing. The sonnet "How soon hath Time" (Sonnet 7), probably written at the start of this period, records the apprehension Milton felt in having nothing to show. "I look younger than my 23 years," he starts by saying; "I don't have the physical signs of maturity. Likewise, I don't have the worldly accomplishments that are commonly taken for maturity. But if physical appearances can be deceiving, so can the signs of maturity!" In the last six lines, Milton doesn't really solve his problem; he dismisses it, as he does in "Nightingale." He appears determined that whatever his progress and eventual destination, it will be what God set out for him. What's imperative, the sestet asserts, is to stay "in my great Taskmaster's eye" (14), not to go anywhere. This is a point made in the late lines of *Paradise Lost*, when Adam resolves "to walk / As in his presence" (12.562–63). One of Milton's final works, *Paradise Regained*, returns to this theme: Jesus, idle, in the desert, waiting for God to lead him. But the waiting is more important than the "full career"—more important than the goal.

While the precise date of the companion poems "L'Allegro" and

18. Stanley Fish, "The Temptation to Action in Milton's Poetry," *English Literary History* 48, no. 3 (Autumn 1981): 527.

"Il Penseroso" is uncertain, I believe they were composed in this period of anxious aimlessness. They are about knowing different ways of life. "L'Allegro" celebrates the active life, "Il Penseroso" the contemplative. One hard-to-resist way of reading these inventive, beautiful catalogs of images is to take them as oppositional, as depicting Milton's imagined onward development to maturity: the poet *is* Allegro now, and *will become* Penseroso. Myself, I find the opposition versus development argument unpersuasive. Is Allegro young and Penseroso old? They're both young and dreamy. Penseroso fancifully projects a future life, just as a youth would do. Is one detached, the other involved? Both are detached. True, Penseroso favors contemplation, but his image of it is not realistic. Surely we are to take his "hairy gown and mossy cell" as a superficial idea of the religious life (169). Is one character good, the other bad? Unlikely, for the poems have no moral vocabulary. Is it pleasure versus work? No, both are pleasure lovers. Is one real, the other ideal? No, both are idealizers. If Allegro's name suggests a simpler being, still one cannot say the style that represents him is any simpler than Penseroso's. Even so, though the poems appear to have no intellectual program, it is hard to resist some edification where one finds, as one does here, a sophisticated strategy involving obvious oppositions in Milton's life. As both Leslie Brisman and Peter Herman suggest, these poems invite us to see the necessity of choice, and then maneuver us into recognizing a reconciliation.[19] In taming the oppositions into art, the poet denies that either can force an exclusive demand on him. The two poems constitute a duality, and we end up longing for a wholeness that includes both characters. If this is right, then these poems, like "Nightingale," heal by inclusion. They present together, deliberately, the idea of partnership and paradise. Here, as Gordon Teskey rightly observes, Milton "begins to become a poet of the world."[20]

19. Leslie Brisman, *Milton's Poetry of Choice and Its Romantic Heirs* (Ithaca, N.Y.: Cornell University Press, 1973); and Peter Herman, *Destabilizing Milton: "Paradise Lost" and the Poetics of Incertitude* (New York: Palgrave Macmillan, 2005).

20. Gordon Teskey, *The Poetry of John Milton* (Cambridge, Mass.: Harvard University Press, 2015), 93.

Throughout his early career, Milton read and made various kinds of poems without really defining himself as any single category of poet. He wrote sonnets, both of self-examination and idealized love (the latter in Italian). He wrote poems that employed elaborate, "metaphysical" conceits, such as "On Shakespeare" and "The Passion." He wrote pastorals. He wrote in the occasional manner of Ben Jonson. The "Vacation Exercise" outlines his epic ambitions; the "Nativity Ode" partially realizes them. Milton's desire to be a varied poet—to be at once lyric, epic, *and* dramatic—would drive him to classical epic, which he viewed as multi-generic, bridging a gap between the inner and outer worlds. In this last respect, *A Masque Presented at Ludlow Castle, 1634* (known as *Comus*) is representatively many works in one. Its genre is that of a masque, that is, a semi-dramatic court entertainment that typically features a lot of song, dance, and spectacle—not exactly what you'd expect a future Puritan to write. Yet it hardly qualifies, as masques typically do, as light entertainment. It is lengthy. The verse is often grand and ambitious. In taking up and not exactly resolving fraught subjects such as chastity, the operation of heavenly grace, the relation of body to soul, and the capacity of earthly virtue to earn salvation, it puts an intellectual burden on the audience. Characters are ambiguously presented. Like Satan, Comus is a seducer, but his argument to the Lady isn't without its merits. The Lady, though she has virtue on her side, is—except when she sings—rather shrill. Both speak like philosophers, and offer a dualism that is contrary to the spirit of the masque, whose patron deity is Hymen, the god of marriage. The opening lines—

> Before the starry threshold of Jove's court
> My mansion is, where those immortal shapes
> Of bright aërial spirits live ensphered (1–3)

—give off a rather epic flavor to a work that one expects to be polite and local. *Comus*, though frequently lyrical, ravishingly so, is not lyrical on the whole. Maybe the poet has overshot the mark by making his work too ambitious, too severe. Such overshooting is everywhere in Milton's work; it is what gives it distinction. (Imagine an epic about the eating of an apple!) But perhaps in *Comus* it is a miscalculation. That miscalculation, if that is what it is, may be the originating point of one of the masque's strangest inclusions: Sabrina, who represents the merging of two worlds of chastity and charm. Yet this merging makes her Miltonic.

By the mid-1630s, Milton had determined he wasn't going to be a member of the clergy. His Latin poem "Ad Patrem" ("To His Father") makes it clear that poets are hardly distinguishable from priests, a notion that offers a preemptive self-exoneration should he eventually choose poetry over the priesthood. The poet-as-priest was on Milton's mind when he wrote his best "minor" poem, the pastoral *Lycidas*. It was prompted by the 1637 drowning of his classmate Edward King in the Irish Sea. It's impossible to know if Milton really knew King well. My guess is that he did not, but that King nevertheless became a symbol to Milton of a life with noble and difficult aims cut short by a heartless natural world, one from which God feels absent. Following a pastoral tradition that deploys the figure of the shepherd to explore the devoted life, the poem poses a universal question: Why strive after anything difficult? In this, *Lycidas* is Milton's first attempt at a theodicy, his avowed purpose in *Paradise Lost*. Inquiring into King's death, he draws in the nymphs, the elements, and the gods. He asks Apollo to testify in place of God, and summons St. Peter to proclaim divine justice. Some readers (Samuel Johnson comes to mind) claim the various conventions and subconventions of ancient pastoral that Milton follows in the poem trivialize his elegiac task. This kind of reader tends to protest that Milton has immersed himself too heavily in the venerable club of poets who have come before him (from Theocritus to Virgil to Spenser), making the conventions that come with that allegiance rob the poem of its sincerity. Why then does *Lycidas* work so well that so many readers revere it? Robert Lowell, in a fit of mania, was "firmly convinced that he was the author of the original";[21] John Berryman

21. Stanley Kunitz, "The Sense of a Life," *New York Times Book Review*, Oct. 16, 1977.

wrote a singular short story about struggling to teach it, "the greatest poem in English."[22] Even Johnson acknowledges its high repute. In part the answer is the sophistication of the verse: Milton's irregular rhymes and short lines; the extraordinary felicity and originality of the phrasing; the musical interplay of vowels and consonants; the intricately compressed networks of meaning; and the way the poem varies its intensity, rising to an apocalyptic opulence, or falling to a murmur of regret.

But it also distinguishes itself by the sustained intellectual drama, which these stylistic fluctuations serve. His refusal to buckle to authoritative dogma offers a counterweight to the conventionality of the poem's pastoral props. Through the persona of the shepherd-speaker, the poet keeps asking pesky questions of the Powers That Be. Was the shipwreck man's fault or God's? If God's, why did God let it happen? By his indifference to King's fate, has God deserted man and the nature he created? What is the sense or rationale of God's world? What is its narrative? It soon becomes apparent as we reflect on the poem that we are witnessing a drama of intellectual maturation. The poem begins in a petulant complaint ("I'm not ready to write!") and proceeds to accusations. It is hard to read *Lycidas* and not think also of Milton's mother, Sara, who died earlier that same year. Does the tender side of Milton make itself prominent in this poem because of his lingering grief, bringing "tears, as I know it can, to the eyes of more readers than one," as A. E. Housman confessed?[23] Perhaps *Lycidas* tries, in Sara's honor, to give the feminine its part in the order of things, even if, in Amy Boesky's view, the feminine is associated with potentially annihilative forces of water.[24] The consolation passage of the poem entwines the sweet pastoral landscape with the world beyond: heaven is seen as having both "groves" and "streams" (174). Conspicuously,

22. John Berryman, "Wash Far Away," in *The Freedom of the Poet* (New York: Farrar, Straus and Giroux, 1976), 369.

23. A. E. Housman, *The Name and Nature of Poetry* (Cambridge: Cambridge University Press, 1933), 46.

24. Amy Boesky, "The Maternal Shape of Mourning: A Reconsideration of *Lycidas*," *Modern Philology* 95, no. 4 (May 1998): 463–83.

Christ is seen as having "dear might" (173), a gloriously contradictory word pair (*oxymoron*), binding the fond and the stern together, like the passage that depicts Heaven as having "solemn troops, and sweet societies" (179). In the last passage there is nothing left for the poem to do but resanctify the natural world:

> And now the sun had stretched out all the hills,
> And now was dropped into the western bay;
> At last he rose, and twitched his mantle blue:
> Tomorrow to fresh woods, and pastures new. (190–93)

In the concluding language of *Paradise Lost*, "[t]he world was all before" the shepherd-poet, as it was for Adam and Eve (12.646). Whatever is theologically worked out will also now be worked out at the level of the physical realm. The poet doesn't make himself choose between whether nature is charming or cruel, compassionate or indifferent. The world Adam and Eve face upon exiting Paradise will be no less ambiguous. Catherine Belsey gets it right: "If Milton's writing displays one singular quality, it is a remorseless refusal to settle for easy solutions or shallow generalizations."[25]

During Milton's grand tour to Italy in 1638–39, the land of Virgil, Dante, Tasso, and Ariosto must have reaffirmed Milton's longstanding ambition to be, as he puts it in *The Reasons of Church Government*, "a poet soaring in the high region of his fancies with his garland and singing robes about him."[26] (Walt Whitman jeered: "soaring yet overweighted ... Milton soars, but with dull, unwieldy motion.")[27] Milton left behind plans during this time indicating he was going to be a classical epic poet, whether a nationalist allegorical poet in the manner of Spenser or a dramatist. (William Poole notes over one hundred outlines Milton sketched on biblical subjects.)[28] According to his neph-

25. Belsey, *John Milton: Language, Gender, Power* (Oxford: Basil Blackwell, 1988), 14.

26. *The Reason of Church Government*, *CPEP*, 839.

27. Horace Traubel, *With Walt Whitman in Camden*, vol. 3 (New York: Mitchell Kennerley, 1914), 185.

28. William Poole, *Milton and the Making of "Paradise Lost"* (Cambridge, Mass.: Harvard University Press, 2017), 105.

ew, during these years he drafted a few soliloquized lines by Satan, which were later inserted into *Paradise Lost* (4.32–41). But the epic and drama were not to come for nearly another twenty years, delayed by his increasing involvement in polemical politics in the 1640s and the parliamentary government in the 1650s.

While collecting a debt for his father up in Oxfordshire in 1642, Milton met Mary Powell, the first of his three wives. She was a naïve 17-year-old from a Royalist family, half Milton's age, and uneducated. Considering Milton's lack of experience with women, his sheltered life, and his educational and political background, it's safe to call this one a marriage from Hell. The couple split up almost immediately, and Mary didn't return to Milton until 1645. During that intervening period, Milton produced a series of divorce tracts in which he argued, invoking biblical sources and the writings of reformers, that traditional divorce laws were much too strict in adhering to the physical part of marriage, not taking into account the more serious matter of love, mutual respect, and compatibility. While the split with Mary Powell was the immediate motive for the marriage tracts, Milton was also pursuing a general principle that we are not bound by a bad marriage—just as he was to argue a few years later that we are not bound by a bad ruler. Marriage for Milton was an institution of mutual aid and comfort, and only secondarily one of sex and child-bearing. This idea of compatibility is a vital component of married life in *Paradise Lost*, yet there are also misgivings: one side of Milton wants Heaven on Earth, another wants to ascend to a higher sphere. In *Lycidas*, nature and grace can be reconciled, but when it comes to sex, the matter isn't so easy for Milton to work out.

In 1644, Milton was involved in more controversy. His great tract of that year, *Areopagitica*, is his most popular prose work, in part because it is so memorably poetic and brilliant. By the standards of any age, *Areopagitica* is a radical document. It proposes truth not as something that can be grasped, but as the process of *seeking* truth. A man, Milton says, may be "a heretic in the truth" if he accepts the truth from someone else, even if his pastor dictates it to him—*"though his belief*

be true, yet the very truth he holds becomes his heresy."[29] The heart of
Milton's oration is as epic-sounding as anything in *Paradise Lost*:

I cannot praise a fugitive and cloistered virtue, unexercised and un-
breathed, that never sallies out and sees her adversary, but slinks out of the
race where that immortal garland is to be run for, not without dust and
heat. Assuredly we bring not innocence into the world, we bring impurity
much rather: that which purifies us is trial, and trial is by what is contrary.[30]

Milton insists that God made us free and capable of finding truth on
our own; therefore, licensing frustrates the providence of God. Adam
and Eve, by God's design, were free to fall. Had they not been free,
they would have been mere puppets. Milton comes just short of say-
ing that the temptation of Adam and Eve was a good thing; among
readers of Milton's poetry, this matter is a crux. There are inconsis-
tencies in Milton's position. (Most notably, Catholics are excluded
from tolerance.) Such inconsistencies speak for a deep ambivalence in
Milton as to how much freedom a society can bear and still be a soci-
ety. In *Areopagitica*, there is a suggestive clash of libertarianism, which
seeks to protect individual striving, with an epic-style nationalism that
reaches out to define a community, a "noble and puissant nation" of
like-minded soldiers of truth.[31] Milton will return to this clash in the
debate between Adam and Eve just before the Fall.

For Milton, "liberty" meant freedom from vice, not self-indulgence.
Milton aligned himself with the parliamentary cause in the Civil War,
which resulted in a victory over the king and the expulsion of Royal-
ists from the clergy. But Milton was becoming more and more fearful
of the Presbyterians, who wanted a church government. On top of
these worries was a greater one: he was starting to lose his eyesight.
He must have felt the darkness closing in, now literally, but later figu-
ratively, as Cromwell's revolution in time gradually failed. Milton was
increasingly drawn into public affairs, and still his early literary am-
bitions were unfulfilled. But he did one indisputably literary thing in

29. *Areopagitica*, *CPEP*, 952, my italics.
30. Ibid., 939.
31. Ibid., 959.

this decade: he published a volume of his *Poems* in 1645. Coming after his unpopular divorce pamphlets, and written in a rather learned and sometimes mighty style that wasn't à la mode, the poems were largely ignored. But I agree with Milton's preeminent modern biographer, William Riley Parker, that Milton was probably induced to publish them because he feared his prose tracts were for naught, and he wanted to establish himself as a literary man, as opposed to a mere polemicist—though that did not mean that he gave up polemicizing.[32]

In his verse of the late 1640s and early 1650s, Milton moved closer to the highly enjambed verse of *Paradise Lost*, in which syntax does not always pause at line ending. The sonnets to Fairfax in 1648 and to Cromwell in 1652 also anticipate Milton's epic in their skepticism about militarism and in their conception of the poet not as a historian but as a prophet.[33] The same freedom with line endings and unexpected development of thought occurs in one of Milton's greatest sonnets, "On the Late Massacre in Piedmont," written in 1655 in outrage against the massacre of the Vaudois, a persecuted sect of Protestants:

> Avenge O Lord thy slaughtered saints, whose bones
>   Lie scattered on the Alpine mountains cold,
>   Ev'n them who kept thy truth so pure of old
>   When all our fathers worshipped stocks and stones,
> Forget not: in thy book record their groans
>   Who were thy sheep and in their ancient fold
>   Slain by the bloody Piedmontese that rolled
>   Mother with infant down the rocks. Their moans
> The vales redoubled to the hills, and they
>   To Heav'n. Their martyred blood and ashes sow
>   O'er all th' Italian fields where still doth sway
> The triple tyrant: that from these may grow
>   A hundredfold, who having learnt thy way
>   Early may fly the Babylonian woe.[34]

32. William Riley Parker, *Milton: A Biography* (Oxford: Clarendon Press, 1968), 1:288.
33. "On the Lord General Fairfax, at the Siege of Colchester," *CPEP*, 152–53; and "To the Lord General Cromwell, May 1652," *CPEP*, 153–54.
34. Sonnet 18, "On the Late Massacre at Piedmont," *CPEP*, 155–56.

Like *Lycidas*, this sonnet opens with an explosion of petulant anger, blaming God for inattentiveness to the welfare of his own people. The sentiment is so strong it pours into the second quatrain. The poet is vehement: *Take care of it now, God! Are you blind and deaf?* The poem then mellows. It doesn't drop its imperatives completely. But it softens them. The last of them, "sow" (10), is not a command, but a prayer. Milton urges God, as if he were a farmer, to "sow" the knowledge of papal perfidy into the consciousness of the Italian people, that they might, like the Vaudois, turn away from the Catholic Church. Now the poet, in a more mature fashion, finds God's justice enacted in natural processes, and he steps back from the brink of crisis. God has ears and eyes, and so do people. Whatever good that comes of this event will come in the future, and not just in Heaven, but on Earth. There is reason to recall here the way *Lycidas* rescues nature from theological might. Or to think of the "Nativity Ode," which relents after first urging on the end of the world—"But wisest Fate says no, / This must not yet be so" (149–50)—resigning itself to the slow medicines of time. If we are not too literal-minded in comparing them, we can see "Piedmont" anticipating the dynamics of *Paradise Lost*, started only three years later, with its loud beginning and muted end, invoking a world not of God's active intervention, but of his permissiveness, and the unfathomable tragedy of the world he created. Here, that tragedy is suggested by the repeated long, low vowel endings: *o, bones, cold, so, old, stones, rolled, moans, sow, o'er, grow, fold, woe*. How this poem groans!

Sometime between 1651 and 1655 Milton wrote his greatest sonnet, sometimes referred to as "On His Blindness":

> When I consider how my light is spent,
> > Ere half my days, in this dark world and wide,
> > And that one talent which is death to hide,
> > Lodged with me useless, though my soul more bent
> To serve therewith my Maker, and present
> > My true account, lest he returning chide,
> > "Doth God exact day labor, light denied?"
> > I fondly ask; but patience to prevent

That murmur soon replies, "God doth not need
      Either man's work or his own gifts; who best
      Bear his mild yoke, they serve him best; his state
Is kingly. Thousands at his bidding speed
      And post o'er land and ocean without rest:
      They also serve who only stand and wait."[35]

It is a more ambitious version of his early Sonnet 7, in that it worries
about lost time and unspent talents. There is also some "Piedmont" in
it; it moves from faulting God to absolving him. Though it is a quiet
poem, it is certainly like the "heroic sonnets" in taking liberties with
the usual eight/six organization of the sonnet form. In line eight, the
figure of "patience" (which you would expect to come in line nine)
breaks—impatiently—in upon the speaker's impatience. The griev-
ance of the first eight lines has some of the anfractuosities of Milton's
prose, constantly resisting simplicity and closure, piling phrase on
phrase "*ere . . . and that . . . which is . . . though . . . and . . . lest.*" Patience
corrects with clear directives: "God doth not need . . . Who best bear
his mild yoke, they serve him best . . . his state is kingly . . . They also
serve who only stand and wait." Christopher Ricks taught Milton's
readers to pay special attention to contrast in Milton's verse.[36] Here we
have the contrast between the octave's vexed inner life and the sestet's
simple demands of God—anticipating Adam and Eve's debate about
how much work is demanded of them in Paradise (9.205–250). Recall
further how the angels in Jesus' stable in the "Nativity Ode" mere-
ly "sit in order serviceable" (244). Whether one thinks the speaker a
trembling slave or a Godly and noble servant, the poem epitomizes
Milton's struggles with the enormous expectations placed on him, and
his desire to do a great deed for God.

Until 1658, Milton worked on various projects, from Latin and
Greek lexicons to a treatise on Christianity, *The Christian Doctrine*
(*De Doctrina Christiana*), which he finished after the Restoration of

35. Sonnet 19, "On His Blindness," *CPEP* 157–58.
36. Christopher Ricks, *Milton's Grand Style* (Oxford: Clarendon Press, 1963).

Charles II in 1660. *Christian Doctrine* contains several heresies, among them Milton's approval of polygamy, his belief in Mortalism (the idea that the soul dies with the body), and his Arianism. The treatise was not published until 1825, shortly after it was discovered in London's Old State Paper Office. There has been some dispute about whether Milton wrote the book or not, with the majority opinion deciding in favor of Milton's authorship. What is at stake is, among other things, Milton's theology. If *Christian Doctrine* is Milton's, its heresies could be an indication of a bold radicalism that survived into Milton's old age, despite the absence of its overt expression in *Paradise Lost*.

Slowly Milton's blindness changed his life. He was relieved of his duties as Latin Secretary. His salary was converted to a pension. Other things changed. Cromwell died in 1658. His son Richard inherited Cromwell's protectorate (Cromwell didn't rule with a parliament any longer) but was too weak to hold it. The army seized it and authorized a new parliament, which invited Charles II back from France. Milton's dream of a revolution was over. Now he had to worry about his life. Until the Indemnity and Oblivion Act was passed in 1660, which excluded most of Charles's enemies from retribution, but provided some exceptions for the most outstanding of those enemies, Milton hid. It is supposed that because of the aid of Andrew Marvell and William Davenant, Milton was not proscribed. Gordon Campbell and Thomas Corns, in their biography of Milton, offer several reasons why Milton was not executed: he was no longer dangerous; he was blind, already punished; he was ineffectual in no longer being a member of government; he was, by virtue of being a superb polemicist, potentially useful to the restored regime.[37] Whatever the cause, Milton came out of hiding in October of 1660. Then, inexplicably, he was jailed, and not released until December of that year. As a political figure, he was superannuated and harmless. But as a poet, he was breaking free.

According to John Aubrey, Milton started *Paradise Lost* in 1658

37. Gordon Campbell and Thomas N. Corns, *John Milton: Life, Work, and Thought* (Oxford: Oxford University Press, 2008), 308–13.

and finished it in 1663.[38] He reportedly composed his verses in his head, and then would allow himself to be "milked" of his lines in midmorning, dictating to an amanuensis, often one of his daughters. *Paradise Lost* appeared in 1667. He was paid five pounds for it. (Marx ironically termed this *"unproductive"* labor, like a silkworm who can't help but spin silk.)[39] It was ten books long, not the customary twelve of classical epic (I think this was an attempt at iconoclasm on Milton's part). I find persuasive Lewalski's supposition that the absence of dedicatory verses and prefatory matter in the book had to do with qualms that other writers had about associating themselves with Milton the radical.[40] The paragraph entitled "The Verse" that comes at the beginning of most modern editions was added in 1668, to anticipate the objections of conservative readers who missed rhyme. (Though, as A. E. Stallings points out, "Rhymes may be so far apart, you cannot hear / them, but they can hear each other.")[41] Given its polemical flavor, "The Verse" was almost certainly written by Milton. The summaries of each book, also appearing in 1668, were probably written by Milton as well. In light of Milton's scandalous reputation (the poem's admirers "dare not publish their opinions," said Johnson)[42] and the lack of rhyme, it is surprising that the poem sold thirteen hundred copies. Even so, Milton's reputation wouldn't truly blossom until Jacob Tonson's illustrated fourth edition of *Paradise Lost* appeared in 1688, at a time when Milton's radicalism threatened less, and when, in Johnson's fascinating words, "the Revolution put an end to the secrecy of love" that readers felt toward Milton's words.[43] Yet the chief poet of the Restoration, John Dryden, boldly proclaimed Milton's poem

38. Helen Darbishire, *The Early Lives of Milton* (London: Constable, 1932), 13.

39. Karl Marx, *Theories of Surplus Value*, 1863, trans. G. A. Bonner and Emile Burns (London: Lawrence and Wishart, 1951), 186.

40. Barbara K. Lewalski, *The Life of John Milton: A Critical Biography* (Oxford: Blackwell, 2000), 456.

41. A. E. Stallings, "Presto Manifesto!," *Poetry Magazine* 193, no. 5 (February 2009): 450.

42. Samuel Johnson, *The Lives of the Poets*, 1779, ed. John Middendorf (New Haven, Conn.: Yale University Press, 2010), 160.

43. Ibid.

as one of the greatest ever written and came to visit Milton in 1667 to get permission to turn *Paradise Lost* into an opera. One would give anything to have a recording of that meeting!

In 1671, Milton published *Paradise Regained* and *Samson Agonistes* in a joint volume. They deserve their own critical books, which they have received. It suffices for me to say that the first is a "brief epic," modeled on the Book of Job, which Milton planned early in his career. In a dialogue between Satan and Christ, it meditates upon the renunciation of action, and the greater heroism of waiting on God instead. The "majestic unaffected style"[44]—concise, austere, yet strangely beautiful—is a world apart from the grandeurs of *Paradise Lost*, a real departure for Milton in his old age. *Samson Agonistes* is a "closet drama" (what Byron would later call a "*mental theatre*")[45] about the biblical hero in the last few hours of his life, submitting to God's terrible providence. Samson is Milton's passive hero *par excellence*, renouncing self and nation, and yet it is hard not to concur with Christopher Hill that Samson in his final violence represents for Milton a secular faith in the eventual resurgence of radical Protestantism, which had been so downcast at the Restoration.[46] (Many have since debated to what extent the poem could be said to endorse suicidal terrorism;[47] Milton's contemporary John Beale continued to harbor suspicions about his radical undertones: "For though he be old & blind, he wilbe doing mischief... [he is] too full of the Devill."[48]) His minor poems were reissued in 1673, augmented by his Latin poems and several English ones, mainly those written after 1645. In 1674, *Paradise Lost* was divided into twelve books, which is the format in which it is now read.

44. *Paradise Regained*, 4.359.
45. George Gordon, Lord Byron, *The Works of Lord Byron with His Letters and Journals and His Life by Thomas Moore*, 14 vols (London: John Murray, 1832), 5:347.
46. Christopher Hill, *Milton and the English Revolution* (London, Penguin, 1977), 425–45.
47. Most notably, Feisal G. Mohamed, *Milton and the Post-Secular Present: Ethics, Politics, Terrorism* (Stanford, Calif.: Stanford University Press, 2012).
48. Cited in Michael Leslie, "The Spiritual Husbandry of John Beale," in *Culture and Cultivation: Writing and the Land*, ed. Michael Leslie and Timothy Raylor (Leicester, U.K.: Leicester University Press, 1992), 162.

In his final decade, Milton had admiring visitors; he had sufficient money; he had a solicitous third wife; his various books were printed, and he must have felt his poetic work was not in vain. Johnson, Milton's most conflicted biographer, speculates on the subject of Milton's confidence in these last years:

Fancy can hardly forbear to conjecture with what temper Milton surveyed the silent progress of his work, and marked his reputation stealing its way in a kind of subterraneous current, through fear and silence. I cannot but conceive him calm and confident, little disappointed, not at all dejected, relying on his own merit with steady consciousness, and waiting, without impatience, the vicissitudes of opinion, and the impartiality of a future generation.[49]

We have no records of Milton's being a member of a church or meeting house for the last three years of his life.[50] Had he become his own "church of one"? He died around Sunday, November 9, 1674, and was interred in St. Giles's, Cripplegate, where his father was buried. A slab later added on the chancel floor is rather plainly engraved:

NEAR THIS SPOT WAS BURIED
JOHN MILTON
AUTHOR OF *PARADISE LOST*
BORN 1608 — DIED 1674.

Without being informed of it, the visitor to the church might miss it. The poet who wrote of Jesus after his victory over Satan that he "Home to his mother's house private returned" would have wanted it so.[51]

49. Johnson, *The Lives of the Poets*, 160.
50. Neil Forsyth, "The English Church," in *Milton in Context*, ed. Stephen B. Dobranski (Cambridge: Cambridge University Press, 2010), 303.
51. *Paradise Regained*, 4.639.

2

The Underworld

(BOOK I)

Few poems begin with the excitement and ambition of *Paradise Lost*. Its first twenty-six lines announce everything to come: the story, the purpose in telling that story, the sources of its material, the poet's reservations in writing about such lofty subjects, and the brief he makes on God's behalf. It's "a big, big statement," as Allen Ginsberg put it.[1] In scarcely six lines we hear of the Fall; the death that punished the Fall; the exile from Eden; the subsequent history of suffering ("all our woe," [3] with its descending vowels, sounds indeed *woeful*); our redemption by Christ; and his restoration of us to Heaven, which regains for us the "blissful seat" of Eden. The verse paragraph offers a self-definition of the poet-narrator (often, but not always, aligned with Milton himself): storyteller, prophet, historian, supplicant, even lawyer, ready to argue God's case. He summons and connects himself with his audience through indirect reference to things they all know: "man's first disobedience" (1), "one greater man" (4), "[t]hat shepherd" (8), "the chosen seed" (8). He draws a circle of fellow Judeo-Christians around him, who—though a few may be offended—are

---

1. Allen Ginsberg, "Basic Poetics," a class taught at the Naropa Institute, April 24, 1980. Transcript of relevant material available at https://allenginsberg.org/2017/10/monday-october-9/.

probably secretly thrilled to hear the rudiments of biblical experience related in the hallowed language of Greek and Latin epic poetry.

His stance curiously mixes confidence and self-doubt akin to that of the speaker of *Lycidas*: bending under the burden of a lost Paradise, and at the same time wondering if he can tell the story of its recovery. He likens himself to Moses, vaunting that he can tell a comparable story of the beginnings of the world, and more. Yet there is some risk: the song is "advent'rous" (13); it "intends" to soar (14), but he confesses there are darkness and lowness within, which he hopes the Muse will illumine and support. But perhaps he isn't ready. He admits he needs "instruct"ion (19). If he sounds boastfully Protestant—claiming that the Muse prefers "Before all temples th' upright heart and pure" (18) —there's an undercurrent of worry about his motives. Is he rising above himself? He alludes to Ariosto's famous boast that his poem, *Orlando Furioso*, will be a *cosa non detta in prosa mai, né in rima*—"a thing never yet uttered in prose, nor in verse." (When classical scholar William Lauder attacked Milton in 1747 for unacknowledged borrowings, he sarcastically included this line as his epigraph!)[2] Milton changes *detta* to "unattempted" (16), a braggart's flourish, but "unat-*tempted*" contains *tempted*, and temptation is what the story of Adam and Eve is about. Does the poet worry that he is, like the first man and woman and Satan himself, overreaching? He has set himself to be God's explainer, and to assert eternal Providence. But what if he fails, and falls? Falls like Satan? What if he cannot defend God, or says in his defense the wrong thing? Dante certainly would have found Milton's claim to justify God impertinent, a galling piece of presumption. In the thousands of lines of the *Divine Comedy*, Dante never attempts to justify God. Why should he? Though he forges ahead, Milton surely feels that sense of presumption. Alone in his task, Milton wonders if his pride will see him cast into darkness like Satan. Even if we know that Milton has been trying and acquitting God often in his poetry, we are shocked at the baldness of his statement.

2. William Lauder, "An Essay on Milton's Imitations of the Moderns," *Gentleman's Magazine* 17 (1747): 24.

T. S. Eliot once commended the "breathless leap" of Milton's poetry,[3] here in a dazzling suspension that doesn't identify the verb until line 6! Milton is dealing with a large extent of time, and so his suspension is an echo to the sense. We are in a poem, we realize, that, though it is "tuneful and well-measured,"[4] doesn't measure things only by lines, but by *sentences*, and verse paragraphs (indicated by an indentation). It is written in movements of different intensities. Book 1 starts out on a level note, then rises to "sing" (6). It falls, and then rises again to "things unattempted yet" (16). It falls yet again, and then works its way up to "justify the ways of God to men" (26). Henry Wadsworth Longfellow likened this dynamic to ocean waves "Upheaving and subsiding":

> So in majestic cadence rise and fall
> The mighty undulations of thy song,
> O sightless bard, England's Mæonides![5]

The same variety that may be heard in Milton's different voices may also be found in his raising and lowering of intensity. These varying intensities, these hills and valleys, are an integral part of Milton's technique. We saw them as early as the "Nativity Ode" and *Lycidas*. Milton's practice of carrying syntax over line endings to give emphasis to size or extent may be seen in Book 1 of *Paradise Lost* when he speaks of his song

> That with no middle flight intends to soar
> Above th' Aonian mount, while it pursues
> Things unattempted yet in prose or rhyme. (1.14–16)

The lines themselves burst: "soar / Above"; "pursues / Things." Another common Miltonic practice here involves the creation of an attractively thick texture through the repetition of "t" in "support," "that," "great," "argument," "assert," "eternal," and "justify" (23–26). Milton deploys repetition to different ends; here, it hammers determination.

3. T. S. Eliot, "Milton," *Proceedings of the British Academy* 33 (1947): 73.
4. Milton, Sonnet 13, "To Mr. Henry Lawes," *CPEP* 150.
5. Henry Wadsworth Longfellow, "Milton," in *The Sonnets of Henry Wadsworth Longfellow*, ed. Ferris Greenslet (Boston: Houghton Mifflin, 1907), 56.

After posing the conventional epic question—who seduced mankind?—Milton begins with the story of Satan's fall. Once again, there is a stylistic ascent (38–43), one that parallels Satan's failed uprising against God in Heaven. Satan's plan comes to a rude ending: "With vain attempt" (44). Coming after lines that have no pauses in the middle, this line is powerful. It stops syntactically, imitative of the way that Satan's rebellion stops in the face of God's might. In his defeat, Satan is sent to "bottomless perdition" (47), the adjective "bottomless" having a figurative meaning that we might not at first appreciate. It is mental as well as physical. Likewise, lines 50 to 83, describing Satan's initial perception of Hell, put an emphasis on mental suffering: it is the "*thought*" of "lost happiness" that is his main torment (54–56, my italics).[6] He is faced with "*sights* of woe" and "Regions of *sorrow*" (64–65, my italics; Olaudah Equiano invokes these very lines to convey the horrors of slavery).[7] The culmination of this passage is the oxymoron "darkness visible" (63), a darkness that is all the more awful because it can be seen. Total darkness would have been a relief. Once again, *cognition* of Hell, rather than hellish pain, is the punishment. This cognitive suffering is emphasized in the enormous sentence that begins "Nine times the space," and runs down to where the tone becomes suddenly pianissimo and elegiac: "O how unlike the place from whence they fell!" (50–75). Milton is a poet of power, but he is also one of loss and pathos. That loss is made especially poignant here by the brevity of its expression, coming after the lengthy sentence. Milton never tires of reminding his readers that these fallen angels were once unfallen. When Satan sees, he sees with "angels ken" (59); when he cries, "Tears such as angels weep burst forth" (620). And yet here, as elsewhere, Satan's angelic powers are aggrandized.

While Milton does provide some setting, it's not long before we

6. See Angus Fletcher, "Standing, Waiting, and Traveling Light: Milton and the Drama of Information," in *Colors of the Mind: Conjectures on Thinking in Literature*, 68–80 (Cambridge, Mass.: Harvard University Press, 1991).

7. Olaudah Equiano, *The Interesting Narrative of the Life of Olaudah Equiano*, 1789, ed. Angelo Costanzo (Peterborough, Ont.: Broadview Press, 2001), 114–15.

encounter a speech. This is a truth of the first importance: *Paradise Lost* is a dramatic poem as much as a narrative one, which is in keeping with the fact that Milton initially drafted a biblical drama on the fall of man (sketched out in his notebooks as "Adam Unparadized"). There are many speeches in *Paradise Lost*. Satan, here prone on the burning lake, addresses Beelzebub, "Breaking the horrid silence" (83). Silence? In the midst of "whirlwinds of tempestuous fire" (77)? Here is yet another feature of Milton's writing: he is constantly making us reconsider his apparent meanings. I call it the Miltonic "double take." In this instance, we go from description to psychology without warning, another example of Milton's impatience with boundaries, with either/ors. The silence here isn't the silence in the setting, but the unspeakable anguish between two who have lost Heaven: the most "horrid silence" of all time.

At this point, Satan interrupts a planned speech's syntax with an outburst that records his horrors at seeing Beelzebub in ruin. The planned speech that he resumes contains a curious cluster of adjective-noun constructions: "mutual league" (87), "United thoughts and counsels" (88), "equal hope / And hazard" (88–89), and "joined / In equal ruin" (90–91). When Milton repeats himself in this way, there is usually a reason, often something beneath the narrative. Why does Satan keep harping about equality and partnership? Milton wants us to remember the line about Satan's desire to "set himself in glory above his peers" that led to the revolt in Heaven (38). Now that he has lost that revolt, Satan seeks, at least for the time being, to pass the responsibility around: *we did it together!* In other words, there is guilt as well as bad decision making lurking in his mind, suggested in his "till then who knew / The force of those dire arms?" (93–94). Milton makes this guilt explicit later in the lines "Millions of spirits for his fault amerced / Of Heav'n" (609–10). Yet Satan admits nothing. On the contrary, in the scene on the Lake of Hell Satan shows undeniable strength of mind—something that Milton venerated in all his heroes—and, like a good leader, Satan is able to forge sustaining beliefs and conceptions. He establishes a way of understanding their predicament: there's the outward and the inward aspect of their fall. We may have lost our "outward luster" (97), Satan concedes, but we are still strong inside. Only superficial things are changed. We have lost the (mere) "field" (105), but we have not lost "All" (106). There is the "low" that we are in now (114), but there is a lower that we can fall into (116). We have learned our lessons, Satan claims. We have "the unconquerable will," the "study of revenge," and "courage never to submit or yield" (106–8). Moreover, Satan has a plan: eternal war, which he works up to as he speaks. The reader notices again the crescendo of the passage from line 95 to line 105. Satan rises up to what is—we will learn later though we suspect it now—a lie: that Satan's armies "shook" God's throne. The volume drops, then rises again.

Fish, in his famous book *Surprised by Sin*, argues that the reader is carried along by Satan's bombast here, only to be let down by sudden reduction of Satan's courage to "deep despair" (126). The reader is reduced and then severely rebuked by the narrator, who is considerably more attentive to evil than the reader and who finds nothing admirable in Satan. Is Fish right? Many readers think so. In the 1970s and 1980s, Fish started a virtual school of Milton criticism that made the reader and his reactions to the text of *Paradise Lost* part of the poem's meaning. Milton, who in the eighteenth century was the preeminent poet of the sublime,[8] now in Fish's view becomes a preacher seeking to turn indifferent Christians back to zealous ones. Even as the reader is carried along by Satan's zeal, he or she knows it is false, and doesn't need any guidance to make that clear. It would not be the only time that *Paradise Lost* asks us for a double response, a contradiction-balancing response. Satan is a leader we can admire; Malcolm X in prison identified with him.[9] While he is also less than honest, we are

8. See Sanford Budick, *Kant and Milton* (Cambridge, Mass.: Harvard University Press, 2010), and Leslie Moore, *Beautiful Sublime: The Making of "Paradise Lost," 1701–1734* (Stanford, Calif.: Stanford University Press , 1990).

9. Malcolm X, with Alex Haley, *The Autobiography of Malcolm X* (New York: Grove

equipped to take that opposition in. Fish underestimates our ability to hold mutually hostile ideas in our heads at the same time. Satan asks "what though the field be lost?" (105). The "field" is Heaven, and therefore the sentiment is preposterous wishful thinking. Yet the courage and, yes, fortitude in these lines is remarkable. Milton isn't rebuking us so much as he is stretching our minds about Satan, and dissuading us from making them up too soon, one way or another.[10] In this passage, Milton is adding to Satan, not subtracting. Above all, Milton's narrator is not "a redundant pedant,"[11] unerring, more eager to preach than to evoke. Quite simply, Milton learned from the great tragedians how to make bad people magnificent.[12] The portrait of Satan is part of the poem's classical panache. It doesn't render a solid belief.

With its long grammatical suspension, Beelzebub's speech (128–55) resembles Milton's sonnet to Fairfax. It opens in praise, but the praise is grammatically appositional. When the meat of the sentence comes, it reveals Beelzebub's ability to see things as they are (134); its defeatism qualifies the root-ti-toot of the praise he has just uttered. His first speech is almost humorous in the way it depicts a character whose critical eye sees the situation for what it is and who mostly speaks his mind, and therefore keeps saying the wrong thing. His devotion to Satan is touching. He affirms that Satan's war endangered God, but he also affirms that the war was led by Satan. Satan doesn't want to hear that now, and so when he answers Beelzebub his speech is full of "ours" rather than "I's" (156–191). Beelzebub sees the war ending in "sad overthrow and foul defeat" which "Hath lost us

Press, 1965), 186; see also Reginald A. Wilburn, "Epilogue: Malcolm X, *Paradise Lost*, and the Twentieth Century Infernal Reader," in *Preaching the Gospel of Black Revolt: Appropriating Milton in Early African American Literature* (Pittsburgh, Penn.: Duquesne University Press, 2014), 327–34.

10. See John Rumrich, *Milton Unbound* (Cambridge: Cambridge University Press, 1996), 21–22

11. Ibid., 21

12. Gordon Teskey, *The Poetry of John Milton* (Cambridge, Mass.: Harvard University Press, 2015), xiii.

heaven" (135–36). He sees "horrible destruction" (137) and "endless misery" (142), and though he wishes to adhere to the official line, which is that "the mind and spirit remains / Invincible" (139–40), he can't help but see that God has left the fallen angels with their energy and spirit just "Strongly to suffer" (147), a fascinating phrase with the true Miltonic flavor. We shall become God's servants, and, in a great line of lacerating r's, he envisions "Here in the heart of Hell to work in fire" (151).

Outlining the speeches in the whole of *Paradise Lost* reveals that they tend to respond to each other, often point by point. Beelzebub has listened to Satan's first speech carefully and Satan listens to Beelzebub's. Satan hears Beelzebub conjecture that the devils must end up serving God either actively or passively. Satan's response is to call Beelzebub "weak" (157) and, with respect to their punishment, he says it is "miserable / Doing or suffering" (158). His exquisitely balanced lines "To do aught good never will be our task, / But ever to do ill our sole delight" (159–60), while borrowing Beelzebub's antithesis, changes the active-passive one to a good-evil one. Here commences what is to be a powerful public stance: if God seeks to bring good out of evil, then Satan will bring evil out of good. It is an infernal providence to match God's Providence. Satan's speech here begins to slide into uncertainty ("may," "perhaps," "if I fail not," 166–67), but then he turns to action as he often does in the rest of the story. Action makes thinking go away, for thinking in Hell hurts, even if it sometimes exhilarates.

God has withdrawn his forces, and it is time to move from the lake to the land. Milton's style in 170–191 is grand, but not without subtleties: "Seest thou yon dreary plain, forlorn and wild" (180) presents an endless desert of long vowels, yet most of them different. There is an attractive internal half-rhyme in the next line with "seat" and "light," an example of the half-rhyming music in *Paradise Lost* that affects us even when we don't take conscious notice of it. As always, Milton plays long words ("desolation," "glimmering," "afflicted," "calamity," "re-assembling") off of short ones ("save," "casts," "void," "rest") and the passage is full of pleasing repetitions: "these," "rest," "how," "we," "our" are all repeated (181–89). The verse paragraph closes with a resounding epigram from Satan that calls up in our minds the great speeches of Churchill, FDR, and JFK:

> What reinforcement we may gain from hope,
> If not what resolution from despair. (1.190–91)

But there is no hope, and that despair cannot lead to resolution (that is why it is despair!). Hearing such lines uttered in such circumstances, how could we not rise up and follow? This is the first sloganeering of history, and it is powerful. Milton's God can, as we shall see, speak gracefully and movingly, but he never thrills us with his oratory. Is it any wonder that Satan has inspired so many of Milton's readers?

What follows is an epic simile (197–209) of resplendent indirection—embedded within a Leviathan-sized sentence, the longest in the entire poem.[13] The function of Milton's similes has been an object of interest since the poem's publication; they often appear digressive and irrelevant. One rather old-fashioned way of dealing with this irrelevance is to compare it to the irrelevant material found in Homer's similes and to regard it as an entertaining digression. Another more modern way is to regard this material as relevant to the subject at hand but not in an obvious way. The similes, if not appearing immediately relevant, may look forward to future events or they may be obliquely relevant to present events. But, whatever they do, they don't make themselves fully explicit. They require agility on the part of the reader to see strange likenesses.[14]

This much is certain: they almost always expand the context of the action of the poem, or the poem's implications. The Leviathan simile conveys just how long and large Satan is (192–209), but it does more. Indirectly it equates Satan and his rebellion to that of the

---

13. Brian Cummings, "Revolutionary English," in *The Literary Culture of the Reformation: Grammar and Grace* (Oxford: Oxford University Press, 2002), 422.

14. See John Leonard, *Faithful Labourers: A Reception History of "Paradise Lost," 1667–1970* (Oxford: Oxford University Press, 2013), 1:327–33.

Titans, a Satanic pattern in ancient mythology that Milton believes is a corrupt retelling of *Paradise Lost*'s "original" story. Mentioning it is a way of aggrandizing his story, as the model story from which all other stories derive. This is one meaning of Milton's desire to "soar / Above th' Aonian mount" (14–15). Just when one thinks the simile is done, however, Milton adds an extension to the story in the medieval legend of Satan as a sea monster who attracts desperate sailors to moor by his side as if he were land. The situation here is highly relevant to Satan's historic deceptiveness as our enemy. We "anchor" (206) on him and he, our false savior, destroys us. The simile also, and more obviously though not explicitly, alludes to the situation of the fallen angels who will put their trust once again in Satan, who now, on the lake, is their Leviathan. Coyly, though, Milton closes out the simile "So stretched out huge in length the Arch-Fiend lay" (209), as if to say that size, and size only, is his interest here. The idiom of this passage is compelling. "Titanian" (198), the adjective, is kept from its partner noun "Briareos" for an entire line (199). By forcing what this Titan did—that is, war on Jove—between two huge names, Milton makes those names greater in magnitude than the deed. Milton makes us wait for another two lines for the largest creature of all those that "swim th' ocean stream" (202). Epic poetry typically inflates a word like "ocean" to "ocean stream," but Milton's "stream" is a highly original way of emphasizing the creature's immense size, in that it reduces the ocean to a "stream."

Now Satan rises from the lake. We notice the historical present in line 221 ("he rears from off the pool"), which, when it appears, helps persuade us, if subliminally, that we are witnessing an eternal, not temporal, action. Satan's "chains," it turns out, are metaphorical only, just like those concentric spheres around the world that we are told of in Book 3. God gives his permission to make an attempt on man—a permissiveness that gives some readers trouble when they attempt to make sense of Milton's defense of God, because it appears that God sadistically exposes man to harm. The next passage makes Satan out to be a Titanic figure, as he fearlessly makes his way to the shore, though the passage's seriousness is deliberately compromised by privy humor (231–37). Likewise, when we read that the two devils are "Both glorying to have scaped the Stygian flood" (239) we experience another Miltonic double take: It is glorious to raise oneself off a burning lake, and yet how can there be glory of any kind if the angels are in Hell and if God rules everything they do (238–41)? The next lines, as Satan reaches land, shake with grandiloquence—repetition and alliteration and symmetrical phrasing thrill the reader but invite, again, a double response. In two words that don't quite match, Satan is a "lost Archangel" (243), at once both grand and pathetic. Is it really, as he insists, "Better to reign in Hell, than serve in Heav'n" (263)? The phrase has intoxicating power in its parallelism. It will make many adherents, but is it true or absurd? In the vicinity of this phrase we run into another one of the poem's most quotable formulations, with the same doubtful validity:

> The mind is its own place, and in itself
> Can make a Heav'n of Hell, a Hell of Heav'n. (1.254–55)

In the second line, notice the AB|BA chiasmus (Heaven Hell | Hell Heaven), suggestive of Satan's moral inversion. These lines (set off for emphasis) take us to the core of *Paradise Lost*'s complexity. They are sometimes cited as being subversively inspiring by those who see Milton as a closet Satanist. The lines affirm our power to interpret and hence to make our own worlds, but they also describe a perversion of common sense that Satan, in a saner, less self-inflating moment, might grasp. Making a Heaven of Hell is absurd, because Hell is fixed in its awfulness as a place of punishment. The best one can do is to adjust. If you make a Hell of Heaven, well, that is what, with predictable results, Satan has already tried to do, and why would he want to try it again? Not even Milton knows the answer. There's panache, even nobility in these lines, yet they gloss over two futile ambitions while affirming an undeniable power that humans have to make their own world.

Beelzebub once again tries to be affirmative but ends up, once again, acknowledging the devils' plight for what it is, though—hilariously—he thinks that that plight is the result of a literal fall rather than a defeat (272–82). Satan ignores him and moves toward the shore. He carries his shield, which is of "Ethereal temper" (therefore made in Heaven), and "massy, large, and round" (285). The narrator surprisingly compares it to the moon as seen through Galileo's telescope, and then draws in the real moon, the "spotty globe," which Galileo saw through that telescope (285–91). Almost without pause, Milton next compares the spear to a Norwegian pine, except that it is many times longer. Together the two similes extend the implications of the poem, giving it a multi-geographical ambiance. Both similes also have the effect of putting the poem in touch with the present. If *Paradise Lost* feels short on event and long on presentation, with divagations into history and geography, over many times and places, it is to suggest that much of what happens in the poem *is always happening*. Moreover, the telescope might reflect upon the technique of poetry itself: moving always between a close-up view of Satan, which tends to be flattering, and a long view, which isn't. In this respect, the passage would be somewhat like the first lines of the poem, in which the narrator calls attention to himself while telling the story. Milton felt a kinship with Galileo, and it's fascinating to consider that he may have seen a resemblance between his poetic craft and Galileo's astronomical one. (You may be distant, and I may be blind, but I can see you!) David Loewenstein claims that this passage, hedged as it is by qualification, speaks for Milton's great ambivalence toward the new science, which he sometimes embraced and sometimes didn't.[15] As Satan moves toward the shore, Milton, in irregular limping meter, shows us how the heat of Hell punishes Satan: "SMOTE on him SORE beSIDES, VAULTed with FIRE" (298). We are meant to sense this pain in the falling rhythms "SMOTE on" and "VAULTed." The verse limps, another of many examples of Milton's "kinetic" art.

15. David Loewenstein, *Milton: "Paradise Lost"* (Cambridge: Cambridge University Press, 1993), 56.

The passages that follow represent Milton's associational art at its greatest and most intense. Milton updates an ancient simile as he compares the devils fallen in battle to fallen leaves:

> His legions, angel forms, who lay entranced
> Thick as autumnal leaves that strow the brooks
> In Vallombrosa, where th' Etrurian shades
> High overarched embow'r (1.301–4)

The eighteenth-century commentator C. Falconer observes how appropriate the simile is, expressing the number of the devils, and their posture "lying confusedly in heaps"; moreover, says Falconer, "the falling of a Shower of Leaves from the Trees, in a Storm of Wind, represents the Dejection of the Angels from their former Celestial Mansions; and *their faded Splendor wan* ... is finely expressed by the paleness and witheredness of the Leaves."[16] What Falconer might also have noticed is the dignity that Milton's eloquent lines give to these perverse sinners. The same dignity attaches to "Busiris and his Memphian chivalry" (307). In part it derives from the high expression (compare "Pharaoh and his troops"), in part from the recitation of proper names, and in part from the long sentences and enjambment that sweeps all the particulars into a tumultuous kaleidoscope of history that follows from Satan's warfare in Heaven and subsequent fall. From the parting of the Red Sea, to the biblical plague of locusts, to the barbarian invasions—all alluded to in quick succession—we are invited to connect what is inside *Paradise Lost* to what is outside it, over all time. Has poetry ever known such ambition and triumphant evocation? Perhaps only in Homer, one of Milton's favorite poets.[17]

"Awake, arise, or be for ever fall'n," Satan adjures his dejected warriors (330). The phrasing is deliberately and effectively short and pungent after a paragraph of run-on lines; it stirs us, but once again we

---

16. C. Falconer, *Essay on Milton's Imitations of the Ancients with Some on the Paradise Regained* (London, 1741), 23; cited in Ricks, *Milton's Grand Style*, 124.

17. See Gregory Machacek, *Milton and Homer: "Written to Aftertimes"* (Pittsburgh, Penn.: Duquesne University Press, 2011).

are conscious of a subtle misgiving, for Satan's followers, whether they awaken and rise or not, *are* forever fallen. Two things must immediately be said about the fallen angels. Whatever they were in Heaven, now, after their fall, they are abject. Though Satan has mistakenly led them into battle, they are still pathetically obedient to his leadership; they still dread Satan, a dread that Satan does not completely deserve and of which he is partially unaware. Notice that the devils are not punch-drunk from their fall, but well aware of the "evil plight" of their condition, even though they choose not to think about it because it is so painful (335–36). As such, they deserve to be the tools of Satan, and appropriately despised. Their master conducts them ashore with his spear just as Moses summoned up a "pitchy cloud / Of locusts" against the Pharaoh (340–41). It makes sense that the followers of Satan could be reduced to locusts, but it is counterintuitive that Milton compares Satan to Moses. Ricks recognizes this problem throughout Milton's work, and he cites Thomas De Quincey (1839) to help him explain it. De Quincey's point is that there is a "subtle and lurking antagonism" in Milton's work that the reader must learn to explicate in accordance with what he knows to be Milton's values.[18] I have called this the Miltonic "double take": Satan is both like Moses and not like him. He is not like Moses in that Moses was pious; he is like Moses in that he is an inspiring leader. He is the Moses of the damned, forever exiled from the Promised Land. If we return to the opening lines of the poem, in which the narrator invites us to see a connection between Moses ("the shepherd") and himself, we will once again be amazed at the subtlety of this deservedly grand poem. Later, in Book 3, Satan's exile will once again be subtly and outrageously likened to the exile of the Israelites from the Promised Land (528–33).

Milton now catalogs the fallen angels who have no names. They once had them, but were stripped of them in Heaven. They have yet to acquire new ones. They will get their new names when

18. De Quincey, "Milton," 1839, reprinted in Thomas De Quincey, *Works* (Edinburgh: A. and C. Black, 1862–63), 6:321–22, cited in Ricks, *Milton's Grand Style*, 15.

wand'ring o'er the Earth,
Through God's high sufferance for the trial of man,
By falsities and lies the greatest part
Of mankind they corrupted to forsake
God their Creator. (1.365–69)

They will become tempting heathen idols, which Milton's God will allow to happen because he believes that mankind needs temptation to attain salvation. This was behind God's permissiveness in allowing Satan to rise off the burning lake. Milton insists on this permissiveness now, just as he did in 1644, when he wrote *Areopagitica* and in it justified God for suffering Adam to fall.

Milton is in a somewhat awkward position when it comes to the large catalogue occupying the middle of the book. He must give the devils names they will acquire, not ones that they had, because they were stripped of those names in Heaven. Moreover, writing in the epic tradition, it is sometimes said, Milton was obliged to write a catalogue. (His similes are explained in much the same way.) But Milton is always writing catalogues, so many that one is sure that he was not acting solely out of literary obligation to a genre when he wrote them in *Paradise Lost*. Catalogues help define his poetic practice. They inform his early works, whether in Latin or in English, from the elegies, to *Lycidas*, to the "Nativity Ode." "Allegro-Penseroso" is one big catalogue. These works are not epics, though they have some epic features. There is reason to look for other motives in the catalogues besides literary conformity. There is something "catalogic" about Milton's poetry generally, and that extends through *Paradise Regained* and *Samson Agonistes*. If catalogues had not been a literary precedent, Milton would have invented them!

In the middle of Book 1, the catalogue offers a genealogy of evil, tracing the fallen angels to the heathen idols they eventually became. Generally speaking, Milton's catalogues, even in his other poems, offer connections between his story and other stories from the Bible or from pagan lore. As such, they serve an expansive function. In this respect, Milton's practice is like Joyce's in *Ulysses*: here the story is connected to all stories and that gives the primary story its significance. Milton, no less than Joyce, is an artist of inclusion. The catalogues are learnedly full of names of places and people. They are as such subject to the charge of pedantry. In Milton's defense, they establish his credentials to tell "the story of all things,"[19] which must perforce have linkages in world history and geography. But granting that to be the case, there is still an aesthetic problem with these long catalogues. Milton's shorter catalogues often enhance his story, but the longer ones risk being too detailed (and too often poetically dull) to hold a reader's interest for their entire length. I'd venture to guess that Milton's contemporaries found them a trial too, though they would have been more interested in their subject matter than we are. The catalogue in Book I (376–506) is better than those that come in the last books of the poem. Even so, despite some bright passages, the reader is inclined to skip it, or gloss over much of it. Milton is so often an entertaining and challenging poet that we are continually surprised that he writes as dully as he does here:

> The pleasant valley of Hinnom, Tophet thence
> And black Gehenna called, the type of Hell.
> Next Chemos, th' obscene dread of Moab's sons,
> From Aroar to Nebo, and the wild
> Of southmost Abarim; in Hesebon
> And Horonaim, Seon's realm, beyond
> The flow'ry dale of Sibma clad with vines
> And Eleale to th' Asphaltic Pool. (1.404–11)

Except for the lyrical and surprising next-to-last line, this is pedestrian. We know Milton can do better. Yes, it expands the implications of the central action and characters and gives evidence of Milton's belief that poetry must teach its "great argument" (24). Even so, its rote quality begs the reader to ask whether Milton would have been better

19. Michael Lieb, "S.B.'s '*In Paradisum Amissam*': Sublime Commentary," *Milton Quarterly* 19, no. 3 (October 1985): 71.

off evoking the history of idolatry rather than setting it forth in literal detail. I have heard it argued that the proliferation of names in Book 1 is meant to give a Tower of Babel effect to Hell and its various deities. I'm doubtful, because there are so many catalogues in *Paradise Lost* where profusion is not meant at all to render such an effect. Besides, it is Milton's art to fuse rather than confuse. It would be more persuasive to say that Miltonic catalogues reassure the reader of his didactic-historical purpose. As such, his catalogues serve a legitimizing function. He may be, unavoidably, a poetic entertainer, but he does not want to give the impression that he's an entertainer who shrinks from some of the required tasks of epic.

However, there are some fresh, exciting passages in Book 1's major catalogue. Every reader can find them. There is Moloch at the beginning, introduced in powerful lines, with a repeated roaring "r" sound: "First, Moloch, horrid king besmeared with blood / Of human sacrifice, and parents' tears" (392–93). The verse settles back to its business, then picks up again in 423–31, an artful passage informing us that angels are sexless. We can see the way Milton plays lines with *caesurae* (pauses) off lines that are unbroken. It constitutes a rhythm in itself, and it is another facet of *Paradise Lost*'s variety. I have italicized lines unbroken by pauses:

> For spirits when they please
> Can either sex assume, or both; so soft
> *And uncompounded is their essence pure,*
> *Nor tied or manacled with joint or limb,*
> *Nor founded on the brittle strength of bones,*
> Like cumbrous flesh; but in what shape they choose
> Dilated or condensed, bright or obscure,
> *Can execute their airy purposes,*
> *And works of love or enmity fulfill.* (1.423–31, my italics)

The transsexuality of the angels has implications for Milton's ideas about human gender. There appears to be no strong division of sex or gender in Heaven, and there is a suggestion that angels, like humans, can love. They are "pure," but, as we will ascertain later, they can enjoy sex. Just as remarkably sensual are the dubious attractions of Thammuz, or Adonis, which passage, in spite of the poem's overt disapproval, contains a delightful couplet about the worship of Astarte among the Phoenician virgins:

> To whose bright image nightly by the moon
> Sidonian virgins paid their vows and songs (1.440–41)

Lest we let down our moral guard, these lines are followed by a particularly harsh and brutal one about the harm Thammuz did to Israel's faith, and that one is followed by the brashest passage in the catalogue, about Dagon (457–66). Here Milton sounds like Fish's moralist preacher.

The last remarkable passage is that condemning Belial (490–505). The portrait of Belial is evidence of what Robert Pinsky calls Milton's ability to open "new emotional registers."[20] It depicts the height of evil, which takes something away from even Satan's evil, who is never referred to as "lewd" (490). Satan's evil serves an end; Belial loves vice not for its appearances, which would make him like us, but for "itself" (492). He is so pure of the accoutrements of evil that he has no temple or altar; he is a purist of wickedness, pursuing its essence. And he is the most contemporary. After his pedantic Azotus-Ascalon-Abbana-Pharphar-Osiris-Bethel-Dan-Jehovah passage (465–90), Milton explodes with his pulpit tone:

> Belial came last; than whom a spirit more lewd
> Fell not from Heaven, or more gross to love
> Vice for itself. (1.490–92)

And then, remarkably, Milton ascends into the heroic mode in words that unmistakably give grandeur if not goodness to this awful spirit as he is brought forward into contemporary London:

20. Robert Pinsky, "The American John Milton: The Poet and the Power of Ordinary Speech," *Slate*, August 2008, https://slate.com/culture/2008/08/milton-s-400th-anniversary.html.

In courts and in palaces he also reigns
And in luxurious cities, where the noise
Of riot ascends above their loftiest tow'rs,
And injury and outrage: and when night
Darkens the streets, then wander forth the sons
Of Belial, flown with insolence and wine. (1.497–502)

While Milton doesn't take the part of the fallen angels, the "due"
he sometimes gives them is a mark of the moral capaciousness that
characterizes his poem, and this capaciousness has always accompa-
nied epic poetry. This arresting opulence gains its power from the
pedestrian lines of the catalogue that set it off. The remainder of the
catalogue—Titan, Saturn, Rhea, and Jove—feels like an afterthought
(506–21). Nothing those deities do "Darkens the streets" as does the
specter of Belial.

When the devils are on shore, the narrative picks up activity. Sa-
tan's demeanor in front of his troops dominates the next few pages
of the poem. His words may offer only "Semblance of worth, not
substance" (529), but at the same time, they are at once gentle and
commanding. He has become a sanctuary of sorts. Now that the lead-
ership is settled, the trumpets play, standards are unfurled, the "orient
colors" wave (546), the "imperial ensign ... [shines]" (536), "Ten thou-
sand banners rise into the air," and there is a parade (545). These things
are presented as happening as if by magic, without effort, though
one gathers that powers working behind the scenes are responsible.
In fact, little has changed from the angels' recent life in Heaven. The
defeated warriors, operating on instinct and training, pick up their
weapons and flags and continue. No twentieth-century reader can ex-
perience this stunning passage (522–71) without thinking, as David
Daiches did, of Hitler's monster rallies at Nuremberg.[21] It's uncanny
foreknowledge, as if Milton were a Nostradamus. The purpose of this
display is to settle the minds of the fallen angels, who are suffering
from "Anguish and doubt and fear and sorrow and pain" (558). This

21. David Daiches, *Milton* (London: Hutchinson University Library, 1957), 166.

remarkable repetition of conjunctions (called *polysyndeton*), making the psychological physical, is another sensational syntactic effect that, fortunately, Milton does not repeat too often. The narrator may invite a cynical interpretation of this entire spectacle, as he exposes its manipulative purpose. Yet the close-up description conveys some indirect admiration. One can hear a marching music in the meter as well as in the deft repetition of adjective-noun combinations: "united force," "fixèd thought," "soft pipes," "painful steps," "horrid front" (560–63). Coming in such concentration there's an almost HUP-two-three-four MARCH rhythm.

As Satan reviews the troops, his heart "Distends" (what an original word!) with pride and "Glories" (572–73). Once again, we are impressed by Satan's recovery and resolve, though we suspect that only God and his son can achieve glory. What follows demands an even more complex response from us: the troops assembled in Hell surpass all of the greatest armies of history. In this respect, Satan's troops are aggrandized at the same time that they represent a corruption that has infected all armies since. A fine, small catalogue lists some of the armies: those that fought at Thebes; the Arthurian knights; Charlemagne's troops (573–87). The passage is at once both lovely and corrupt, with resonance of the medieval opulence that Milton once aspired to poeticize, but which he now holds in contempt. *You think these armies of legend and history are great? They are only debased descendants of the paradigm of hell.* Yet we quiver at the sonic beauty of

Jousted in Aspramont, or Montalban …
Or whom Biserta sent from Afric shore
When Charlemagne with all his peerage fell
By Fontarrabia. (1.583–87)

But Milton—at least for now in his narrative—makes their appeal suspicious, just as he makes Hell suspicious.

The passage describing Satan in front of his troops is curious (589–615), almost wholly external. Milton withholds what is going on in his mind, suspending syntax:

> he above the rest
> In shape and gesture proudly eminent
> Stood like a tow'r. (1.589–91)

"Stood" is emphasized by its position as the first syllable of its line. "Stood" and "standing" are key words in Milton's vocabulary. We might remember the last line of the sonnet "On His Blindness": "[they] also serve who only stand and wait" (14). Satan has not "stood," but fallen. Yet he is like a tower, a term of approval. But it is an appearance. It doesn't mean he *was* a tower, but that he "stood" *like* one. He's wounded by thunder, but "care / Sat on his faded cheek" (601–2). Does this mean he cares, or is it only an image he projects? Satan's "eye" is cruel (604), but is that because leaders need to look cruel? He shows "Signs" of remorse (605), as he should, but is that remorse real? Satan, we will learn, and we can already infer, does feel some remorse, but here he engages in image-making. We hear that his words are "interwove" with sighs (621), which suggests art. What complicates the matter is that the narrator is elsewhere inclined to tell us precisely Satan's deepest passions, as when Satan is "racked with deep despair" (126). Milton was not obliged, as a modern narrator would be, to keep a steady perspective. More audaciously, we may have a fallible "character" in the narrator, who sometimes sees into things and sometimes takes appearances at face value. Likewise, as suggested earlier, we have in Satan what Leonard sees: an ambivalent character, an archangel, and a devil at once.[22] Maybe what lurks behind Milton's portrayal of Satan is "L'Allegro" and "Il Penseroso," torn between two worlds and systems of valuation. Leonard insists we can't dismiss Satan by merely laughing at him, and we can't dismiss the allegiance paid to him as merely specious.[23] Like several modern readers of Milton, he's trying to find a middle ground between Satan as saint and Satan as scoundrel.

When Satan speaks his position emerges clearly: (1) I am not to

22. John Leonard, *Faithful Labourers*, 2:393–94.
23. Ibid., 442–44.

blame for our loss, because nobody could have known just how powerful God was; (2) we will recover our losses and will regain Heaven; (3) we are better off for having lost because we have learned to transcend the use of force; (4) we are still a viable force and, if we choose the right course of action or strategy, we can prevail (621–63). Satan has a leader's way of turning loss into victory. We have learned something from this loss, he says: "who overcomes / By force, hath overcome but half his foe" (648–49). A fine sentiment, we might think, but we don't want to hear it from General MacArthur! Even so, though its expression may look like a feeble rationalization, the sentiment is dear to Milton, as we know from his sonnet to Fairfax, with its memorable refusal to celebrate General Fairfax until he completes the work of peace, or in Milton's words, "For what can war, but endless war still breed"?[24] It is curious, complex, and really quite remarkable of Milton to put so many of his favorite ideas into dubious contexts, or into the mouths of figures he detests. And this practice, as well as anything else, has prompted some readers, with Blake, to conclude that Milton is "of the Devil's party." Satan's peroration—"War then, war / Open or understood must be resolved"—is open to question (661–62). He has no interest in further combat (643–49); he wants a battle of guile, that is, war "understood" (662). But he makes it sound as if he's open to debate. We shall see soon if that is so. In the meantime, "War then, war" is meant to give a stirring militarism to the proceedings, which is good for morale. His armies respond with enthusiasm. In an imaginative passage, the blaze of their swords, drawn from their "thighs"—one of many rather overt sexual images in Book I, such as Satan standing like a tower—illuminate Hell "far round" (664–66).

Though Mammon, "the least erected" of the devils (679), set an example in Heaven for architectural leadership, nobody gives orders here. The devils know what to do next; as they search for metals to build a city, they "rifled the bowels of their mother Earth / For treasures better hid" (687–88), and "digged out ribs of gold" (690),

---

24. Sonnet 15, "On the Lord General Fairfax, at the Siege of Colchester," *CPEP*, 152, line 10.

a passage that troublesomely anticipates the creation of Eve from Adam's "rib" (8.466–69). Milton unequivocally condemns this exploitation and materialism—"let none admire / that riches grow in hell" (1.690–91)—but we notice that Heaven has a rich pavement of "trodden gold" (682), one of many apparent contradictions that should trouble us. We notice as well that in spite of the condemnation, Milton denigrates all subsequent earthly attempts at grandeur as poor imitations of the engineering genius of Hell, just as he does with Hell's military prowess. That Pandaemonium will be built out of the fires of Hell is an allegory of evil *par excellence*: the very structures the devils (and humans) live in are hellish to the core. Yet it is impossible to read this passage (700–751) without admiration for the technical genius of Hell and the marvelous vigor that put it all together. It is a vigor that Milton praises throughout his work. The passage is full of felicities: the smelting procedures of lines 700–710, culminating in the comparison of the fabric of the building to organ music, is impressively specific. Lines 740–46 about Mulciber are justly famous for Milton's frequent *caesurae*, as well as for the two remarkable reversed first feet—"DROPPED" in line 745, and "ERRing" in 747. The first gives the effect of kinetic power, the second a snarl of cynicism as the narrator tears down his own romanticized conception of Mulciber, now harshly effaced by enjambment. Again, we may choose to see here a narrator who is manipulating and teaching the reader, or a narrator who is internally divided in his sympathies and who has a shifting sensibility, always seeking to encompass, rather than condemn or accept.

Hell, like Heaven, is a place of ceremony, and what follows is a description of the hall where the "great consult" will take place (798). Miraculously the devils are reduced to the size of "smallest dwarfs" so that they may all fit within (779), though the lords among the devils stay in their own dimensions. The book ends with two remarkable similes, juxtaposed, but not elucidated. The first, comparing the devils to bees, is a conventional one out of classical epic. It appears to present an idyllic spring scene, with vibrant activity and "fresh dews and flowers" (771). The passage brims with a pleasing sibilance, as in "Brushed with the hiss of rustling wings. As bees / In springtime, when the sun with Taurus rides" (768–69). The artful repetition of long vowels in "Pour forth their populous youth about the hive" (770) gives a richness to the impression. Fittingly, colonies of bees were associated with ideal societies in ancient epic. But what's sunny and natural in the bee simile is taken back—presto!—in the simile that compares the devils to pygmies or elves at a midnight revel, which "some belated peasant sees, / Or dreams he sees" (783–84), as if all of Pandaemonium, even all of earthly life itself were only a nightmare emanating out of superstition, a midnight carnival. These similes cannot be reconciled, just as Pandaemonium presents both a familiar world and one that is inexplicably strange, alternately joyful and fearful, like our world.

Milton characteristically elevates, then reduces. Pandaemonium begins as a mighty structure, but ends up a beehive. Mulciber is celebrated, then revealed as a fraud. What Milton inherits from the poetic tradition, he changes. What he writes, he rewrites. It is this elusive quality that David Quint has in mind when he calls Milton a revisionary writer.[25] It is not an outrageous opinion to say that the Milton of *Paradise Lost* starts his poem as a militarist, yet ends as a poet of domestic love.

25. David Quint, *Inside "Paradise Lost": Reading the Designs of Milton's Epic* (Princeton, N.J.: Princeton University Press, 2014), 199.

3

Hellish Speechifying

(BOOK 2)

Book 2 opens on a gaudy note. Satan is like an Eastern potentate sitting on his throne: literally "High," while also carrying connotations of luxury, arrogance, and despotism (1). Milton's language is tension-ridden: Satan "exalted sat" is an oxymoron of sorts; Satan is raised by "merit" to a "bad eminence," one of Milton's great phrases (5–6). The phrase that follows is likewise complex: Satan is "from despair / Thus high uplifted beyond hope" (6–7). This may mean that Satan is now hopeful where once he was despairing. But "beyond hope" suggests some intoxication of high spirits that compensates for, and is fed by, Satan's despair. Satan's first speech should be familiar (11–42): we can't be held down; Heaven is not lost; our adversity will feed our celestial virtue and make us better. (Is Satan proposing a perverse "Fortunate Fall"?) Satan then turns to what is a compulsion, his claim to power. He says he was made leader according to the "fixed laws of Heav'n" (18), that is, he believes he has divine *right*. But he was also, he says, *elected* leader in Heaven by his followers. He has achieved *merit* in battle as that elected leader. Finally, and most strangely, his leadership is cemented by the eminence he has already achieved in Hell, which makes him most vulnerable to God's punishment. In a remarkable couplet, "Where there is then no good / For which to strive, no strife can grow up there" (30–31), Satan has achieved the *ne plus ultra* of badness: he has no rivals in his wickedness. His logic is patently preposterous, but nobody contradicts him. Satan here comes off better than his followers.

The debate in Book 2 is one of the poem's greatest accomplishments, a brilliant series of impersonations. There is no better testimony to Milton's speech-writing ability than George Steiner's judgment that Milton had an almost "sensuous apprehension of the tone of politics in high places" (or, less exaltedly, in any bureaucratic meeting).[1] Moloch speaks first in the debate, and rightly so, for his speech is the simplest, the most urgent. The language that introduces him is harsh and military, like Moloch himself. Lines 46–50 march in a stark rhythm. As is commonly the case with Milton, repetitions adorn this passage: the *l* words (eterna*l*, *l*ess, a*ll*, *l*ost), and the near-rhymes of Hell, less, lost, and worse.

> His trust was with th' Eternal to be deemed
> Equal in strength, and rather than be less
> Cared not to be at all; with that care lost
> Went all his fear: of God, or Hell, or worse
> He reck'd not (2.46–50)

Moloch is an army "lifer." His solutions are all military because he doesn't know of any others; he likes to fight wars for their own sake. His "sentence is for open war" (51) because he's an open, if vacuous, creature. He has no patience with guile. He characterizes his followers as "Millions that stand in arms" (55), that is, ready to do battle again, though it soon becomes apparent that his solution is the least popular and that nobody wishes to stand with him. His root claim is that nothing is "worse" than the indignity of Hell and of losing (85). This hatred of losing deludes him into thinking that losing runs contrary to the devils' nature, and that re-ascending to Heaven and winning is natural to them. But underneath that, his real argument is that Hell

1. George Steiner, *The Death of Tragedy* (New York: Hill and Wang, 1961), 61.

is unbearable and that anything—even being totally destroyed by God—is better. Moloch gives away his ruling passion, and the contradictory nature of his speech emerges when he concludes that spending the rest of eternity fighting Heaven—"with perpetual inroads to alarm"—without any prospect of victory is good enough (103). This, we see, doesn't square with his earlier stated belief that the ascent to Heaven would be easy. His "Heaven," it turns out, is perpetual fighting, an eternal means to no end. His speech ends abruptly because he has nothing more to say.

Belial is a perfect foil to him. Belial's speech is one of the greatest in *Paradise Lost*. It is quite long, twice the length of Moloch's. It is not simply an utterance. It has a life of its own; it breathes. It's the speech of what we would call an intellectual, who knows, despite his "peers" (119), that he is smarter than anyone else present. It is full of derisive, clever humor, but it also has splendor: we notice the highly Latinate vocabulary: "dissuade," "persuade," "ominous conjecture." His lines,

> the Tow'rs of Heav'n are filled
> With armèd watch, that render all access
> Impregnable (2.129–31)

are sublime and sublimely true, whatever their evil origins. The speech epitomizes Milton's practice of making poetic hills and valleys: it starts slowly, then surges, then subsides. Belial's position is that renewed war is dangerous and futile, and that it's desirable for the devils to accept their lot in Hell. Playing off Moloch's "What can be *worse* / Than to dwell here?" (85–86), Belial imagines a conflagration of God's vengeance that would be much *worse*. In putting down Moloch's stance, Belial nearly argues from God's own heights, which is the counterpart to his sense of intellectual superiority. Some think that Belial is Milton's voice, or at least a voice to which Milton is sympathetic, evinced by Belial's superior manner, but also his ostensibly reasonable logic. In making Belial sympathetic, Milton risks subverting his project of justifying God and condemning Satan. So Milton must put him down. But is the put-down convincing?

Fish is partially persuasive when he argues that Belial's speech is *not* reasonable, mainly because it is inconsistent.[2] Out of one side of his mouth, Belial argues that he doesn't want to lose his intellectual being, while out of the other, he posits that Hell can become tolerable to the devils by making them too numb to feel its flames. Belial's speech contains an even more fundamental contradiction that exposes his unreasoning fear. Belial initially holds that God wishes to "punish endless" (158–59) the angels, yet he eventually suggests that God may in time "much remit" his anger (210–11)! Belial will say anything to win over his audience to inaction, to an eternity of conversing. Fish claims that Milton lures us into sympathy with Belial, only to show that Belial is wrong; this makes Milton out to be a tricky preacher, not truly sympathetic to the devil's cause. Nevertheless, Belial's speech is exhilarating, and Milton, as a revolutionary and as a man who thought he was a lot smarter than his peers, could certainly have regarded it just as he distrusted it. It should be observed as well that Milton was dubious of exclusively military solutions to political problems, and would have found Belial's anti-militarism in some degree sympathetic. There is a lot of John Milton in Belial.

Mammon's speech almost wins the day. It certainly gets an enthusiastic reception (284–90), which a truly strange simile compares to the hum of hollow rocks in a bay harboring a ship. Why does Mammon get this response? Because he understands, *contra* Moloch, that the fallen angels don't want to do any more fighting. He also intuits that they don't find especially appealing Belial's promise that Hell could be an eternal graduate school seminar. Mammon turns what is a negative in Moloch and Belial into a positive. Hell isn't a bad destiny but a promising opportunity! Heaven is boring: a place—in Mammon's brilliant phrasing—of "Forced halleluiahs" (243) and of "splendid vassalage" (252). Mammon may be oblivious of the irony in the latter phrase, but his speech is catchy, and he has picked up Satan's

2. Stanley Fish, *Surprised by Sin: The Reader in "Paradise Lost"* (Berkeley: University of California Press, 1971), 15–17.

habit of turning bad news into good and moral loss into political gain. Here in Hell, he says, we shall prefer

> Hard liberty before the easy yoke
> Of servile pomp. Our greatness will appear
> Then most conspicuous, when great things of small,
> Useful of hurtful, prosperous of adverse
> We can create (2.256–60)

The balanced phrases—"great things of small / Useful of hurtful, prosperous of adverse"—carry Mammon's assertion: the industrious life, even in Hell, makes sense. The poem will eventually revise this language to invoke the good life—

>   by small
> Accomplishing great things, by things deemed weak
> Subverting worldly strong, and worldly wise
> By simply meek (12.566–69)

—suggesting a striking interconnection of apparent opposites in *Paradise Lost*. For Mammon, Heaven is (and was) only a place of "Magnificence," and magnificence can be created in Hell (2.273). Even so, refuting Belial and Moloch as offering unrealistic hope, Mammon nevertheless does repeat their sentimentalities when he claims that Hell could be a superior version of Heaven. (Does God speak out of thick clouds and darkness? Hell has those things too!) He says as well that the fallen angels can acclimatize themselves to its brutal temperatures. It is up to the next speaker, Beelzebub, to disabuse every one of such hopes.

Beelzebub is described as a building, with a face constructed to make what today we would call an "image" of power. He seems a "pillar of state" (302). Deliberation is "engraven" (302) on his front, along with "public care" (303). As with Satan earlier, he is seen from the outside, again suggesting his attempt at image-making. He enters the debate because things are getting out of hand, and he needs to set things on their proper course, as dictated by Satan (see lines 378–86). His opening lines, in which he refers to the fallen angels as "imperial

Powers" and "offspring of Heav'n" (310), speak to them as warriors and realists. The other speakers have been skirting the truth, whereas Beelzebub sees loss as "Irreparable" (331). We are doomed forever, he says, to God's jail. There can be no peace, and no war. But there is one possible course of action. There is terrorism, which is what one carries on against a country that one can't defeat and with whom one cannot be at peace. Heaven is lost, but God's new rumored created race, called "Man," located in another world, can be the target of revenge (348). Nothing will be gained but the interruption of God's joy, yet that is enough, and it is certainly better than, in Beelzebub's witty phrasing, "to sit in darkness here / Hatching vain empires" (377–78). The scheme is submitted to the assembly and approved unanimously. The venture appeals because it recaptures the warmth of glory for the devils, and costs them nothing. Given the options, it makes sense.

Having won the vote, Beelzebub describes the mission out of Hell through Chaos. His phrase "the palpable obscure" (406) is remarkable as an oxymoron. Beelzebub piles it on, describing a perilous journey that no rational being would undertake—and we notice that by describing the proposed journey in the third person singular he is already ruling out a commando group raid. As we could have predicted, Satan accepts this mission, making it look as if the task chooses him, and he obsessively and cleverly ties his acceptance into his assumption of royalty. Much of Satan's language ("imperial sovereignty," "splendor," "power," "royalties," "reign") has to do with kingship (446–51), lending credence to those readers who have seen Satan as a stand-in, not for Milton the revolutionary, but for Charles I. It becomes clear that Satan wants to leave Hell because staying in any one place bores him, but there is also a desperate impulse on his part to reach for some residue of power. How can I reign, he reasons, if I refuse to go on this mission? Satan knows that his followers don't want to fight. He calculates that if he offers to do the work of battle, his followers will grant him kingship as a precondition. The narrator is conscious of the ironies. Satan's followers fear Satan the way one might fear God—or perhaps the Son of God, since Satan is about to make a self-sacrifice in journeying to another world. This is a relief for the fallen angels. Their relief is figured in a lyrical excursion into the pastoral, depicting the sudden and welcome emergence of the sun in a stormy summer landscape. It is a passage that is rather refreshing and not in itself problematical, but that serves to naturalize the underworld, drawing it into relation with our own (488–95).

The similarity of the underworld to our world is one of the implicit themes of Books 1 and 2, and never so much as in the passage that tells of the activities of Hell while Satan is gone (506–629). Hell, we have already learned, has music, architecture, building, politics, pageantry, and ceremonies. Now we learn of choral societies, athletic competitions, war games, a school of philosophy, exploration, and so forth. Hell is an image of our own world (an idea that wasn't unfamiliar in Milton's time among Christian radicals)[3] and that world is epitomized in the passage that follows Satan's election as the devils' redeemer. There, we are told how the devils pass "the irksome hours" until Satan's return (527). "Irksome" tells everything. Punishment, as observed earlier, isn't so much physical as it is psychological, and that punishment isn't so much one of horror as of a modernistic *ennui*. In Milton's Hell, the devils are required to make choices, all of them sad. It is a place where they seek "sweet forgetfulness" (608), not from physical torment, but from their fall from grace. Hell is a metaphor for a world of separation from God and righteousness. That makes it our world. It is a place of "restless thoughts" (526). The Great Debate was part of that Hell because throughout it, whatever was argued, everyone missed the point—rather like the philosophers of Hell, who despite their mastery of the traditional arguments concerning "providence, foreknowledge, will and fate" (559), are lost "in wand'ring mazes" (561). "Wand'ring" (12.648) is the last thing we see Adam and Eve do as they leave the Garden to come to our world. Their situation is not unlike that of the fallen angels, different though they are.

3. Christopher Hill, *Milton and the English Revolution* (London, Penguin, 1977), 75.

It is true that Milton's Hell also contains some of the traditional hellish features of Dante's Hell (e.g., 570–629). But for all of its insistence on the physical horrors of Hell, from Gorgons to raging fire, to ice beds, to prodigious monsters, to the stunning monosyllabic catalog of "rocks, cave, lakes, fens, bogs, dens, and shades of death" (621), there is something unconvincing in the generality of Milton's physical Hell, as opposed to the specificity of Dante's. We have already witnessed in Books 1 and 2 the psychological aspect of Hell: its half-lunacy, the obsessions of its central characters, the horrific and unsurpassable guilt of losing Heaven. Reading Milton's description, we feel that he is insisting too much, such as when he writes "bitter change / Of fierce extremes, extremes by change more fierce" (598–99), which is a half-chiasmus that doesn't enhance, just as "dark and dreary vale" is an uninspired alliteration (618). "Where all life dies, death lives" is a shrewd inversion (624), but the following lines

> all monstrous, all prodigious things
> Abominable, inutterable, and worse
> Than fables yet have feigned, or fear conceived (2.625–27)

are telling versus showing. Repetition alone can't convince. In the interest of inclusiveness, Milton is trying to enclose a traditional Hell inside his rather more original Hell, but it doesn't scare us. And the speed with which, after the description, he moves on to the next segment of the book is telling.

Satan, in a famous simile, is next seen from a distance, "As when far off at sea a fleet descried / Hangs in the clouds" (636–37), a comparison that William Wordsworth thought a stunning example of the power of Milton's imagination: his ability to see things from unusual and sublime perspectives and to reduce the many to the one.[4] The imagery and the names of places along the Indian Ocean ("The Ethiopian"), as well as merchants and spicy drugs, give a fresh and exotic air to the poem, but be suspicious when Milton lulls us with

---

4. William Wordsworth, "Preface of 1815," in *The Prose Works of William Wordsworth*, edited by W. J. B. Owen and Jane Worthington Smyser (Oxford: Oxford University Press, 1973), 3:31.

the promise of such escape (636–44). The "spicy drugs" (640) may be equated with mortality itself, which the second line of *Paradise Lost* tells us was "brought" into the world by a merchant of death, that is, with "man's first disobedience" (1.1–3). Such indirection is altogether typical of Milton.

The Sin and Death scene (2.648–884) is not, surely, to every reader's taste. Contemporary students tend to find it strange after the realism of the narrative thus far. It was condemned by Joseph Addison, who in most respects appreciated Milton's epic art. He thought the episode detracted from the poem's dignity; there was no precedent for such grotesqueries in ancient epic.[5] (Addison also didn't like Milton's wordplay, or his display of learning.)[6] There is nothing like the episode prior to it, though we have seen Milton's subtle humor in the flatulence passage (1.230–37), and in the way he quietly satirizes the fallen angels by making them utter preposterous sentiments even while they swagger heroically (2.221–41). But that may be the point. Nothing here has really changed. Nobody who reads *Paradise Lost* should miss Joseph Summers's sardonic account of this episode.[7] For Summers, the Sin and Death episode is simply an exaggerated version of what we have seen heretofore in the poem: a constant invitation to entertain epic majesty that is then undercut by the grotesque and ridiculous nature and behavior of the characters, the comedy of "the ceremonious tone and the appalling content."[8] The plot of the episode is full of such incongruities: Satan's high-toned, snobbish dismissal of Death as "hell-born" (2.687), Death's condemnatory rebuttal, as if he were qualified to sit in judgment of Satan's rebellion, and the promise of an imminent apocalyptic battle between them—a battle that is made absurd by the sudden intrusion of Sin, the wife of Satan and mother of his rapacious, rapist son, Death. Also incongruous is Sin's long pious

5. Joseph Addison, "Addison's Papers on *Paradise Lost*," 1712, reprinted in *Milton: The Critical Heritage*, ed. John Shawcross (London: Routledge and Kegan Paul, 1970), 212.
6. Ibid., 158–62.
7. Joseph Summers, *The Muse's Method* (London: Chatto and Windus, 1962), 46–54.
8. Ibid., 49.

narrative of her birth, life, and betrayal. So is Satan's subsequent and hilarious pseudo-gallant reference to Death as "the dear pledge / Of dalliance had with thee in Heav'n" (818–19), and his pompous promise to be the providential father to them, giving them a new world in which to dwell. A final irony is Sin's affirmation (rather like the Apostle's Creed) of Satan as her provider and husband, and her consent to open the doors leading out to Chaos and to Earth.

At the same time that this scene amuses us, it draws us in. It is an allegory, of course: Sin comes from Satan's head. In narcissistic love, Satan has sex with Sin (who is Satan's image, and therefore Satan makes love to himself) and out of Sin comes Death, in that our sin led to God's sentence of death. Death rapes Sin in the same way that consciousness of death leads to desperation and hence to more sinning, which can be equated to the howling monsters that devour their mother daily.[9] The rough outlines of an allegory are there (underlined by an allusion to Spenser's *Faerie Queene*, I.i.14–15), but as several readers have observed, the allegory is not neat. Satan himself is not allegorical, and the encounter of Satan, Sin, and Death is probably not either. Moreover, militating against an allegorical reading, the story of Sin's exploitation, rape, and agony is affecting in a strange way. We find it hard to think of Sin as merely "sin," that is, an abstraction of evil. Sin sounds like a suffering human being, due some sympathy. These incongruities, Summers convincingly argues, are deliberate confusions, part of Milton's constant practice of forestalling either/or thinking, encouraging us to resist dualisms while reading the poem.[10] Sin is a pathetic victim, but she is a faithful spouse and ally to Satan; as such, she is a force of evil. Death is an idiotic monster, a pious son, and a formidable epic force, a Homeric Titan. The story is part allegorical, part realistic. We must respond as human beings, and yet our response is partly literary. This confusion isn't Milton's failure, but his "rejoicing."[11] Milton's

9. F. T. Prince, ed., *Milton's "Paradise Lost" Books I & II* (Oxford: Oxford University Press, 1962), 165–66.

10. Summers, *The Muse's Method*, 41.

11. Ibid., 40.

most outrageous linking is that of Sin and Eve. When Sin opens the door out of Hell (864), she sounds like Eve when Eve disobeys God. In Book 9, Eve's action is a fall that precedes the Fall. The passages are joined by their marvelous suspended verbs. Here are the lines from Sin: "Thus saying, from her side the fatal key, / Sad instrument of all our woe, *she took*" (871–72, my italics). And from Eve: "So saying, her rash hand in evil hour / Forth reaching to the fruit, she plucked, *she ate*" (9.780–81, my italics).

The gate of Hell opens wide. In a scene that is *echt* Milton, Satan, Sin, and Death stare out into the abyss. Notice that Milton rarely simply transports a character from one place to another. He moves slowly, always careful to offer us, through the character, a perspective. Milton's characters typically preview, then see, then encounter experience. They don't simply go to their destinations. The repetition of the phrase "into this wild abyss" (910, 917) enacts Satan's pause before he commits himself to flight. What Satan sees is Chaos, the apparently boundless space out of which God created the universe, and Hell, which lies below the universe. The passage depicting Satan's flight is full of Miltonic complication. Satan is buffeted by the air; he is at its mercy. Clearly he doesn't know what he's gotten himself into. And yet, in the middle of this hubbub, he is "undaunted" (955). He may be obliged to obey the elements, but he endures. He comes strangely close to being a Miltonic passive hero, who waits on the powers above—like Jesus in *Paradise Regained*, and like the angel Abdiel in *Paradise Lost* (see 5.896–903), who alone heroically resists the pressures of the bad angels before the War in Heaven.

Paradise Lost is a book of meetings. The last meeting in Book 2 is Satan's encounter with Chaos and with other "Powers / And Spirits of this nethermost abyss" (968–69). Satan requests a way to some part of Chaos that is close to Heaven. The speech is not remarkable in itself, except insofar as there is humor in Satan's swift mastery of a diplomatic tone, which Satan had to learn in his encounter with Death. He reveals himself an insincere statesman, offering Chaos a piece of his former empire back, an empire that was reduced by the creation of Earth. Chaos speaks mournfully of "That little which is left so to defend" (1000), which, considering the boundless dimension of Chaos, is hilarious and meant by Milton to be so. Chaos's speech, *caesurae*-ridden, full of senectitude and weariness, comes to life only with the phrase "Confusion worse confounded" (996). Satan sees Chaos as a self-pitying, traditionalist fool. Quickly, he gets the directions he wants and departs without either thanks or goodbye. Milton, having populated the most unruly part of his poem's geography with personified powers, promptly, like Satan, forgets them.

Next, Satan is compared to Ulysses (1019–20), which is suitable because Ulysses was notorious for his deceit. More broadly, Satan is compared to a mariner, a metaphor that begins in the Indian Ocean passage (636–43) and is carried through the poem until the Fall (see 9.513–15). Satan's flight into the confines of the universe is one of the great stylistic triumphs of the poem (2.1014–55). The passage offers a sense of exhilaration that comes from the experience of new vistas and privileged insight. It is elegant too, so much so that it leaves us to wonder if Milton is offering us a brief respite from the weight of his moral condemnation. There are innumerable felicities, including the deft alliteration in "God and good angels guard by special grace" (1033). This line has an attractive off-balance meter which is trochaic and top heavy—"GOD and GOOD ANGels GUARD by SPECial GRACE"—and that offers a near-rhyme along with its alliteration: *God, Good, Guard*. In reference to the light of Heaven, there is the explosive "Shoots" (1036) and the way it plays off the soft "glimmering dawn" in the next line. In 1040–41 there is the repetition of "less" until just that point when it threatens to cloy, and then it disappears and the line can relax, just as Satan now can relax from his toil. The entire passage is a congress of *w* sounds from "*w*ith" to "*w*aft" to "*w*eather" to "*w*aste" to "*w*ay" to "*w*ings" to "*w*ide." Satan is now free to survey God's world with its gorgeous "opal towers" and "battlements adorned / Of living sapphire" (1049–50). Finally, gloriously, there is

"This pendant world, in bigness as a star / Of smallest magnitude close by the moon" (1052–53). But just as we are about to swoon, Milton changes perspective, and we are stringently reminded of Satan's destructive mission:

> Thither full fraught with mischievous revenge,
> Accurst, and in a cursèd hour he hies. (2.1054–55)

The last word obtains its power by releasing energy that is built up in the words that precede it. Milton tantalizes with "thither," and then pours out participles ("fraught," "accursed," cursèd") as he holds off his verb, and then hits the reader with the present tense: "hies." "Hies" reminds the reader, in a poem full of adjectives and participles, that *Paradise Lost* is about actions.

4

Heaven to Earth

(BOOK 3)

Book 3 is not many readers' favorite book. But why is that? Granted, it is not as exciting as Books 1 and 2, but it starts with an invocation that contains some of Milton's most affecting poetry. The Dialogue in Heaven (as it is known) that follows, in addition to its genuine poetry, presents an epitome of the major themes of *Paradise Lost*. The travel narrative that concludes Book 3 gives a surprising look into Milton's sensibility, a sensibility that runs contrary to the stereotype of him as a primarily moral and theological poet. Overall, Book 3 is regarded as mainly doctrinal, but it is more.

The book starts out on an intellectual note, pondering the origin of light (1–12). Did it come after Heaven in time, an "offspring" of Heaven? Or was light co-eternal with Heaven, "Bright effluence of bright essence increate" (6)? Or is light simply a "pure ethereal stream" (7), whose source is unknown? Milton raises these questions, giving his poem a stamp of theological learning, but then he dismisses them. The important thing, he says, is that light came before the creation of Earth and the universe, and was used by God to create them. It is altogether typical of Milton, in his poetry at least, to simplify any theological or philosophical dilemmas he raises, while making the human ones more complex than they at first appear.

In the invocation (1–55), the poet speaks of himself as a blind man suffering the burden of God's yoke. But he also implicitly compares himself to Satan. How so? He rises and returns to the world of God, just as Satan is only now flying into the purlieus of the creation. Like Satan, the narrator has "Escaped the Stygian pool" (14). We understand that he is talking about the imaginative trip that he had to take to Hell to write the first two books, yet still the connection to Satan is there. He sees himself, like Satan, as a wanderer and an exile. He was "detained" like Satan (14), which suggests he was for a time held in Hell as if jailed (as Milton was in 1660). His blind eyes "roll in vain" (23), as Satan in Book 1 was seen "rolling in the fiery gulf" (1.52). Like Satan, he thinks about his repute. Both he and the villain of the poem are exiles. Both have a "complaint"; both have been wronged. Both, in their own way, speak great poetry.

> Thus with the year
> Seasons return, but not to me returns
> Day, or the sweet approach of ev'n or morn,
> Or sight of vernal bloom, or summer's rose,
> Or flocks, or herds, or human face divine;
> But cloud instead, and ever-during dark
> Surrounds me, from the cheerful ways of men
> Cut off, and for the book of knowledge fair
> Presented with a universal blank
> Of Nature's works to me expunged and razed,
> And wisdom at one entrance quite shut out. (3.40–50)

The narrator rises from Hell, but he also presents himself, again like Satan, as having fallen from his "Heav'n," that is, Earth, and the visible changing seasons and the changing times of day. All of these things have enchanted him, in what was his normal life, when he was not blind and walked "among the cheerful ways of men"—ways that still go on, without him. When Lewis speaks of the "Satan in Milton" and when he says that "we have all skirted the Satanic island," and broadens the conception of Satan to include us all, he must have been thinking about this passage, among others.[1] In Book 1, Milton linked his attempt at epic to Satan's "attempt" on Heaven. Here he worries that his own darkness is God's punishment, and he is only an inch away from saying that it is unjust, a notion he also flirted with in his sonnet on his blindness: "Doth God exact day labor, light denied?"[2] Those like Blake who say that Milton was an unconscious antagonist of God may take encouragement from this passage. But there remains the strong possibility that Milton did know he was potentially of the devil's party. He could see it in his own work.

The entire proem to Book 3 that follows is highly original in its personal lament, without precedent in ancient epic. It contains memorable turns of phrasing. "Day" comes stressed at the beginning of line 42, when the context would call for a season—"Seasons return, but not to me returns / *Fall*" (41–42). I am not merely missing a season, the narrator insists, but a thing as basic as *day*. In 1775, Thomas Sheridan marveled at the suspension enacted by the enjambment "returns / Day"—the line

stops you unexpectedly and strikes the imagination with the immensity of his loss. He can no more see—what?—Day!—Day and all its glories rush into the mind.[3]

He longs for the "sweet approach" of evening or morning (42), where another poet would have simply said that he misses night or day.[4] This is a difference that matters, for Milton never misses a chance to celebrate natural process. The word "obscure" (see "obscure sojourn," 15) connects, in its oppositional semantic meaning, with "renown" (34), reminding us that Milton wishes to serve God but also to gain a reputation, and not an infamous one, doing so. When he says he visits Zion "nightly" (32), we understand that he speaks of drawing noc-

1. Lewis, *A Preface to "Paradise Lost,"* 101, 103.
2. Sonnet 19, *CPEP* 157, line 7.
3. Thomas Sheridan, *Lectures on the Art of Reading*, Part II: *The Art of Reading Verse* (London, 1775), 246–47.
4. Christopher Ricks, *Milton's Grand Style* (Oxford: Clarendon Press, 1963), 42.

turnally and regularly upon Hebrew poetry and scripture, but also that he draws something out of his darkness that fosters him. He will "Sing[s] darkling" (39). He will sing a "nocturnal note" and make poetry out of darkness if he has God's help and the celestial light that he hopes will "Shine inward" (40, 52). He may, like Satan, be "shut out" (50), but, like God, he will endeavor to see what others cannot see. "Cheerful ways of men" is an arresting phrase considering that Milton writes in part to lament the loss of Eden (46). Are we cheerful now in spite of that Fall? Apparently we are. Are these "ways" meant to chime with the phrase "justify the ways of God to men" (1.26) from the poem's beginning invocation?

God makes his appearance now, and we encounter other revealing phrases. As God looks down on Adam and Eve (3.64–69), they are the "only two" (65): a *one-ly* two, a unit. We see that their love is "unrivalled" and that they are placed by God in "blissful solitude" (68–69). They are not yet in a society; their love is not rivaled by children, or others. But solitude also means away from God. It is as if they are on their honeymoon, but there is also something of long-term importance: God is not a puppet master, Milton asserts in *Areopagitica*. One gift Adam and Eve have is that they are not (yet) dependent on God, but, at least before the Fall, dependent only on each other. They are close to being autonomous. The poem does not quite insist on this condition, but it comes up again in the Dialogue itself.

God sees Satan heading toward Earth. He acknowledges that Satan cannot be held by bonds. It is a curious concession, for in Book 1 we learned that God *allowed* Satan to rise up from the lake. In an exposition of the theology of the poem, God goes on to predict the following: that man will fall, though he was—in a key phrase—"sufficient to have stood" (3.99); that the Fall is man's fault, not God's; that he made man free to disobey so that man wouldn't merely serve necessity; that his foreknowledge of man's fall isn't the same as his willing that fall; that once he ordained man's freedom, he could not turn around and change his own high decree; that because man is tempted by another—Satan—man will find grace; Satan, self-tempted, none. "But mercy first and last shall brightest shine" (134)—"Not only last, but first," as Robert Frost underlined.[5] God's speaking hardly has the panache of Satan's (or the narrator's) speech, but he is not by any means dull (see Chaos for that!); if anything, he is imposing, even pushy.

The Son "responds" to God by seeking to correct God or, alternatively, to speak God's other side, his merciful side. The dialogue between them is strangely like that between Satan and Beelzebub in Book 1 in that both speak the same thing while emphasizing different aspects of it and adopting a different tone. The Son is not quite God's equal, though God is expressed through him. But the distinction is blurry. The Son sounds as if he is criticizing God when he asks God plangently if Adam and Eve shall be damned. But then just as quickly he tells God that such an act would be against God's nature: "That be from thee far, / That far be from thee" (153–54). Yet only a few lines later, he admonishes God toward right doing (165–66).

God's response (169–216) makes it clear he's in something of an unavoidable partnership with the Son: "All hast thou spoken as my thoughts are" (169–70). Man will receive grace and be renewed, but for now he will be upheld by God; he will know the frailty of his position and know how much he owes God. Milton departs from Calvinism, which dictated that man's salvation was predetermined. It is true that God declares that some are elected by "peculiar grace" to salvation (183–85), but his position is Arminian and liberal: The rest of mankind may attain salvation by "prayer, repentance, and obedience" (191), and *all* shall have within them a conscience placed there by God. Only those who turn away from God will be excluded from mercy. But still, man is disobedient in eating the apple and he must die, and all of his progeny must die as well—or justice must die, unless

5. Robert Frost, "A Masque of Mercy," in *The Poetry of Robert Frost: The Collected Poems, Complete and Unabridged*, ed. Edward Connery Lathem (New York: Henry Holt, 1979), 493–524.

someone can "pay / The rigid satisfaction, death for death" (211–12). We must keep in mind that the price is not only death, but the ruin of history and the futility of human aspirations: "all our woe." We may feel that the deal is unfair; sometimes Milton does, too.

Someone in Heaven must come forth. But, astonishingly, not one of the entire angelic multitude does: "*silence was in Heav'n*" (3.218, my italics). The line verges on the sardonic. The silence is deafening, and the parallel to what happened in Hell is troubling (see 2.417–29). Is Heaven more like Earth than what we imagined? Even if one answers this troubling question by positing that the Son must, after all, give up something of enormous value in order to be a hero, something beyond even the reach of angels—even so, there is trouble. Can there be cowardice in Heaven? But before the matter can come to a head, the Son advances and offers his life for man's. He will give up his privileged status to do so. He then expresses faith (or is it certainty?) that he will rise to Heaven after death, though he will be "long absent" (261). It is difficult to tell what the Son knows in this scene. Milton was an Arian, or, if not one, at least was a person who believed that the Son was subordinate to God. If we believe that the Son in *Paradise Lost* is equal to God, then his sacrifice doesn't carry as much weight as it would if he went into it not quite knowing what his fate will be, but trusting that he would be taken back to Heaven by God.

The latter, I believe, is the case: the Son knows less than God. When he says he will rise again, it is hard to know if he refers to the Resurrection, which happened three days after his death, or to the Last Judgment, which was to occur at the end of time ("long absent"). The Son is uncertain about Christian doctrine, though strong in faith. God praises him, and significantly says that "man, as is most just, / Shall satisfy for man" (294–95). This is the second reference to God the Son as "man," the first occurring in the opening lines of the poem—"one greater man" (1.4). But God also proclaims that the Son will not degrade his own nature in assuming human form, and he adds that the Son is "Equal to God," affirming a rather more Trinitarian and traditional view of the Son (3.306). The matter is complicated! In his *Christian Doctrine*, Milton affirms that the Father is greater than the Son, but this document was not published in Milton's lifetime, and it is likely that in *Paradise Lost* Milton made the matter less certainly Arian-sounding and even orthodox-sounding in some places because he didn't want to distract the pious. Arianism for Milton's readers would have been heresy. Milton wanted readers. But for the most part, we are given the impression that God is somehow superior to the Son. Regardless, the Son renounces Glory for Love. He puts down his higher nature, whatever that is. He is in this respect unlike the self-aggrandizing, glory-seeking Satan. If the Son is great, it is not because of his birthright, but because of his merit (309–10). He is exalted by his humiliation, which he chooses to endure. God then offers praise to the Son, crowns him highest in Heaven (below God), quietly corrects his account of the Last Judgment (pointing out that the Son will initiate that event after he has returned from Earth to Heaven), and announces the eventual closing up of Hell. Finally, he proclaims for the future the dissolution of hierarchy in Heaven, as God will become "all in all" (340–41), an allusion to 1 Corinthians 15:28 that has endeared Milton to radicals and egalitarians. A celebration of the Son follows.

The presentation of God is one of the two most controversial issues of *Paradise Lost*. While there are many readers who find Milton's God an acceptable figure, both in his presentation and in the theology he espouses, there is probably an equal number who wish Milton had not chosen to present God at all, either because presenting God is inevitably awkward or because this God's theology is objectionable or even indefensible. What is at issue? Those who, with Blake, believe that Milton was of the devil's party argue at least one of several things: God as presented in *Paradise Lost* is petty and tyrannical. He is like a king. He is as jealous of his power as Satan is. His "deal" for man is unfair. He knows the Fall will happen and yet insists, falsely, that he had nothing to do with its happening. He doesn't equip man for the Fall (Adam and Eve are no match for Satan), and then blames them when it happens. His punishment for the Fall is cruel and unusual, out of proportion to the transgression. God is cold and uncaring. Some of these readers, like William Empson, a non-Christian, see the poem as precisely the opposite of what it intends. It isn't a defense of God but an indictment of him, whatever Milton set out to do. "The reason why the poem is so good is that it makes God so bad," says Empson, reaching back to the liberal Romantic reactions of Shelley and Blake.[6] There are other charges. Lewis contends that God (whose case is otherwise a good one) shouldn't be made to sound so human.[7] He shouldn't be made to argue his case. Milton made a mistake in putting a face on God, something that Dante never tried, because it would expose his narrative to so many absurdities. God should have been "made sufficiently awful, mysterious, and vague."[8] For some readers, God simply protests too much. He is too much like his own lawyer— which is what the narrator ought to be!

In considering a defense of Milton's God, it is probably best to follow the advice suggested in Denis Danielson's *Milton's Good God*, that Milton presents only part of God's "truth" in Book 3: his legal side.[9] We see a rather bossy God here and a defensive one, but soon, when we are witness to his creation of the world or his two primary beings (Adam and Eve)—that is, when we see his goodness in action and deed—we will feel differently. This "revision" of God's harsh side begins with the Son's insistence on mercy shown to man—that is, in soft language opposing his "good cop" nature to God's "bad cop." The entire poem works that way, luring you into one position, then making you modify it as you find out more.

With respect to the presentation of God, Milton would probably have found strange the objection that his God is too cold and isn't fully human. Milton wanted God to be more than a doctrine, as is

6. William Empson, *Milton's God* (London: Chatto and Windus, 1965), 13.

7. Lewis, *A Preface to "Paradise Lost,"* 130–31.

8. Ibid., 130.

9. Denis Danielson, *Milton's Good God: A Study in Literary Theodicy* (Cambridge: Cambridge University Press, 1982), 107.

revealed in places when God speaks with emotion, such as referring to Adam as an "ingrate" (97), or when he continuously refers to his "Son" in an affectionate, proud, possessive way that serves to humanize him. Milton's instinct generally is to humanize and to see the human as the paradigm of all things. He could have made God entirely "other," that is, something like a flashing or quivering light show that we might idolize. "Dark with excessive bright thy skirts appear," writes Milton (3.380), and Lewis seizes upon this lovely line (sung by the angels) as setting a standard by which God should be presented; when we read it, we are "silenced,"[10] meaning we accept God and his doctrine and authority as he presents it. Lewis argues that the flavor of Olympus weakens Milton's presentation of God. To which we might reply: possibly, yes, in that his God is humanized, as Milton felt he must be, but Milton's God is not a power beneath fate. Neither is he above fate or the law. Milton wants to ensure that his readers will not see God as Charles I, or as an autocrat arguing that whatever the president does becomes the law, whatever the law might be. Milton's God makes the laws, but then he puts himself on an equal footing with those laws. He is a lawgiver and, given those laws, a constitutional monarch: a thinking monarch. Michael Bryson asserts that Milton's God is presented as a king as imagined by some in Milton's day.[11] But for me, Milton's God does not simply *declare* divine privilege. He thinks he must make his case in court.

Once God has made his laws, he does not feel at liberty to modify them, as he argues he cannot revoke the "decree / Unchangeable" by which he made Adam and Eve free (126–27). This fixity comes up again after the Fall, in Book 11, lines 48–49. God assures the Son that he can't go back on his plan to expel Adam and Eve from Paradise, because he has already dictated that Paradise's element remains pure and Adam and Eve are no longer chemically pure. The key line is "The law I gave to nature him forbids" (11.49). God can't go back on his

10. Lewis, *A Preface to "Paradise Lost,"* 130.
11. Michael Bryson, *The Tyranny of Heaven: Milton's Rejection of God as King* (Newark: University of Delaware Press, 2004), 11–12.

decrees, such as the decree that Adam and Eve must leave the Garden. God isn't an absolute potentate. One ventures to say that Milton's God, if he has ruled absolutely, is weary of absolute rule. Early in Book 10, after the Fall, God tells the Son that "to thee I have transferred / All judgment" (10.56–57), as if he were seeking retirement. Whatever God's official position about his own power is, by arguing his own case, he leaves Heaven and enters our world of law, proof, and argument.

God's claim that foreknowledge is not foreordination looks like question-begging to us; to Milton, it was a reasonable position that could be argued. To turn God into a mere spectacle, without the power to reason or speak and to defend, would be to foster in the reader an unquestioning attitude. Milton expects the reader to embrace reasoning as a value, even if the reader does not accept God's reasoning. As *Areopagitica* argues, "A man may be a heretic in the truth" if he simply takes everything on faith, even if that faith is "true."[12] This semi-constitutional God I have presented, whatever his deficiencies, is a far cry from Christine Froula's God of *Paradise Lost*, who is mysterious, distant, and decidedly male, an invisible oppressor. Froula's God argues nothing and keeps himself hidden. This God will later, after the Fall, become the spiritual (and male) authority of the church that Milton rejected.[13]

After the plangent humanity and concreteness of the introduction to Book 3, the dialogue strikes many readers as dull, a mere piece of the poem's "business," a place where it unloads its doctrine. Many readers have found the calm, rational guidance of this moment disappointing. It is true that the dialogue hasn't the colorful, dynamic, kaleidoscopic mode of Books 1 and 2, yet it is capable of moving us. Here I must take issue with W. H. Auden's assertion that

12. *Areopagitica, CPEP*, 952.
13. Christine Froula, "When Eve Reads Milton: Undoing the Canonical Economy," *Critical Inquiry* 10, no. 2 (December 1983): 321–47.

The most obvious characteristic of [Milton's] style is its uninterrupted grandeur, which is incapable of any lighter tone, and the number of themes to which such a grand style is suited is strictly limited.[14]

Indeed, various styles *within* the grand style can be found. God, as you might expect, has grandeur. Listen to this long arc of sound in God's speech, so long that it contains both Satan's crime and his punishment:

> Only begotten Son, seest thou what rage
> Transports our Adversary, whom no bounds
> Prescribed, no bars of Hell, nor all the chains
> Heaped on him there, nor yet the main abyss
> Wide interrupt can hold; so bent he seems
> On desperate revenge, that shall redound
> Upon his own rebellious head. (3.80–86)

If God sounds like a magistrate here, a few lines later he sounds like an enraged dockworker: "whose fault? / Whose but his own?" (96–97) and he goes on: "Ingrate, he had of me / All he could have; I made him just and right" (97–98). Then, he sounds intellectual—as well he might be, since he is trying to say (after arguing that Adam is free) that man's fall was certainly foreknown:

> they themselves decreed
> Their own revolt, not I: if I foreknew,
> Foreknowledge had no influence on their fault,
> Which had no less proved certain unforeknown. (3.116–19)

Book 3 has these varying voices, then, including those that strike a beauteous note, such as "Dark with expressive bright thy skirts appear" (380) and "Beatitude past utterance" (62) or "Dwells in all Heaven charity so dear?" (216) or "In whom the fullness dwells of love divine" (225). There is also an appealing repetition of words and phrases in the Dialogue, one that is too pervasive to need lengthy quo-

14. W. H. Auden, introduction to *Poets of the English Language*, vol. 3, *Milton to Goldsmith*, edited by Wystan Hugh Auden and Normal Holmes Pearson (New York: Viking Press, 1950), xvi.

tation. Let one passage suffice. Notice, in addition to the repetitions in the passage below, the rhymes and near-rhymes, something that also pervades the poem in spite of Milton's excoriation of rhyme in the poem's preface:

> O Son, in whom my soul hath chief delight,
> Son of my bosom, Son who art alone
> My Word, my wisdom, and effectual might,
> All hast thou spoken as my thoughts are, all
> As my eternal purpose hath decreed:
> Man shall not quite be lost, but saved who will,
> Yet not of will in him, but grace in me (3.167–74)

The presence of these repetitions imparts for a moment an almost lyrical quality to the Dialogue, anticipating the angelic song that follows and reminding us that Heaven is a place—as it always is in Milton—of musical celebration, even when there is theological business to enact. The Dialogue, as these last two monosyllabic lines reveal, also has an epigrammatic wit that is in excess of its argumentative purpose and that gives it sumptuousness. There is an aesthetic appeal in "Sufficient to have stood, though free to fall" (99); or in "So Heav'nly love shall outdo Hellish hate" (298) or "the Heav'nly choir stood mute / And silence was in Heav'n" (217–18); or "By merit more than birthright Son of God" (309); or "Though now to Death I yield, and am his due" (245) or "Love without end, and without measure grace" (142). This sense of elegant coherence could be seen as a preemptive strike against the wobbly, question-begging theology that it expounds. Poets tend to make things look especially neat when they know they are messy. But that these lines among many others please us in the hearing, even if we are not conscious of them, there can be little doubt. We should mention their beauty more often.

We rejoin Satan on the outside of what Milton calls the "world" (419), which isn't the earth, but which contains the earth as well as all the planets, the sun, and the moon inside of its round shell. It is what we today would call the universe. Outside of the universe is chaos, the abyss. If the world is finite, this abyss is infinite and immeasurable. From the material of this abyss, God made the world. It is altogether typical of Milton to put an orderly, limited world next to an infinite one, but also to make them connect, to make one dependent upon the other.

The world hangs from Heaven by a golden chain, as we were told in the last lines of the previous book. We are tempted to think of this chain as metaphorical, but Milton doesn't say as much. He leaves the issue open. Are spheres metaphorical too? Or are they the fancies of mere old-fashioned, Ptolemaic friars satirized in lines 481–83? Leonard argues persuasively that Milton's universe is Copernican, not Ptolemaic, as was previously thought.[15] Satan flies right through the spheres when he flies to the sun and then to Earth, indicating that the spheres are not literal dividers. That Satan must seek directions to the earth suggests that the earth is not the center of the universe as it was in the Ptolemaic system. Outside of and on top of the shell of the world, Satan—vulture-like by now and hungry for prey—finds himself in an eerie place: a "windy sea of land" (440), half-illuminated by the light that shines down from the purlieus of Heaven. This place, we are told, will become the Paradise of Fools in future times, occupied by vain, superficial people "who in vain things / Built their fond hopes of glory or lasting fame, / ... All who have their reward on Earth" (448–51), and who seek "Naught ... but the praise of men" (453). The place is notably occupied by Catholics, and the passage closes out in a burst of severe anti-Catholic raillery beneath the dignity even of this free-speaking narrator, especially when he has the "fools" tormented by a childish St. Peter holding keys from Heaven's gate (485). But it is altogether typical of this poem's complexity that the narrator rails against what he himself covets, earthly fame, as is revealed in the opening passage of Book 3, when he tells us of his desire to equal the ancient bards, "So were I equaled with them in renown" (34).

15. John Leonard, *Faithful Labourers*, 2:705–9.

At this place, Satan looks up and sees a staircase, which attracts him with its light and visual magnificence. In one of the most technically subtle passages in the poem, it's compared to Jacob's ladder (510–15). We pause to regard the passage's beauty (Satan ought to ponder its lesson), but there's strange mischief afoot: someone in Heaven chooses this moment to let the stairs down (523). The idea is to torment Satan, but since the stairs are let down just over the hole in the top of the world, the action of teasing Satan also directs him toward the earth and Paradise located inside the globe. Is this God's plan? If so, God makes no mention of it. And surprise: the passage, when Satan finds it, is wide! It is wider than the path from the Promised Land to God. If Heaven is exclusive, this way downward is broad, inviting, and inclusive.

A prominent strain of Miltonic criticism is the kind that sees *Paradise Lost* as a preacher's document. Fish, as I have already related, argues that *Paradise Lost* is aimed at rousing the moral sense of the religionist whose faith needs activation. Leonard holds that if *Paradise Lost* can't successfully defend God (which it intends to do) then it is a failure. Empson argues that *Paradise Lost* successfully indicts God; Denis Danielson that Milton defends a God who is fundamentally "good." These perspectives, different though they might be, are often traced back to Lewis's famous use of Milton's poem to lecture the reader corrupted by modernism and pseudo-sophisticated morals that came with it. Whether it lines up against or for God, then, *Paradise Lost* has become a moralist's poem. But Lewis, as if to contradict himself, later emphasizes what I will call the entertainment value of *Paradise Lost*. The poem, unlike Dante's *Commedia,* is not a devotional one; it isn't really religious in the sense that it promotes, primarily, piety and self-examination. Instead, we look at the poem's events "from outside," and note its attention to "the objective pattern of things."[16] The reading of the poem isn't like hearing a sermon. It is rather an "epic holiday" from the serious moral occupations that weigh readers

16. Lewis, *A Preface to "Paradise Lost,"* 132.

down.[17] Lewis may overstate his case, but these early books support him, with their evocation and presentation of exotic and unseen places. After the Dialogue, Book 3 picks up the travel motif from Book 1, recalling the sailors on the Indian Ocean as seen from a distance, or Satan's journey from Hell through Chaos. Here in the middle of Book 3, Milton imagines how Satan "Looks down" on the world, as he once looked at Chaos before leaping into it. The vista is dramatized by the enjambment suggesting the scope of the world: "the sudden view / Of all this world at once" (542–43). We experience with Satan a sense of expansion, taking in the measure of God's universe, which he sees as a scout sees a metropolis "With glistering spires and pinnacles adorned" (550). Although, as we find out presently, Satan doesn't yet know his way in this world, he can see all of its intoxicating, heaven-like beauty, which he covets. Milton is so impressed by this phenomenon of Satan looking down on the entire world that he repeats it just as magnificently a few lines later:

> Such wonder seized, though after Heaven seen,
> The spirit malign, but much more envy seized,
> At sight of all this world beheld so fair. (3.552–54)

The poem pauses with Satan, as it paused for him when he surveyed Chaos. Note Milton's deliberate care here to honor impressions and perspectives and pauses, remembering that we are all perceivers as well as actors; even God is first seen looking down on his creation (59). When Satan first encounters Eve before the temptation, he *sees*, appraises, and appreciates Eve from a distance.

What Satan sees is vast, and he sees all of it at once, again disproving the notion that Milton's universe contains Ptolemaic spheres. Isabel McCaffrey memorably compared this view of Satan on the top of the universe to God's view of history as seen by Christian writers, who aspired to this view. In God's view, there is no narrative history. All times are one: past, present, and future. The point McCaffrey

17. Ibid., 126.

makes is that this "long view of time as illusory" helps make clear the impression *Paradise Lost* claims on the reader.[18] That is, the purpose of *Paradise Lost*'s constant and shifting references to other times isn't to distract the reader so much as to concentrate the reader on the single recurrent event, and to assimilate all events to one event. We participate in a moving narrative in the story of our falling, but our falling is also a constant thing. We are always falling. It may seem an unlikely conception, but there are passages in *Paradise Lost* that offer evidence of it.

Paradise Lost is nowhere more like an "epic holiday" than in the latter part of Book 3. Satan pitches himself down full speed through the universe, taking the reader on an exhilarating journey, past "innumerable stars" (565) like "other worlds" (566), or like "happy isles" (567), past constellations that dance, past magnetic beams of light from the sun. What is preeminent about Milton's universe, in addition to its serenity, is its motion and vitality. We notice how Milton's narrator pursues this paradox in depicting how the sun

> gently warms
> The universe, and to each inward part
> With gentle penetration, though unseen,
> Shoots invisible virtue even to the deep (3.583–86)

There is both gentleness and force in the eroticism of the sun, an eroticism that we will see enacted elsewhere in both the human and non-human agents of the poem.

Satan lands on the Sun to ask for directions to Earth. There he meets the angel, Uriel, who, not knowing Satan's real identity or what he intends, gives him the directions he seeks. The scene runs over one hundred lines (3.621–735). Why is it there at all? Could Satan as a supernatural being not have found Earth on his own? The scene appears to carry no essential information, and yet it does, because in it we see a being (Uriel) of angelic power falling blamelessly for a lie out of in-

18. Isabel McCaffrey, *"Paradise Lost" as "Myth"* (Cambridge, Mass.: Harvard University Press, 1959), 7.

genuous inexperience, something we shall see Eve do later in the poem. But the scene also offers an instance of Satan's perspicacity, his ability to read people quickly, and his capacity to charm, as he later will show with Eve. He sees Uriel "on some great charge employed" (628), "fixed in cogitation deep" (629), staring in appreciation at God's creation. Uriel, Satan perceives, is a naïve Creation geek. Satan dresses accordingly. Milton's description of him is precise:

> And now a stripling Cherub he appears,
> Not of the prime, yet such as in his face
> Youth smiled celestial, and to every limb
> Suitable grace diffused, so well he feigned;
> Under a coronet his flowing hair
> In curls on either cheek played, wings he wore
> Of many a colored plume sprinkled with gold,
> His habit fit for speed succinct, and held
> Before his decent steps a silver wand. (3.636–44)

All he needs is a little powdered sugar on top! Satan's strategy with Uriel is perfectly judged. As a stripling, Satan wants to study God's creation first-hand, and chiefly man, God's "chief delight and favor" (664). His purpose is "admiration" (672). He already knows that God has created this new race of people to repair the loss of the fallen angels, in order that these new creatures might serve God better. Satan reveals in these lines that he has picked up the Heavenly gospel, the official "line." He closes with a pious shibboleth: "Wise are all his ways" (680).

Uriel falls for it; who would not? He assures Satan that his desire to learn about the creation in order to glorify God leads as such to no excess; he even goes so far as to find fault with those fellows angels, couch potatoes, who learned about the creation in Heaven, "Contented with report" (701). Uninvited, Uriel launches into a lengthy account of the Creation. It is only after some time that he answers Satan's question. There is much of Milton in his response:

> Look downward on that globe whose hither side
> With light from hence, though but reflected, shines;

That place is Earth the seat of man, that light
His day, which else as th' other hemisphere
Night would invade, but there the neighboring moon
(So call that opposite fair star) her aid
Timely interposes, and her monthly round
Still ending, still renewing, through mid-heav'n,
With borrowed light her countenance triform
Hence fills and empties to enlighten th' Earth,
And in her pale dominion checks the night.
That spot to which I point is Paradise,
Adam's abode, those lofty shades his bow'r.
Thy way thou canst not miss, me mine requires. (3.722–35)

Imagine two angels, standing in the sun, one asking directions, the
other giving them, with digital help. The scene perforce has grand-
ness about it, but it is deliberately and profoundly homely and funny,
right down to the universally mundane act of giving directions: "Thy
way thou canst not miss." For Milton, Paradise *was* literal, but it was
also largely figurative, so evoking a world where one can point to it is
magnificently nonsensical and charming, not only for our age but for
Milton's.

5

Paradise on Earth

(B O O K 4)

Book 4 is a major book in *Paradise Lost*, if only for the sake of its extraordinary variety, synoptic in both character and importance. It goes from high dramatic utterance and character study to description, to personal incident, to lyric song, to action or near-action. As we start Book 4, suddenly we are in an Elizabethan play. The book opens with one of the greatest passages in the poem: Satan's speech to the Sun as he stands on Mount Niphates. He has finally landed on Earth—in Milton's rich, fresh, ceremonial expression, "His journey's end and our beginning woe" (3.633). The book's prelude is in what John Keats called "a Grandeur of Tenderness":[1] the anguished voice of the narrator, wishing that he had a prophet's voice to transcend time, that he might warn Adam and Eve, whom he perceives as "frail" (4.11). Does "frail" mean that Adam and Eve are *not* created "sufficient to have stood" (3.99), or does it merely express the anxiety that "our first parents" (4.6) haven't the strength of Satan? *Paradise Lost* will never let us rest our minds in certainty.

Some readers think the Satan we meet here is a humbler, less char-

1. John Keats, *The Poetical Works and Other Writings of John Keats,* vol. 5, ed. Maurice Buxton Forman, Harry Buxton Forman, and John Masefield (New York: Charles Scribner's Sons, 1939), 302.

ismatic one than in Books 1–3. His despair, which earlier "slumbered," is now awake (4.24). The sun's height and brilliance make him realize how he has fallen through his own pride and ambition. He sought to be the highest in Heaven, thinking that he would be relieved of his debt to God, but now he realizes what he always really knew and what we remember from Milton's sonnet on his blindness: God's generosity being what it is, indebtedness to God is self-canceling; merely to owe God is to see that debt paid. Satan also believes, or rationalizes, that if he hadn't rebelled, another angel would have, and he, Satan, would have joined him. He now recognizes the truth of what he said in front of Beelzebub: the mind *is* its own place. Satan's utterance here is driving and forceful: "Which way I fly is Hell; myself am Hell" (75). If you have a hellish mind, then you are in Hell. What's more, Satan apprehends that his future is bleak: he thinks he might repent, but he can't; his disdain and dread of shame make that course impossible. If he did repent, he knows he'd only fall again. He hates God, and that hatred has decided his irrevocable fate. He can only make evil his good. Therefore only a "lower deep" can await him (76).

Like so many things in *Paradise Lost*, Satan's speech to the sun has given rise to controversy. Over a half-century ago, A. J. A. Waldock argued (with some verve) that the Satan we meet in Book 4 isn't the one we met in Books 1 and 2. *That* Satan became too attractive for the poem's good, and had to be reduced in stature retroactively. The soliloquy serves that function, as do the references to Satan as a "wolf" (4.183), "vulture" (3.431), and "cormorant" (4.196), which *degrade* him. Milton tampers with his own creation to make it more orthodox.[2] But there are problems with Waldock's reading. First, according to his nephew, Milton drafted some of Satan's speech years before he started *Paradise Lost*, when he was contemplating writing a biblical drama on the fall of man. The Satan presented in this speech has an aura of nobility that the Satan of Books 1 and 2 doesn't come close to

2. A. J. A. Waldock, *"Paradise Lost" and Its Critics* (Cambridge: Cambridge University Press, 1966), 83.

having. He is ruthlessly direct and honest. It is true that he rationalizes throughout, making himself a victim of his own fixed attitudes, but he doesn't bluster, bloviate, or sloganeer. For one of the few times in the poem, he sees most things as they really are, and this candor and ruthless self-criticism gives his speech a degree of dignity. We will see this Satan again in Books 5 and 6. Setting forth as he does here the "law" of his own nature, he resembles God earlier in the poem, promulgating his own law, which he is not permitted to violate. The sun here (Satan might have had this self-examination while hiding in a dusky grove) is emblematic both of his perspicacity and his splendor. This speech is one of his greatest moments, not only because he justifies God, but because he acts like an archangel. He may be condemned, but he is not reduced. I can't agree with every element of Bryson's scathing attack on Milton's God, but he is right to see Satan in Book 4 as a "tragic, and in some degree noble figure," at least at this stage in the poem.[3]

These pages teem with felicities of phrasing. My favorites include the passage introducing Satan (19–39), which has a pugnacity and vigor that comes from the repetition of blunt words like "wakes" and "what" and "worse," and from frequent *caesurae*, pauses that make Satan sound anguished, for instance:

> now conscience wakes despair
> That slumbered, wakes the bitter memory
> Of what he was, what is, and what must be
> Worse; of worse deeds worse sufferings must ensue. (4.23–26)

As Sheridan admired: "What an amazing force does this position give to the word *worse!*"[4] The passage is flooded with harsh plosives: "blood," "boils," "devilish engine," "threw me down," "battle," "bold," "horror." By contrast, the elevation and elegance of some of the lines can seem rich: "The debt immense of endless gratitude," with its meter regulating its long words (52). The same is true of the rather less regular and yet no less regulated line "Infinite wrath, and infinite

3. Bryson, *The Tyranny of Heaven*, 78.
4. Sheridan, *Lectures on the Art of Reading*, 2:248.

despair" (74), which suggests the four-stress line of *Beowulf*. We notice how the verse gains a sense of drama by the constant repetitions: "hadst thou," "thou hast," "whom hast thou?" We appreciate the way Milton follows metrically irregular lines with regular ones: "Under what torments inwardly I groan / While they adore me on the throne of Hell" (89–90). "Adore" is aptly sardonic; the word never sounded so hollow. "Groan" and "throne" are sneaky rhymes that reflect Milton's anti-royalism. Sometimes otherwise arbitrary phrasing on Milton's part, such as Satan's assertion that "Disdain forbids me" reveals subtlety of behavior (82). Satan appears addicted, ruled by an inner "law," determined by a hardened heart. Now his condition is such that "Disdain" forbidding is stronger than God forbidding. He is ruled by his transgressions—again, just as God is ruled by his own decisions. Everywhere we look, we find unsettling parallels, repetitions, and echoes. In this respect, *Paradise Lost* is a rich and strange work.

The rest of Book 4 can be divided into easily sectioned parts: the trip by Satan to Paradise; the description of Paradise; the introduction of Adam and Eve; the narration of a day with Adam and Eve, including Eve's dream and culminating in their going to bed; and the fracas between Satan and the angelic guards. These parts are characterized by Milton's constant reviving of our curiosity. We are impelled forward, Lewis observes, by a narrator who shrewdly doesn't give us Eden all at once.[5] Likewise, when we are there, we are driven by curiosity about our first parents; that partially satisfied, we want to know what they will do together at night. In the book's conclusion, we are eager to learn what will come of the strife between angel and angel. Milton tantalizes us all along the way. He makes us want what is to come.

When we encounter Milton's Paradise, it turns out to be an elevated garden in the east of Eden, itself an elevated place. The narrator makes a lot of this elevation; he says Paradise "crowns" the wilderness around it, as if it were a royal enclosure (133). Is there an allusion to royalty? Yes, royalty of the natural kind. Yet Milton also endows Par-

5. Lewis, *A Preface to "Paradise Lost,"* 48–49.

adise with the suggestion of the coming drama of the Fall, with words like "theater" (140) and "scene" (141). (Since Paradise is round and woody, it is not unlike Shakespeare's "wooden O," the Globe Theatre.) There is an emphasis on protection, walls, and angelic guards, which is curious, since Satan easily leaps over Paradise's boundary, and since God has already adopted a permissive policy toward evil, allowing Satan to do what he wants. God is presented in a simile here as protecting his "cash," like "some rich burgher, whose substantial doors, / Cross-barred and bolted fast, fear no assault" (188–90). We love the linkages of sound in these lines, but we wonder: Is Milton putting the reader on? Are Adam and Eve cash? Is God simply an avaricious, self-deluded hoarder? Are not riches unholy? There is no escaping such questions. Later the flowers of Eden are "vegetable gold" (220); the garden represents nature's "wealth" (206), and Milton insists that Heaven is a place of jeweled riches. It is hard not to conclude, whatever we may say about it, that Milton was no more bothered than Shakespeare was by the implications of money. About God's self-delusion concerning protection in Eden, we can only be stymied, and suggest that part of the openness of the epic style is the entertainment of unusual perspectives. Is there a side of Milton that thought that God, in not foiling Satan, is at fault, his locks and bars a merely ceremonial security? What else may we conclude from the foiled protections? But then, we might add, there is no necessity to equate God with the burgher. The simile is culturally broadening, and might not be directed toward a moral point. But do we believe that?

The broadest and yet most meaningful term to characterize Milton's Paradise is that it is in several senses an *inclusive* place—what Keats lauded as "a grand Perspective of all concerned"[6]—which may be a reason why God makes it penetrable from the outside. Paradise is full of "Nature's whole wealth" (207). "All" is a key word in Book 4 (as well as in the entire poem), occurring repeatedly: "Flow'rs of *all* hue" (256), "*All* trees of noblest kind" (217), "*all* kind / Of living crea-

6. Keats, *The Poetical Works and Other Writings*, 300.

tures" (286–87), "*all* these delights" (367), "*all* these joys" (411), "*All* other creatures" (431), "*all* things clad" (599), "*All* these with ceaseless praise" (679), and so forth. For Albert Labriola, "all" represents "the essence of *Paradise Lost* i.e., the profound unity of the poem"[7] This point about "all" is worth making, because we are liable to think of Paradise as virginal, a place of beginning, of absence, of purity, a place that is emphatically exclusive, a fenced off compound for our first parents. But the trees of Paradise are "loaden" (147), and the vine is "Luxuriant" (260), and nature is "boon" (242). Words that are associated with Paradise suggest thickness, muchness, tangledness, unboundedness, linkage, and overlap: "undergrowth" (175), "diverse" (234), "error" (239), "wand'ring" (234, 531), "various" (247, 423, 669), "divided" (233). Another way of expressing this quality is to say what Paradise is not: it's not single, or straight; it isn't all visible to the eye. Though its rivers do unite, it is not severely ordered, and yet it is loosely unified; it represents an artist's vision, a vision of muchness and fecundity.

Hence, Paradise is "A happy rural seat of various view" (247), a "landscape" full of variety (151), often thought to be the model for the English pleasure garden of the eighteenth century. Peter Herman takes a different view. He emphasizes the presence of "or" in *Paradise Lost*; it occurs more than seven hundred times, edging out "all," which occurs almost as often. "Or," Herman contends, is like "the DNA of the poem's competing narratives";[8] it inscribes the incertitude that is "at the heart of *Paradise Lost*,"[9] an incertitude that, according to Herman, comes from Milton's uncertainties after the Revolution collapsed.[10] That uncertainty occurs everywhere we look. Herman and many other contemporary readers who strongly resist seeing Milton as a doctrinal poet hold that it is hard to take in all of *Paradise Lost*'s contradictions and smooth them into a consistency, and it is at least worth consider-

---

7. Albert C. Labriola, "'All in All' and 'All in One': Obedience and Disobedience in *Paradise Lost*," in *"All in All": Unity, Diversity, and the Miltonic Perspective*, ed. Charles W. Durham and Kristin A. Pruitt (Selinsgrove, Penn.: Susquehanna University Press, 1999), 44–45.

8. Herman, *Destabilizing Milton*, 43.

9. Ibid., 57.

10. Ibid., 21, 58.

ing that Milton made *Paradise Lost* as a place to display his doubts and speculations, as well as his affirmations. Herman contends that the presence of "or" in *Paradise Lost* counteracts the totalizing influence of the word "all," and that the two instincts are at war with each other. But it may also be true that "all" doesn't contradict "or," for "all" may signify something that capaciously holds contrarieties without forcing them into a rigid uniformity, just as Milton envisioned a perfect state: all unified in disunity, in contention, in disagreement—various, but also happy.

This sense of healthy tension can be found in the presentation of Paradise. As we see and shall learn, it's a place of joy, sunshine, abundance, and delight, if not simplicity. The "air" becomes a song and the very breeze inspires (264–66). At the same time, words like "fell" (230), "divided" (233), "wept" (248), and "darksome" (232) gloomily anticipate the coming Fall. The brooks run with "mazy error" (239): though "error" may literally hew to its original etymology of "meander," it can't help but wander into its modern meaning of "mistake." The description of the garden culminates in an extraordinary simile, foreshadowing not only the Fall but the misery of the world to follow: "all our woe" (1.3), as we heard in the Invocation.

> Not that fair field
> Of Enna, where Proserpine gathering flow'rs
> Herself a fairer flow'r by gloomy Dis
> Was gathered, which cost Ceres all that pain
> To seek her through the world (4.268–72)

Prosperine stands in for Eve here, and Dis for Satan. But is Ceres Adam, or Jesus, or God, or the poet?... or all of us, seeking to recover what we had before the Fall? Whatever we think, these instances of post-lapsarian misery and pathos, falling, and division are not accidental, but a part of Milton's Paradise, and the effect of them is to make Paradise not self-contradictory, but richly and strangely inclusive. Paradise is unfallen, yet simultaneously contains the fallen world. Just as he deliberately confuses literal and figurative, so Milton is disinclined to accept an either/or anywhere in his poem. Everywhere he finds unity out of opposition, *concordia discors.*

Consider the lengthy description of Adam and Eve in lines 288–311: Adam and Eve are "Godlike erect," yet they are with "native honor" clad (289); they have connections in both this world and the world above. They are "lords," yet they are under God; they have "majesty," yet they are "naked" (290)—a word not associated with majesty in Milton's world or our own. They are naked, yet "clad" (289), another reconciled opposition. They are "Severe" (294), yet placed in "filial freedom" (294). Only in the description of their capacities is there dissonance. Adam is formed for "contemplation" and "valor" (297), Eve for "sweet attractive grace" (298). These are lines that indicate fixed gender bias, with stark contraries. Adam is a heavy thinker, Eve a graceful charmer. The differences in their hair also indicate gender parts for our first parents. Yet there are complications: Eve's "disheveled" (meaning "let down") hair appears to be out of Adam's control, as do her "wanton ringlets" (306). "Wanton" here means "sportive," but there is a suggestion, if not of lewdness, then sensuality. If these words appeared alone, we might not think so, but Eve's "sweet reluctant amorous delay" denotes a sexual technique that everybody associates with post-Fallen sexuality (311). Eve is sexy, she plays sex games, and in this sexuality she "rules" Adam as well as being ruled by him. The passage teems with oxymorons: "gentle sway," "coy submission," and "modest pride" (308–10), all of which suggest a mature relationship in which Eve holds her own, and even has liberties. That these blatant sexist and then non-sexist terms exist side by side is what persuades Wittreich to assert that *Paradise Lost* "maps patriarchal, misogynous, and feminist discourses within a cacophony of competing …voices."[11] *Paradise Lost,* to put it more simply, may be a poem with a doctrine, but it doesn't always keep that doctrine under strict control. The persistent recurrence of reconciled opposites in the poem is hard

11. Joseph Wittreich, "'Inspired with Contradiction': Mapping Gender Discourses in *Paradise Lost,*" in *Literary Milton Text, Pretext, Context,* ed. Diane T. Benet and Michael Lieb (Pittsburgh, Penn.: Duquesne University Press, 1994), 157.

to deny. If there can be said to be one central rift dividing Milton's readers in recent decades, it is between those favoring unity and those favoring cacophony.

Having already presented Adam and Eve as naked, Milton even so does not miss an occasion to repeat that they are naked, that their private parts are not covered, and that they feel no shame. Linked in "nuptial league" (339), they experience "love's embraces" (322) and "youthful dalliance" (338), which, along with "hand in hand" (321), enforces a sense of Adam and Eve as affectionate newlyweds. Though it won't, we anticipate, always be such. Now the work they do makes their eating and drinking more delightful. It is not yet a burden, but a pleasure. Speaking of pleasure, with the mention of their romance, the reader becomes curious about what they will do when they go to bed. Milton doesn't tell us, yet he carefully makes reference to the passing hours of the day. Is he teasing us?

Satan is soon on the scene. His response to Adam and Eve is powerfully fraught. He sees divinity about them. They are hardly inferior to divine creatures, and their residence is "Heav'n" (371). He almost pities their upcoming change, seeking "league" (375) with them, and inviting them to Hell:

> Hell shall unfold,
> To entertain you two, her widest gates,
> And send forth all her kings (4.381–83)

Though these lines have something sinister about them, they are stately as well, and I agree with readers who find them sympathetic to Satan—even though scarcely a second later Satan rationalizes his malicious plan against Adam and Eve by calling it necessary, an excuse-making that the narrator manifestly condemns. I don't wish to turn Satan into a hero, but he was an archangel, whose most recent address was Heaven. Moreover, to attribute generosity to him here is to give credit to the god-like stature of Adam and Eve, after all.

Adam is the first to speak. (Eve, in Book 12, will be the last.) His speech (411–39) is rather bland and unexceptionable: a boy's speech.

It praises God for his liberality and bounty and for his easy single command, which is not to eat the fruit of the tree. It emphasizes what has been given to them, "power and rule" (429). Adam insists that the toil of paradise is "sweet" (439). The speech is a plot device, however. From it, Satan finds out what he must know: what it will take to ruin Adam and Eve. Eve's response is both formal and direct. The opening lines brim with chiming words and phrases, alliteration and full or near-rhyme:

> O thou for whom
> And from whom I was formed flesh of thy flesh,
> And without whom am to no end, my guide
> And head, what thou hast said is just and right. (4.440–43)

These four lines unfold elegantly: *for whom ... from whom ... without whom*. They defer their point (that Adam is "right") until the very end. Eve's association with the "w" sound is evident a few lines later in her birth story (449–92): *wondering ... where ... what ... was ... whence*. It has an echoing effect. The story she tells is familiar to all lovers, especially young ones: *The Day We Met*. It confirms that she believes herself in need of Adam as the "preeminent" consort—a valuation that will be modified later in the poem. In the minds of some, the story might record a dangerous brush with narcissism, though to others the story reveals youthful excess. "Her fascination with her own image," says Summers, "is a natural and inevitable potentiality for any free creature of perfect beauty."[12] Eve's image charms her, but she does not say she loves it; the image rather presents "looks" of love (464). Eve is guided away both to Adam and to the task of bearing "Multitudes like thyself" (474), a substitute narcissism.

I don't believe Milton is revealing some general depravity in Eve. She was tempted by her own beauty, as who wouldn't be? But, shown the right way, which is the way of relationship, she corrects herself, much as God does in Book 3. Milton's God likes to test people, and

12. Summers, *The Muse's Method*, 98.

this is a test, which Eve passes. Part of Eve's perfection is indeed her ability to fall, which is true of Adam as well. Milton is not interested in a Robot of Goodness. Eve has the power to fall and also to ascend, to change. In connection with this idea of change, we notice that Eve had "fixed" (4.329) her eye on her own image—in this fixing, she is temporarily like Satan, who has a "fixed mind / And high disdain" (1.97–98). In Eve's case, to be irremovably fixed is to be damned, but it is only temporary. Coming from a different direction, modern feminist criticism might be tempted to see here Eve's encounter with her "self" (see line 4.468) as we use that word now, that is, her inner, independent being—which could be rebellious to God's hierarchy. But that would in Milton's view make Eve semi-Satanic.[13] The scene closes with a typically Miltonic juxtaposition: Adam's "gentle hand / Seized mine" (488–89), Eve relates, a complicated image of potentially consensual power, as she "yielded" her hand. We notice, by the way, that whereas Eve was the possessor of grace when we first met her, now Adam is endowed with "manly grace" (490). Milton's ground sometimes shifts, imperiling facile categories and stereotypes, even his own: for instance, in Book 9, Eve comes off as an efficiency expert, Adam as a love-stricken romantic.

Milton tells us again that Satan is driven mad by the sensuality of Paradise, as he sees Eve is "naked" with her swelling breast on Adam's chest. Satan's envious response tells us that Eden is a place of fulfilled love and Hell a place of celibacy where "fierce desire" (509) is one of the punishments: "Sight hateful, sight tormenting!" he exclaims,

> Thus these two,
> Imparadised in one another's arms
> The happier Eden, shall enjoy their fill
> Of bliss on bliss (4.505–8)

Observe the affirmation of a Miltonic principle: if the mind is its own place, then Hell can be Heaven and Heaven Hell, and Paradise can

13. Froula, "When Eve Reads Milton," 328–29.

be found in two lovers' arms. Maybe Adam and Eve never needed a garden to begin with! In the remainder of his speech, Satan insists that God's prohibition of the Tree of Knowledge is "reasonless" (516), even tyrannical. It is hard to believe that Satan doesn't understand God's prohibition, and there is no indication yet in the poem that God wishes Adam and Eve to be ignorant. What is more likely here is that, like a Shakespearean villain, Satan is thinking aloud about what his strategy of temptation will be: "Hence I will excite their minds / With more desire to know" (522–23). With that plan laid, Satan starts roaming the woods, lest he be spotted by the angelic guard. It is now evening (Milton records the process of the day's change carefully, from noon to late afternoon, to dusk, to evening) and Uriel has flown down to Earth to warn Gabriel that "on the Assyrian mount" he saw Satan "disfigured" (125–26)—a moment Keats relished for its "dramatic vastness and solemnity fit and worthy to hold one amazed."[14]

Dusk approaches, and the tone of the poem mellows as Adam and Eve prepare for bed. In a passage that stands behind so much English pastoral poetry (589–609), Milton records the process of the evening's arrival, from the appearance of "twilight gray" (598) to the silencing of the birds, to the glowing of the sky with stars, to the rising of the moon. Set to music by Charles Ives in 1921,[15] the passage has a quiet incremental power, and with phrases like "rode brightest," "clouded majesty," "Apparent queen," and "peerless light" it suggests a royal procession (606–8). Odd, for a Puritan regicide! There are some fine suspended verbs, such as "She all night long her amorous descant sung" (603), suggesting time, and in "o'er the dark her silver mantle threw" (609), suggesting space. Altogether the passage indicates that the natural and the elegant are reconcilable. Now Adam delivers a little lecture on work. We see an evolution in this book of the idea of work, from something that enhances pleasure to something that con-

14. Keats, *The Poetical Works and Other Writings*, 304.
15. Charles Ives, "125. Evening," 1921, reprinted in *129 Songs*, ed. H. Wiley Hitchcock (Middleton, Wis.: American Musicological Society, 2004), 291.

fers dignity, to an absolute necessity lest the garden become a jungle.

Eve responds here with elaborate consent. She sounds as if she's reciting a catechism; somewhat naïve, even childlike. Without being at all cynical about it, we sense that Eve's tone will change from this to another as she grows up:

> My author and disposer, what thou bidd'st
> Unargued I obey; so God ordains,
> God is thy Law, thou mine: to know no more
> Is woman's happiest knowledge and her praise. (4.635–38)

(Note that "author" has already been used for Satan [2.864], the fallen angels [3.122], God [3.374], and will chime another ten times in the poem—what does this mean for Milton's own authorship?) This avowal is followed by a "delay" of love-making in the form of a charming poem:

> With thee conversing I forget all time,
> All seasons and their change, all please alike.
> Sweet is the breath of morn, her rising sweet,
> With charm of earliest birds; pleasant the sun
> When first on this delightful land he spreads
> His orient beams, on herb, tree, fruit, and flow'r,
> Glist'ring with dew; fragrant the fertile earth
> After soft showers; and sweet the coming on
> Of grateful evening mild, then silent night
> With this her solemn bird and this fair moon,
> And these the gems of heav'n, her starry train:
> But neither breath of morn when she ascends
> With charm of earliest birds, nor rising sun
> On this delightful land, nor herb, fruit, flow'r,
> Glist'ring with dew, nor fragrance after showers
> Nor grateful evening mild, nor silent night
> With this her solemn bird, nor walk by moon,
> Or glittering starlight without thee is sweet. (4.639–56)

Milton never wrote anything more dulcet, with the possible exception of the flower passage in *Lycidas* (141–51). It is the poetry of youth. The two parts of the poem are almost stanzaic, though without rhyme. Though they are repetitive, they are repetitive with variation. The repetition is guided by the syntax. The first half is adjectival and positive: "sweet," "pleasant," "fragrant," "sweet," followed by an antithetical pattern: "but neither," "nor," "nor," "nor." It is framed in a long chiasmus: "sweet is ... is sweet." Eve's utterance, set for a certain time of the day, is both ritualistic and spontaneous. In the beginning of her life, we might say, Eve speaks in song. In Book 9, later, we will see she is a little more grown up, speaking in something closer to prose, though she is still innocent. Youth aside, however, this lyric is complex: while it celebrates her affection for Adam, Eve sets down her love of the garden as almost its equal. She forgets all time when she speaks to Adam and says that all "seasons" (times of the day) are alike, but she also celebrates variation and change. Just as Milton's depictions of the universe were in Book 3, her words here are full of references to process in the garden ("rising," "spreading," "glist'ring," "ascending," "glittering") and to time ("time," "season," "first," "after," "coming on," "evening," "night," "rising sun," "after"). Milton knows how to marshal a featured saturation when he wants to urge on our sentiments.

Eve's question that follows, about the economy of starlight, reveals a developing maturity. Adam's first answer, that light nourishes the earth and makes it more receptive to the sun's light, is rather well improvised. It's hard to tell if Milton believes it. His second answer, that light provides a show for those "millions of spiritual creatures [who] walk the earth," almost rivals Eve for its poetry (677), particularly the idea that Adam and Eve can hear "Celestial voices" singing to "the midnight air" (682). It appears that Milton has in mind not only the celestial guard, but more generally a population ("millions") of angels who simply appreciate earth's nightly show. *Paradise Lost* is remarkable for its constant return to aesthetic pleasure as a good in itself.

Adam and Eve are ready to retire. Now we learn that they enjoy sex before the Fall—and by extension, we learn that the Fall is about something other than a transgression into sexuality. (Or maybe, as Millicent Bell long ago suggested, they were already fallen.)[16] In this celebration of pre-lapsarian intercourse, Milton proves himself a liberal-minded and controversial author. He resists the medieval tradition of depicting Eve as a wicked seductress. Milton's portrayal of Eve is sexual, but not lascivious. The controversy about pre-lapsarian sexuality is one that Milton especially welcomes, altering his tone from the placid to the polemical. Unlike us, he insists, Adam and Eve don't wear "disguises" (740) and their sex is open. Coming so closely after their evening prayers, prayer indistinguishably blends into sex. Lewis finds Milton's pre-lapsarian sexuality unconvincing in its literal-minded presentation: a mistake on Milton's part. Sex in *Paradise Lost*'s Garden is too much like ours in the fallen world, and Milton's addition of a few phrases like "mysterious" and "rites" and so forth doesn't persuade us otherwise.[17] I used to resist Lewis's take, but now I believe it has some validity.

The love of Adam and Eve is too reminiscent of fallen sexuality to be accidental. This merging of fallen and unfallen is made clear in the passage after "Hail wedded love" (750–75). Previous to this moment, Milton celebrated the specialness of love inside the state of innocence, but now he segues into praise of marriage. At first, marriage is celebrated for what it historically brought into human relations (it drove lust away, brought charities into families, and so on), but when it's called a "Perpetual fountain of domestic sweets" (760), we might well be talking about our modern world. Likewise with the subsequent lines about "harlots," "court amours," "Mixed dance," and "wanton masque" (766–68), the text becomes turbulent with irregular stresses: "REIGNS HERE and REVels; NOT in the BOUGHT SMILE/ Of HARlots." Line 766 that follows is nominally iambic, but because of the strong break after "harlots," the rest of the line has an

16. Millicent Bell, "The Fallacy of the Fall in *Paradise Lost*," *PMLA* 68 (1953): 863–83.

17. Lewis, *A Preface to "Paradise Lost,"* 124.

insistent, harsh, falling rhythm: "LOVEless, JOYless." Now the poet is celebrating good marriages, reminding us that Puritans believed the original innocence of Eden could be restored in our own lives. In Milton's mind, marriage is what we have remaining of our unfallen state. Milton closes the section with a "loaded" passage:

> Sleep on,
> Blest pair; and O yet happiest if ye seek
> No happier state, and know to know no more. (4.773–75)

It is a merry benediction, with a playful jingle on an admonitory "no" ("No ... know ... know no"). But it makes a key statement about Adam and Eve, one contradicted by a passage later, about the desirability of striving for more. Why? Because here, at least, Adam and Eve ought to have all that they need. And their satisfaction, Milton implies, ought still to be open to us now.

With one last arresting reference to passing time, "Now had night measured with her shadowy cone / Half way up hill this vast sublunar vault" (776–77), we shift our attention to Gabriel's response to Uriel's warning about Satan (782–96). Gabriel, presumably ignorant of God's permissive policy toward Satan, expresses surprise that an infernal being could escape Hell. He leads his squadron of followers to the Bower, where Satan is found, whispering into the sleeping Eve's ear things that might plant a seed of discontent in her—diminished to being "Squat like a toad" (800; a phrase William Cullen Bryant summoned in mockery of John Calhoun).[18] Ithuriel touches Satan with his spear, and we find out that Satan is not simply *like* a toad but *is* a toad, for now he resumes his former shape. It is a curious confusion of the literal and figurative—not an unusual thing in Milton, as we know. The exchange between Zephon and Satan (844–50) is one of many fascinating meetings in *Paradise Lost*: we immediately think of Satan and Beelzebub after their fall, or Satan, Sin, and Death, or Uriel and Satan.

18. William Cullen Bryant, "Calhoun's Diminished Stature," September 20, 1837, reprinted in *Power for Sanity: Selected Editorials of William Cullen Bryant, 1829–1861*, ed. William Cullen Bryant II (New York: Fordham University Press, 1994), 74.

There will be more. For Milton, there is something in meetings that reveals and dramatizes who people essentially are, especially how they are creatures who change.

What charges this meeting is Zephon's inability to recognize Satan. For his part, Satan is incensed not because he is caught, but because, since his fall from Heaven, he has declined. He has lost his looks, his reputation, and his distinction. When he is reminded of as much by Zephon, he is crushed. While Satan is "Undaunted" (851), Zephon is "Severe" in his "youthful beauty" (845) a phrase admired by Felicia Hemans;[19] his grace is "Invincible" (846); his goodness "awful" (847), which Milton knew meant both impressive and frightening. *Fear, invincible, awful, undaunted, weak*: these are terms from warfare, but it becomes clear, just as it did in the Sin and Death episode, that there will be no battle. The battle here is one of wits, of getting the verbal upper hand. In this, Satan, though not defeated physically, and still unafraid of harm, loses. He is "overcome with rage," as if he were losing in combat (857). While the angelic guard could have expelled Satan from the Garden, Milton enforces this pattern of meetings and verbal combat by having the guard conduct Satan to Gabriel. Gabriel sees Satan from a distance, "And with them comes a third, of regal port, / But faded splendor wan" (869–70), meaning that Gabriel isn't sure at first who it is either. Now comes the Miltonic intellectual contest: Gabriel asking Satan why he has left Hell, Satan sarcastically responding that, as Gabriel ought to know, he left Hell because it was too painful. At this thoughtless, gain-temporary-advantage response, Gabriel directs what must be a crushing weapon at Satan: a smile. If you escaped Heaven because it is so awful, he asks then why do you persist in thinking of yourself as a hero, and why were you not joined by others? In response to this question, Satan, appearing trapped, begins to waffle and delivers what is almost certainly his worst speech in *Paradise Lost* (925–45). It is long-winded, tired, flabby in syntax, and

19. Felicia Hemans, *Selected Poems, Letters, Reception Materials*, ed. Susan J. Wolfson (Princeton, N.J.: Princeton University Press, 2010), 115.

devoid of wit. And in this feeble defense, Satan is guilty of something worse in Milton's world than cowardice: inconsistency.

Book 4 rises to what promises to be a certain battle. By now, however, taught by the Sin and Death episode in Book 2, we ought to suspect it will not take place. Here, instead of escalating into a fight, the confrontation becomes instead a Miltonic choice: God holds up his scales, which indicate that it would not be prudent for Satan to fight, and it is Satan who flees. In the run-up to the battle-that-doesn't-actually-happen, there occurs a simile (980–85) that is stranger than most in a poem full of slightly askew analogues. The spears of the angels (and, by extension, the angels themselves) are compared to ears of grain, ripe for harvest, waving in the wind. So far so good, one supposes. There are several angels present, and a man ready for battle might sway with anticipation—but who is the "doubting" plowman? A famous eighteenth-century editor of Milton, Richard Bentley, dismissively ascribed many of the curiosities of *Paradise Lost* to Milton's blindness, positing a malignant transcriber.[20] Bentley audaciously revised Milton's passages to conform to his own sense of rightness. The consensus about Bentley (dating back to Jonathan Swift)[21] is that he was wrong about Milton more often than he was right, and that his edition represents an aberration of scholarship. At the same time, Bentley has been given credit for reading *Paradise Lost* with the close care that it deserves and demands.[22] Whatever the errors of his judgment, he has a sharp eye, and asks the right questions. As for the plowman, Bentley simply removes him from the poem as being not applicable. Empson takes a different tack, arguing that the simile of the plowman *is* applicable—to God, and the passage reveals God's fecklessness, whether Milton intended it or not. This interpretation conforms to Empson's reading of Milton's poem as an exposé of a weak, tyrannical, and non-omnipotent God. Or, Empson says, if the plowman is Satan, then Satan is still the

20. Richard Bentley, *Milton's "Paradise Lost": A New Edition* (London: Jacob Tonson, 1732).

21. Jonathan Swift, *Milton Restor'd, and Bentley Depos'd* (London: E. Curll, 1732).

22. See Sophie Read, "Rhetoric and Rethinking in Bentley's *Paradise Lost," The Cambridge Quarterly* 41, no. 2 (June 2012): 209–28.

ruler of the angels, which, again, hardly speaks favorably of God.[23] Criticism of Milton is hard to separate from polemic. But the plowman who, seeming to doubt them, puts his angels to the test is rather like the God we will meet in the next few books.

23. William Empson, *Some Versions of Pastoral* (London: Chatto and Windus, 1935), 172.

6

Life in Paradise

(BOOKS 5-6)

This chapter's title is an apparent misnomer for two reasons. The depiction of life in Paradise begins in Book 4, with the introduction of the Garden, then of Adam and Eve, then of their conversation, and at last of their ritual of going to bed. And life in Paradise continues until the final book of the poem, when Adam and Eve are expelled from the Garden. Moreover, these middle books reach beyond life in the Garden. They take up the War in Heaven (Books 5-6) and the story of the Creation (Books 7-8). Even so, to segregate this middle section as I have done is to emphasize that *Paradise Lost* has a beginning (1-4), a middle (5-8), and an end (9-12), which may explain why Milton later expanded *Paradise Lost* from ten to twelve books, making a tri-partite poem possible, if not certain. This division also emphasizes the legitimacy of paradisal innocence as a subject worthy in itself, regardless of its end in the Fall. *Paradise Lost* is not simply a story about the fall of Adam and Eve, but of their origin, their growth, their acquiring of experience, and the decisions they must face as adults. These are matters of no interest to the author(s) of Genesis. Consider how many things, in Milton's account, fill in the bare bones of Genesis: the description of Adam and Eve and of the Garden; Eve's creation story;

Adam and Eve's conversations and speculations; Eve's song to Adam; the consciousness of the passing of time in Eden; the near-battle of the good and bad angels within Paradise; Eve's dream; Adam's explanation of dreams; the arrival of Raphael; the meal; Raphael's explanation of angelic nature; the story of the War in Heaven, the extensive account of Creation; the long quarrel Adam and Eve have before their fall, and more. Throughout these books, we watch Adam and Eve become adults. The people we meet in Book 4 are different from the ones we will see in Book 9, though they are "innocent" and unfallen in both (at least in the early part of Book 9). Raphael makes this clear in his speech to Adam midway through Book 5: "God made thee perfect, not immutable" (524). Adam and Eve can rise from their present status. As I have argued, God even attributes mutability to the divine being when he says that his nature will change, the deity becoming "all in all" (3.341). Change, including growth, can be part of perfection. When Milton rewrote Genesis, he became an evolutionist of sorts.

The beginning of Book 5 is fascinating. We have been moved into a new realm of innocence. Eve wakes up with her hair discomposed, her cheeks glowing. Adam has awakened before her, and is admiring her as she sleeps. His speech is honeymoonish: "My fairest, my espoused, my latest found" (18). It is the language of new lovers, and there's an element of both *carpe diem* and aubade as Adam encourages Eve to seize the morning (21–25). There is an undertone of time passing, too, with words like "last," "ever new," "fresh," and "lose the prime" (19–21), just as there is an undertone of darkness and error earlier in the description of the Garden. The Fall is never far away. Eve addresses Adam as "sole" (5.28), as Adam did to her earlier (4.41), and even God did to the Son (3.276)—"sole" mates all. This reassures us that she is still a devoted spouse, but there's a note of panic in her voice because of her dream. Satan's temptation in that dream is multifold: it makes the fruit desirable because it is forbidden, and suggests that the prohibition is unjust because there is no reason for it. Satan also turns the fruit into an idol by calling it "fruit divine" (5.67), and in doing so makes an appeal to Eve's curiosity about Heaven and her worshipful affection for Adam. Satan appeals to an innocent vanity in Eve. The temptation has a lot going for it!

Is it a sign of Eve's fallenness that she has had the dream at all? The poem's doctrine, as expounded by Adam, that evil may come into and exit the mind without stain, may settle the issue. Yet readers often suspect that there is something inherently depraved, or at least not wholly innocent, about someone who has entertained these temptations, especially since they are present again at the climactic temptation in Book 9, the temptation that succeeds. But this is the temptation that Eve resists (successfully? the syntax of "I, methought, / Could not but taste" comes across as deliberately evasive [5.85–86]). Whatever in her appears to give way to the temptation is in fact forced upon her. Why does Milton add this dream to the story told in Genesis? Why does Eve need to be tempted before she is tempted? Perhaps Milton isn't putting Eve under suspicion, but endowing her with experience, so that when she encounters Satan face to face at the Fall she won't be a neophyte—making a fairer fight between Eve and Satan. He wants the Fall to matter. More importantly, he wants the Adam and Eve we encounter in Book 4 to mature as we get to know them: they are not static beings. Adam, we notice, is tempted here too; like Eve, he passes the test well. He keeps his composure; he comforts Eve, affirming her virtue; he expounds what he can; he gives her hope; he turns her to action (95–128). His explanation of how dreams work makes him like a rather more sophisticated, older character than he was in Book 4. Even so, the first line of Adam's neat almost-couplet, "That what in sleep thou did'st abhor to dream" (5.120) is undercut with mild dramatic irony by the disturbed foot of the second line, "WAKing thou never wilt consent to do" (121). Altogether, as Summers observes, the passage, though ultimately upbeat, flirts with darkness by featuring such words such as "fallen," "fell," feared" and "offended" (130–35).[1] Is the Fall unavoidable?

Summers's appreciation of the scene of Eve and Adam's matins is a

1. Summers, *The Muse's Method*, 83.

great example of how to read Milton. *Paradise Lost*, he says, is pervaded by a sense of delight in alteration for its own sake.[2] As we learn in the next book, even in the all-light precincts of Heaven, the angels create "grateful vicissitude" (6.4–8)—a changing-light show in a cave—for no purpose than to amuse themselves. If this is not a sign of the intricacy of Milton's universe, I don't know what is. Likewise, because Milton values change, Adam and Eve pray in "various style" (5.146), that is, in an irregular manner, and the things they praise in God's creation, from the angels circling God's throne, to Lucifer, to the sun, the moon, the clouds, the winds, the falling waters, to the birds, are all in motion—are in fact celebrated *because* of their motion. In keeping with this idea of motion, the song ends by invoking the dispersal of dark at dawn, but the rhythm of the earth dictates that the dark will come back—just as Satan, chased off by the angelic guard, also will return.[3] He has a place in our world, just as darkness and "error" are part of the Garden, and "wanton"ness is an attribute of Eve's hair.

Adam and Eve proceed to their day's "rural work," and, if we are tracking the poem, we notice already another sign of change and growth (5.211). Early in Book 4, we are told that toil in Paradise exists only to make refreshment more refreshing, that nothing is really required of Adam and Eve but that they keep God's one commandment (4.411–39). But then Adam hints that their activity is a little more onerous than he suggested earlier. The garden's alleys, Adam says, "mock" the labors of him and Eve and "require / More hands than ours" (4.628–29). Now in Book 5, we begin to sense something more like real work that Adam and Eve must do:

> On to their morning's rural work they haste
> Among sweet dews and flow'rs; where any row
> Of fruit trees over-woody reached too far
> Their pampered boughs, and needed hands to check
> Fruitless embraces (5.211–15)

2. Ibid., 71.
3. Ibid., 83.

The work among "sweet dews and flow'rs" is pleasant enough, but there is a suggestion of duty here that comes from "haste" and from the implied moralism in "reached too far" and "hands to check / Fruitless embraces." We are moving closer to the Protestant work ethic. Milton certainly had it himself; it is hard to imagine his Paradise as a place of slothful ease. Over the course of Books 4 and 5, as I have suggested, it becomes more than a place of leisure. We see Adam retiring from the heat of toil and needful of "respite" (5.232). Adam soon will want to know some answers about the higher world. That's work too.

God instructs Raphael in how to prepare Adam for what is to come at the hands of Satan (224–45). He tells Raphael to "bring on" "*discourse*," to "*converse* with" Adam, rather than *tell* him that Satan is plotting against him now (230–34). It is a plot of "deceit and lies," and God says that Adam should be ready (243). Milton's desire to justify God here makes both God and the narrator sound defensive, something that is suggested by the insistent and heavy-handed "So spake th' eternal Father and fulfilled / All justice," as if just saying it were enough (246–47). After God's rather legalistic language, the next hundred or so lines evince Milton's typical changing of gears: now he intends to seduce us with beauty. We read of "celestial ardors" (249), and "gorgeous wings" (250). We read of the parting of the choirs in Heaven, and the turning of the gate of Heaven on its golden hinges, and Raphael's flight downward as he "Sails between worlds and worlds" (268), and, flying like a glorious phoenix, "Winnows the buxom air" (270). Then we read of his approach, looking like Mercury, with his colors as if "dipped in heaven" (283), filling the paradisal air with the perfume of his wings, and streaming through Eden's "spicy forest" (298), a "wilderness of sweets" (294), words that aren't usually partnered. Adam, seeing Raphael approach, brings his own punning preciosity into the scene as he addresses Eve:

> Haste hither Eve, and *worth thy sight* behold
> Eastward among those trees, what glorious shape
> Comes this way moving; seems another morn
> Ris'n on mid-noon (5.308–11, my italics)

Adam instructs Eve to open their stores to entertain the angel, but Eve, correcting Adam, tells him there is sufficient store on the stalks themselves, ending her speech "here on earth / God hath dispensed his bounties as in Heav'n" (329–30), one of many passages in *Paradise Lost* that equate the two paradises of Heaven and Earth and that insist on bounty and inclusion.

The meeting of Raphael and of our first parents is under-celebrated by Milton's commentators (350–91). Milton presents Adam as a natural aristocrat, as man was in his first or "primitive" condition. The verb "walks" connotes forthrightness, and yet Milton also wants us to see Adam's "state" (351, 353), presenting Adam as bearing a sense of stateliness that has nothing to do with accoutrements. He is an anti–Charles I, a Puritan's dream, and yet he is king-like. It is notable here, once again, how the narrator crosses a line easily into the post-Paradise world, the world of regal privilege that Milton so detested. When Adam is presented to Raphael, he is "not awed," yet "submiss" and "meek" (358–59), typical Miltonic opposites. There is the same tension as in the passage in Book 4 describing Adam and Eve's stature with regard to each other. It is hierarchical, and yet not grossly so.

The characterization of the meeting with Eve is similar. Eve, naked, is "Undecked, save with herself," just as Adam wears his naturally endowed demeanor (5.380). Raphael addresses her as Gabriel addressed Mary, but also as one would address the president of a country, not a rural maiden:

Hail mother of mankind, whose fruitful womb
Shall fill the world more numerous with thy sons (5.388–89)

The narrator goes on to associate Eve with Venus and a wood-nymph, as well as with Mary. The ostensible idea is to make Eve stand above the others in beauty, but the passage's real effect is to make Eve an apotheosis of all these celebrated women, at once combining chastity, beauty, and pagan eroticism, plus dignity! If Adam "walks" plainly forth to meet the visitor, Eve "stood to entertain her guest from Heav'n" (383)—a line of majesty and simplicity that is about simple and majestic behavior. But in the vicinity of these lines we find a trove of homely expressions: "grassy turf" (391), "table" (392), "mossy seats" (392), and "no fear lest dinner cool" (396), the second of several reminders that the fare of Paradise is vegetarian. Whatever splendor Adam and Eve enjoy, they thrive in a modest, homely setting.

Adam, offering food to Raphael with apologies, is contradicted for the second time in a few minutes (the first contradiction came when Eve corrected him about the sufficient store of food "on the stalk" in Paradise). Raphael denies any need for apology by observing that angels are part corporeal—and therefore can eat, digest, and presumably excrete—just as man is part spiritual. This is a fact of enormous significance in *Paradise Lost*, for it says that beings of Heaven and Earth are different in degree but not in kind, and therefore all is connected, all matter originating with God, who, we are told later in the poem, creates the world by withdrawing himself from it (7.170). Even though God is of a higher spiritual nature than man, he is of the same substance as matter, and not antagonistic to it. And so it is with the angels. The angels, God, and man live in a monistic, all-inclusive universe. There is degree in this universe; some beings are higher than others, as they are more spiritual, but they are all interconnected by the same "first matter" (5.472). So if angels can "descend" to eating food, and God can descend to become man, man can "rise" to a more spiritual condition over a period of time (493–505). This possibility of ascension is, I believe, in keeping with the emphasis in *Paradise Lost* on the goodness of change, motion, and mutability: we never stand still.

But a problem is raised in Raphael's speech. It invites Adam and Eve to aspire to a higher spiritual state: "Your bodies may at last turn all to spirit"—that is, become more perfect than the supposedly perfect one that they have been given (497). Apparently, some discontent is "wired into" the human condition. But if that is so, does it also mean that Adam and Eve are invited to fall by overreaching? Raphael tells them to "enjoy" their "happy state," and that they are "incapable of more" (503–5), yet hasn't he just implied that there is a *happier* state?

In the meantime, Milton has made Eden truly pleasing to the senses. We shall not easily forget the descriptions of Book 4, or the part telling us (twice!) that Eve is "naked," once in an extravagant and rare lilting meter—"MEANwhile at TABle EVE / MINistered NAKed" (5.443–44)—as he depicts her filling the flowing cups. But then the book, joyous meal and all, takes a difficult turn with Raphael's introduction of the ideas of obedience and of ascension. These bring with them the paradoxical notion that Adam and Eve can be perfect but also mutable, and that their service to God is required but also voluntary. Raphael makes it clear that the angels have the same conditions laid upon them. Paradise is already becoming more complex.

When Adam asks about obedience, Milton emphasizes how much pleasure (and not merely information) Adam gets out of hearing the archangel talk, even finding that speech superior to angelic music (544), which may be Milton's way of indicating that it is acceptable that Raphael is taking over the poem, speaking throughout Books 6 and 7 and dominating Book 8. The story he will tell is that of the first disobedience. The reader now realizes that the epic has started in "the middle of things" with Satan's fall (a practice called by the Romans beginning *in medias res*), and now Milton, through Raphael, is starting at the proper beginning, which is God's elevation of the Son, an event that led to the War in Heaven (Book 6), which in turn led to the Creation (Book 7). In doing this, Milton was following Virgil's *Aeneid*, but also what Virgil did in his poem *Georgics*, setting forth the nature of existence itself. Here, as in Wagner's *Ring*, or Dante's *Paradiso*, we must resign ourselves to some instruction.

This ambitious philosophizing, along with the story of the Fall, is what Milton intends in *Paradise Lost*, even if it sometimes means dulling the aesthetic impact of his work. Before he tells Adam and Eve the story of the War, Raphael makes it sound as if, in order to make the "invisible exploits" (5.565) of angels clear, he will have to resort to aesthetic fictions. Yet as we shall see, most of what happens in Book 6 is literally true: for angels, as Raphael himself said, are corporeal. They are more like humans than we thought. There is another contradiction that has gotten the attention of readers who think that Milton's mark is his incertitude and inconsistency. Herman sees God as making a speech to the angels in Book 5 (lines 600–615) that is quite different in nature from his speeches in Book 3.[4] The episode in Book 3, the Dialogue in Heaven, happens later in the poem's chronology (after Satan has escaped from Hell), though earlier in the narrative. But both passages do essentially the same thing, Herman argues, which leads him to ask why the poem needs both. The answer to that question might be that the scene in Book 5 has to do with an elevation of the Son to co-equal power with God, and so God must employ harsh language, whereas Book 3 has to do with the depiction of the Son's mercy rather than his power, and so here the Father chooses "softer" language. But my defense of Milton here is forced. Milton's God in 5.600–615 is needlessly obnoxious. His phrase "All knees in Heav'n" robs the angels of their dignity (608). It is clear that God wishes to warn the angels, but Milton, in his eagerness to exonerate God here, turns him into a despot. Is Empson's claim true, that Milton in attempting to defend God reveals that God is indefensibly tyrannical?[5] Is Milton simply himself uncertain whether God can be defended? Milton would probably argue that being an all-merciful Father is not inconsistent with a certain toughness and asperity. The discrepancy in presenting God in Books 3 and 5 could be seen as an artistic flaw attributable to Milton's partial lack of confidence in his own logic. There are other examples of such discrepancies in *Paradise Lost*, and they can't be easily argued away. But maybe these many incongruities in Milton's work "are the signs not of Milton's confusion but of his artistic courage, his resolute willingness to enter a space of contradiction and deep disturbance."[6] God is not one-dimensional, nor is his relationship to his angels.

Whatever we might think, in Heaven "all seemed well pleased" (5.617), and most of the angels spend their day in song and dance and

4. Herman, *Destabilizing Milton*, 54.
5. Empson, *Milton's God*, 146.
6. Greenblatt, "The Lonely Gods," 6.

"Quaff immortality and joy" (638). When "grateful twilight" comes, Satan begins his temptation of the other angels (645). There are a few things to notice about this temptation. The first is that Satan is motivated by *pride*, not a sense of injustice; he thinks himself "impaired" (665) by the Son's exaltation by God (the telling word is "begot"—see 603). Second, Satan provokes his followers. He isn't borne on a wave of their resentment; he stirs it up. Later, when Abdiel raises an objection to Satan's words, the other angels don't second him—not because they object for any reason, but because what Abdiel says is "out of season judged, / Or singular" (850–51). (Leave it to Milton to turn rebels into conformists!) Notice that Satan is disturbingly successful, drawing to his side one full third of Heaven's host. The number is scriptural, not Milton's (Revelation 12:4). Nevertheless, the poet didn't need to follow it; in doing so he makes Satan a formidable figure. God could keep loyal only two-thirds in the face of Satan's opposition? This refusal on the part of so many of the "good" angels to follow God is fodder for the Satanist reading of *Paradise Lost*.

But Satan's speech to the angels (772–802) is full of absurdities; even Empson finds it "confusing."[7] Satan, desiring to turn a personal slight into a cause, argues that, yes, there can he hierarchy in Heaven (read: Satan wants to remain number one), but he also wants to make his appeal attractive by saying all the angels are equal, which the poem tells us is not true. Satan can't say that all angels are really equal, because then he would undermine his own claim to power, and so he says angels are God's equals—"if in power and splendor less, / In freedom equal" (796–97). In freedom equal? The angels were always equally free. This claim can be credited only if one isn't listening. Its central contradiction anticipates Johnson's dismissal of Levelers as people who want to level society down to themselves, but who "cannot bear leveling *up* to themselves."[8]

Out of the ugly midnight meeting emerges a Miltonic spokesper-

7. Empson, *Milton's God*, 73–74.
8. James Boswell, *Boswell's Life of Johnson*, vol. 1 (New York: Oxford University Press, 1953), 317.

son and hero: Abdiel (5.809–48, 877–95). Abdiel is a spokesperson because he espouses things that Milton believes—for instance, that God made all things; that there is a benefit that travels downward from God's hierarchical reign, a "trickle-down" of dignity; that creators have power over those whom they create; that hierarchy doesn't oppress, but gives honor to those on the lower end. Abdiel is a Miltonic hero of resistance; he is surrounded by his enemies, but, unlike the rebels, doesn't lose his loyalty to God and to God's unseen presence. His virtues are expressed deliberately by Milton in a stunning series of consecutive negative participles, "unmoved, / Unshaken, unseduced, unterrified" (5.898–99), a quadruple pattern that appears nowhere else the poem (there are doubles and triples, i.e., 2.185, 2.821, 3.68, 3.231, 4.129, 4.629, 5.245, 5.670, 6.404, 7.314, 8.197, 10.595).[9] Milton's past participles throughout *Paradise Lost* lend the action a sense of the present as severely acted upon by the past, which is the point of epic poetry.[10] As such, Abdiel adumbrates the narrator as he presents himself in Book 7, a man "fallen on evil days," but still faithful to his God (25). He is a historical type, as we learn later on in Book 11: "the only righteous in a world perverse"; the "one just man" (701; 830; 902). When we hear in Book 9 about a new type of epic hero, we are invited to remember Abdiel "encompassed round with foes" (876). Book 5 comes to a climax in repetitions ("his," "his," "he," "he," "Faithful," "faithless," "faithful") exploding off the page. The fight is on.

Many readers would agree that the War in Heaven is one of *Paradise Lost*'s off-books. It isn't usually condemned outright, but it is frequently treated with condescension: that is partly because, as Samuel Johnson charged, it appears to confuse spirit and matter. Johnson worried about that confusion, but more fundamentally, in his view, the book was "the favorite of children"[11]—that is, insufficiently se-

---

9. See Daniel Shore, "Milton's Depictives and the History of Style," in *Cyberformalism: Histories of Linguistic Forms in the Digital Archive* (Baltimore, Md.: Johns Hopkins University Press, 2014), 168.

10. Seymour Chatman, "Milton's Participial Style," *PMLA* 83, no. 5 (October 1968): 1392.

11. Johnson, *Lives of the Poets*, 197.

rious, a potentially engaging drama that is spoiled by sensationalism and silliness. In my view, the book suffers from a lack of serious and credible purpose. It doesn't engage Milton fully; it doesn't draw upon his best gifts as a poet. Rarely do readers select their favorite Miltonic passage from Book 6! After the fully satisfying mental heroism of Abdiel in Book 5, and the exposition of Satan's megalomania, Book 6 feels pointlessly action-ridden, undramatic, superfluous. Was it done for show? Perhaps even the poetry is theater. The suspicion is hard to shake that Milton wrote it to make his poem conform to ancient epic, not out of any vocation for martial poetry, and that consequently his heart isn't fully in the book. As he confesses in the proem to Book 9, he was "Not sedulous by nature to indite / Wars" (27–28).

Book 6 opens with a sense of epic excitement as Abdiel returns:

> All night the dreadless angel unpursued
> Through Heav'n's wide champaign held his way (6.1–2)

God greets and celebrates Abdiel, and encourages him to face what will, after the "Universal reproach" (34) he faced in the previous scene, be easier: a physical battle. He is to "subdue / By force who reason for their law refuse" (40–41). He has won "The better fight" (30), and now will fight the lesser, that of arms. God's commands to Michael and Gabriel are likewise martial in flavor:

> Go Michael of celestial armies prince,
> And thou in military prowess next
> Gabriel, lead forth to battle these my sons
> Invincible, lead forth my armèd Saints
> By thousands and by millions ranged for fight;
> Equal in number to that godless crew
> Rebellious, them with fire and hostile arms
> Fearless assault, and to the brow of Heav'n
> Pursuing drive them out from God and bliss,
> Into their place to punishment, the gulf
> Of Tartarus, which ready opens wide
> His fiery chaos to receive their fall. (6.44–55)

Soon the battle is underway, commanded by necessity and sanctioned by God. The lines following, describing the angels trooping across Heaven (evoking the Satanic troops of Book 1), are full of a march of symmetrical adjective-noun phrases: "Ethereal trumpet," "Heroic ardor," "adventurous deeds," and so forth (60–66). Milton is beating war drums. The passage is so loud that we don't at first notice that the battle between Satan and Abdiel is really one of *words*. In this connection, we ought to be confident that Abdiel's belief is right: "who in debate of truth hath won, / Should win in arms" (122–23), but that turns out not quite to be the case; is God intent upon giving a partial victory to the bad angels? Anyway, Abdiel and Satan fight, and Michael call the troops into battle. The poet heightens the language. We notice how the phrases of this passage vary in length, some a half line long, some two full lines, streaming over the line endings, building up excitement:

> whereat Michael bid sound
> Th' archangel trumpet; through the vast of Heaven
> It sounded, and the faithful armies rung
> Hosannah to the Highest: nor stood at gaze
> The adverse legions, nor less hideous joined
> The horrid shock: now storming fury rose,
> And clamor such as heard in Heav'n till now
> Was never, arms on armor clashing brayed
> Horrible discord, and the madding wheels
> Of brazen chariots raged; dire was the noise
> Of conflict; overhead the dismal hiss
> Of fiery darts in flaming volleys flew,
> And flying vaulted either host with fire. (6.202–14)

The weary alliterations "hideous," "horrid," "raged," "fury," and "dire" have by this time in the poem worn out their welcome. And "fiery darts in flaming volleys flew" is an awkward tongue-twister. It is hard not to regard the verse as game-like—and we soon learn that God regards this war as a game. He has limited the might of both sides, overruling what happens from his "stronghold of Heav'n high" (228). The good angels will prevail on the first day; the bad angels on the second; and the Son will prevail, as arranged, on the third. There was never any real war, never any real battle. A real battle is something you can lose. The bad angels can of course lose, but they were defeated, that is, damned, as soon as they rebelled. The good angels, though they don't know it, can't lose. Because, in Michael's words, "Heav'n the seat of bliss / Brooks not the works of violence and war" (273–74), all of the book's militarism is forbidden and illegitimate, which is consistent with Milton's values. Moreover, though the bad angels can suffer pain, they cannot die, and the good angels experience neither pain nor death: there is strangely little at stake. Nonetheless, the good angels go bravely into battle and

> each on himself relied,
> As only in his arm the moment lay
> Of victory (6.238–40)

Everybody except God takes militarism seriously. A Homeric passage that also borrows something from Shakespeare's *Henry V* is one of the book's triumphs:

> Now night her course began, and over Heav'n
> Inducing darkness, grateful truce imposed,
> And silence on the odious din of war:
> Under her cloudy covert both retired,
> Victor and Vanquished: on the foughten field
> Michael and his angels prevalent
> Encamping, placed in guard their watches round,
> Cherubic waving fires (6.406–13)

In fact, the good angels can suffer confusion, humiliation, and disgrace. Milton's readers are all indebted to Arnold Stein for his insight that the war in Heaven is more a war of insult and ridicule than of literal battle, starting with the first verbal battle between Abdiel and Satan.[12] When

12. Arnold Stein, *Answerable Style: Essays on "Paradise Lost"* (Minneapolis: University of Minnesota Press, 1953), 19–22.

he is later wounded by Michael, Satan senses not only pain but "anguish and despite and shame" (340). With that principle understood, Milton's failure to move us with battle scenes makes sense, though there are exceptions to that failure. The most engaging scene occurs on the second day, after the bad angels, routed on the first day, invent gunpowder. They next scoff at the good angels and, though they cannot injure them, confuse them and laugh at them. The humor in this scene, if forced, is nevertheless refreshing, its raillery taking something from the risqué insult often seen in Milton's political tracts.

The temporary defeat of the good angels is, according to Stein, attributable not merely to the invention of gunpowder, but to the fact that the good angels, as we would say today, have "bought into" this war. Each has relied on himself as if the outcome of the war were up to himself alone, rather than God.[13] In such a frame of mind, the good angels have armed themselves to the teeth. When the cannonballs start falling on day two, they are rolled awry,

> The sooner for their arms, unarmed they might
> Have easily as spirits evaded swift
> By quick contraction or remove (6.595–597)

The angels are, Raphael insists, bodily beings, but they are more spiritous than humans. As such, they have an advantage of movement. Armored, they become more like us. The armor and its implications might have been left out of the book, had Milton not wished to suggest that good angels have been put on trial and have erred by subscribing to a belief in the efficacy of war—something Milton deprecated in his heroic sonnets to Vane and Cromwell. It is hard to escape concluding that, just as God put Adam and Eve on trial in the stories of their creations, or put all the angels on trial when he announced the elevation of the Son, so he has put his good angels on trial when he commands them to go to war. God keeps even Abdiel and Michael in the dark, as if they were merely members of the heavenly rank and

13. Ibid., 238.

file. As it turns out, most of the battle is shown to be futile in itself, and no resolution can be found. We notice how the alliteration of the next line gives a sense of meaningless repetition: "War wearied hath performed what war can do" (695). Angelic battle serves only as a foil to the employment of the Son as God's bearer of justice.

The passage describing the Son coming out from Heaven into battle is a divine show, imbued not with Godly persuasiveness but with power. There are shapes, colors, radiances, effusions, flames, and vast numbers of angels in the Son's following. As the Son comes forth, we experience from the mouth of Raphael the showiest, most colorful, most Baroque poetry Milton ever wrote:

> He in celestial panoply all armed
> Of radiant urim, work divinely wrought,
> Ascended, at his right hand Victory
> Sat eagle-winged, beside him hung his bow
> And quiver with three-bolted thunder stored,
> And from about him fierce effusion rolled
> Of smoke and bickering flame, and sparkles dire;
> Attended with ten thousand thousand saints,
> He onward came, far off his coming shone,
> And twenty thousand (I their number heard)
> Chariots of God, half on each hand were seen:
> He on the wings of Cherub rode sublime
> On the crystalline sky, in sapphire throned. (6.760–72)

This is divine display. In the book's climactic passage, the very spectacle of the Son in his chariot drives the bad angels out of Heaven. There is no battle here, just as in the "Nativity Ode" there's no battle, only the revelation of the Redeemer. The angels are not defeated; rather, the Son "infixed / Plagues" in their souls (837–38). The angels are afraid of the Son's "ire" rather than his physical blows (843). As the result of the onslaught, they are "drained, / Exhausted, spiritless, afflicted, fall'n" (851–52)—but not physically, not materially, harmed. In a Miltonic twist, they are not hurled downward by God, but instead throw themselves off of Heaven's brink! As Elizabeth Barrett Browning shrewdly perceived, their fall is accelerated by the unusual meter's two final anapests in line 866: "to the BOTtom less PIT."[14]

By the close of Book 6, Adam and Eve are warned. Raphael tells them that Satan envies them and is now "plotting how he may seduce / Thee also from obedience" (901–2). Fair enough, but has the tale of the War genuinely taught them anything, or is it a diversion? The truly instructive story is that of Abdiel. It models obedience to God under pressure. But the war story does not show God in the best light. As I have pointed out, God disrespects his good angels before the War, when he announces in a hostile manner the exaltation of the Son. Likewise, why would he tempt his good angels when they have already just passed the trial of Satan's rebellion? Or why he would not inform them of a serious rule of Heaven that war accomplishes nothing? In putting the good angels on trial twice, he almost makes stooges of them (precisely Satan's complaint!). Yet trial is the moral principle in Milton's world: even good angels are not exempt; even God must be accountable, and must subject himself to trial by the poet and reader in order to be legitimate. This deference to a higher authority is what Stuart Curran has in mind when he argues that the economy of God's entire universe is "debt," which is what you owe to the being above you, all the way up the chain to the top.[15] Satan resents the debt: "So burdensome still paying, still to owe" (4.53). This debt is dependency and service, the opposite of Satan's fantasy of self-begotten autonomy. This obedience involves taking on sacrifice. God sacrifices the Son, the Son his divine being. Eve and Adam both sacrifice their self-sufficiency. The angels' "victory" in Book 6 is nothing; their final willingness to be in debt to God, and not their success in being so, is everything.

14. Donald S. Hair, *Fresh Strange Music: Elizabeth Barrett Browning's Language* (Kingston, Ontario: McGill-Queen's University Press, 2015), 53.

15. Stuart Curran, "God," in *The Oxford Handbook of Milton*, ed. Nicholas McDowell and Nigel Smith (Oxford: Oxford University Press, 2009), 532.

7

Creation

(BOOKS 7–8)

When Milton revised *Paradise Lost* for the 1674 edition, he made
it a twelve-book poem, more in keeping with Virgil's twelve-book
Aeneid as well as the twenty-four-book Homeric epics. He proceed-
ed with slight revisions, dividing Book 7 into 7 and 8, adding a little
transitional material. Then he renumbered the old Book 9 to Book
10, and split the old Book 10 into Books 11 and 12. I have argued that
the final arrangement of *Paradise Lost* in twelve books permitted it
to be seen as a tripartite poem, with a beginning, middle, and end.
More commonly, the final version of *Paradise Lost* is seen as bipartite,
with Book 7 as the first book of the second half ("Half yet remains
unsung," 7.21)—thereby allowing his poem, after the War, to start over,
as befits the Creation. This shift also has the effect of elevating the
Creation to more than an event in the poem: it could suggest to some
readers a timeless principle of repetition and remembering.[1] As such,
the Creation is something like Christmas in the "Nativity Ode," or like
the Fall: a single event, yet a recurrent one as well. Starting with his
early love of Guillaume de Salluste Du Bartas's *Divine Weeks*, we know

---

1. See Regina Schwartz, *Remembering and Repeating: Biblical Creation in "Paradise Lost"*
(Cambridge: Cambridge University Press, 1988), 2–3, 7.

that the Creation had a special attraction for Milton.[2] The Creation is invoked in his early "Vacation Exercise," as well as in the "Nativity Ode," where it's implied in the story of the poet's gift to the Christ child. This suggests the poet is also a maker, an earthly counterpart to God, who is "the heavenly Maker of that maker," in Sir Philip Sidney's resonant formulation.[3] We hear various Creation stories, or, more broadly, origin stories in *Paradise Lost*: Eve's story, Adam's, and Sin and Death's. In Book 3, we hear of the origin of light. In Book 5, we are taken back to the origin of the rebellion in Heaven. The whole of *Paradise Lost*, of course, is devoted to the origin of our "woe" (1.3), our miserable past. Adam and Eve are in a sense de-created at the Fall, and then are regenerated again, facing a newly created imperfect world. We remember the "fresh woods, and pastures new" that express the regenerated life of the poem's speaker in *Lycidas* (193). But to say all this isn't to arrive at what Milton's creation actually is in our experience of reading it. It is neither complex nor weighty. It is the most cheerful book of *Paradise Lost*, full of activity and high spirits. It is bright; sometimes it is explosive. It affirms Adam and Eve; it also repairs the rather cranky God we saw in Book 5 with an active and benevolent one, one who is associated with the physical world, because God, as we learn, created the physical world out of his own matter.

The narration in *Paradise Lost* is at its most vivacious in Book 7, but the book opens on a dour if beautiful note. If the speaker once (in Books 1 and 2) worried about his trespass into the nether world, here he worries about his trespass into the heavens in the previous two books. His "native element" (7.16) is earth, and he starts by saying that he feels safer there ... then, almost immediately, he launches into one of the most bitter passages in the poem, where he presents himself as an Abdiel figure, or the lonely poet-hero that we see in the invocations to Books 1 and 3, and will see again in Book 9. This is a figure that

2. See Eric B. Song, *Dominion Undeserved: Milton and the Perils of Creation* (Ithaca, N.Y.: Cornell University Press, 2013).

3. Sir Philip Sidney, *An Apologie for Poetrie* (London, 1595), 26.

Stephen Dobranski sees as invented and cultivated by Milton (and imitated by his Romantic and then his modern followers), a myth of the poet, mal-appreciated, suffering amidst enemies, "fall'n on evil days" (7.25), and threatened with "dangers compassed round / And solitude" (27–28).[4] While Milton was not averse to image-making and self-inflation, besides being blind and therefore vulnerable, Milton was in real, and not merely imaginary, danger of losing his life during this period. By virtue of his defense of the deposing and execution of Charles I, he was an infamous regicide, and some of the regicides were brutally tortured and executed in the fall of 1660 after the restoration of the Stuarts. Orpheus, the poetic archetype—invoked here, as in *Lycidas* (58–63)—was torn to pieces in just such a way as some of the regicides were.

The poet's repeated reference to himself as "fall'n" (7.19, 25, 26) underlines that his subject is not only Adam and Eve's fall, but his—and our—own daily repetition of the original Fall. Out of fashion, ignored, living in a "barbarous" age (32), the poet urges Urania to "fit audience find, though few" (31), a line that every reader remembers because of the potent alliteration and the sneer that comes with playing "few" off of "fit." The sudden appearance of "purples" in "morn / Purples the east" (29–30) is an example of Milton's surprising active verbs. He exploits several in this book; an indication that, in a dark world, he has not given up hope. Recall his bittersweet recognition in Book 3 that the seasons "return," even if he cannot see their various manifestations. Perhaps we are always falling, but, as Wallace Stevens posited, "it may be, innocence is never lost."[5] It is tempting to imagine Milton blind in the midst of London's darkness and in the winter of his political discontent, fantasizing about the light-and-motion-show that was the Creation, and about some freshness that remains in God's world, as it

---

4. Stephen Dobranski, *Milton, Authorship, and the Book Trade* (Cambridge: Cambridge University Press, 1999), 8–10.

5. Wallace Stevens, "Like Decorations in a Nigger Cemetery," in *Collected Poetry and Prose* (New York: Library of America, 1997), 127.

does in Gerard Manley Hopkins's "deep down things."[6] This is the Creation as it really matters to our lives. Against the bad story of history, there is the "now" world of animals, a comfort to history's losers such as the poet, and to God, who lost many of his angels, and who will lose his Son. The Creation is not simply a story for Adam and Eve that fills in what they don't know; it offers to them the prospect, though it may mean nothing to them now, of repairing what has been impaired.

Adam and Eve are curious after Raphael's account of the war. They want to know how the world began. Milton's doctrine on what knowledge is permissible to humans is open to some question. In the first part of Book 7 (50–130), the doctrine seems straightforward enough: Heaven permits Raphael to tell Adam and Eve about Heavenly things. The rebellion, war, and Creation are all open to inquiry. In addition, Raphael is commanded to be explicit about the danger Satan represents, and asserts that knowledge is permitted that best serves and glorifies the maker (111–30). Beyond, he stipulates, "abstain / To ask" (120–21). There are some things, he asserts, that are "not revealed" (122), things hidden in night, not even permitted to people in Heaven. Knowledge, Raphael goes on to say, is like food: it sustains you, but too much is not good for you. As G. K. Hunter reads the passage, it makes sense to see Milton's limitation on knowledge as symbolic of a general human limitation.[7] That is, God is not keeping things from us. If he were, Adam and Eve wouldn't have been made witnesses to Raphael's monologue. But God is requiring temperance of us, temperance in all things. Overall in the poem, however, we notice some slippage: some things are forbidden in themselves, some only because we may overindulge in them. The notion will be pursued further in Book 8, where astronomy is the subject. As for now, it appears that God's "knowledge policy" is not terribly restrictive. Adam and Eve may know a great deal indeed.

Why does God create the world? Empson, that nonconformist of

6. Gerard Manley Hopkins, *Gerard Manley Hopkins*, ed. Catherine Phillips (Oxford: Oxford University Press, 1986), 128.

7. G. K. Hunter, *Paradise Lost* (London: George Allen and Unwin, 1980), 174–75.

Milton criticism, thinks it is out of spite.[8] God insists the Creation is a putting forth of his own goodness, to teach the principle that he makes good come out of evil (e.g., 188–91). The creation is not a maneuver to gain the upper hand. Yet God can sound petty and vengeful toward Satan:

> But lest his heart exalt him in the harm
> Already done, to have dispeopled Heav'n,
> My damage fondly deemed, I can repair
> That detriment, if such it be to lose
> Self-lost, and in a moment will create
> Another world (7.150–55)

Whatever one decides, there is at least some question in Milton's mind about the possible motive of spite.

Preeminently, Book 7 celebrates divine energy. Many passages convey that energy through the energy of style:

> One foot he centered, and the other turned
> Round through the vast profundity obscure,
> And said, "Thus far extend, thus far thy bounds,
> This be thy just circumference, O world."
> Thus God the heav'n created, thus the earth,
> Matter unformed and void: darkness profound
> Covered th' abyss: but on the wat'ry calm
> His brooding wings the Spirit of God outspread,
> And vital virtue infused, and vital warmth
> Throughout the fluid mass, but downward purged
> The black tartareous cold infernal dregs
> Adverse to life: then founded, then conglobed
> Like things to like, the rest to several place
> Disparted, and between spun out the air,
> And earth self-balanced on her center hung. (7.228–42)

Milton wonderfully suspends the verb "outspread," giving a sense of God's extent. Line 238 is remarkable for its string of adjectives: "black

8. Empson, *Milton's God*, 56.

tartareous cold infernal dregs," whose cacophony gives a sense of massiveness and effort. Milton crowds the passage with verbs to convey a sense of vigorous action. Nearly every line in the passage contains a felicity, and yet the whole, concluding "And earth, self-balanced on her center hung" (242), conveys a power and force that exceeds the parts with a finality. Earth hangs on its own center, and isn't dependent on anything, even God. This independence is suggested in the eroticized passage depicting the creation of the earth, with the warm "humor" impregnating the globe (279–82). We notice immediately how the mountains "upheave / Into the clouds" (286–87), as if they willed their emergence themselves! This inherent energy, waiting to burst out, is the key to this book: the creation is alive, charged with Hopkins's "grandeur of God."[9] Hunter notices the way the vitality of the vegetation is enlivened by the verbs preceding the nouns:[10] "Forth flourished thick the clust'ring vine, forth crept / The swelling gourd, up stood the corny reed" (320–21). This, we realize, is not so much a description of creation as it is a dramatization of it, one that paradoxically lay dormant in Milton's mind for decades.[11]

At the same time that the earth is independent and vital and, well, *earthy*, it is also like Heaven, a semi-transcendent place "where gods might dwell / Or wander with delight" (7.329–30). Heaven and Earth become indistinguishable. On the fourth day, the bodies of Heaven are sowed "thick as a field" (358). Milton returns yet once more to *Lycidas*, where he speaks of the "other groves, and other streams" of Heaven (174), as if the earth was a paradigm of all creation. On the fifth day, the fish, reptiles, and birds explode from their restraints, and Milton, celebrating the diversity and beauty of the physical world, becomes as playful as he was back in "L'Allegro" and "Il Penseroso." Vigorous double-stresses ("GREEN WAVE," "MID-SEA," "SEA-WEED") sug-

9. *Gerard Manley Hopkins*, 128.
10. Hunter, *Paradise Lost*, 170.
11. See Summers, *The Muse's Method*, 141–44; see also W. B. C. Watkins, "Creation," in *Milton: A Collection of Critical Essays*, ed. Louis Martz (Englewood Cliffs, N.J.: Prentice-Hall, 1966), 121–47.

gest the rapid changing motion of the fish (7.402–4). In lines 430–36, *caesurae* and cacophonous arrangements of words make the big birds sound slow ("the air / Floats, as they pass, fanned with unnumbered plumes," 431–32). In the same passage, short words in a regular meter ("From BRANCH to BRANCH the SMALLer BIRDS with SONG," 433), makes the birds sound diminutive and agile. Everywhere the diction is remarkably fresh: animals of the shores burst their eggs with "kindly rupture" (remember the sun that *"warmly smotes"* the bower, 4.245); whales "Tempest the ocean"; birds "despised the ground" (419, 412, 422). We are told these are "perfect forms" (455): the animals are already as they will be, and they assert their right to be themselves on the instant. Creation comes not "from above," but God allows nature (already formed?) to be what it already is.[12] Who can't see a mode of paganism in Book 7, especially where the poet says of the "Eternal Father *(for where is not he / Present)*" (517–18, my italics). Milton refuses to separate God from his creation, or nature from spirit. And yet, for all the naturalism and paganism, "perfect forms" suggests, with many other phrases in Book 7—"painted wings" (434), "pearly shells" (407), "coats dropped with gold" (406), "shining scales" (401), and "Adorns" (445)—that this creation is as much an *artistic* as a natural event.

The end of Book 7 has perplexed some modern readers in its acceptance of the first chapter of Genesis in depicting the creation of Adam and Eve as more or less equals, as opposed to the story told by Adam in *Paradise Lost* Book 8, which follows Genesis 2, in which Eve is created from Adam's rib, suggesting that she is a lesser, derivative being. Milton accepts both stories. This may be seen as one of many clashes in *Paradise Lost* that have prompted some readers to find Milton's poem a dialogic rather than doctrinal work. What makes this particular contradiction notable is that it is not one imputed to Milton by his modern readers, but one built into Milton's source itself, the Book of Genesis. As such, it is harder to deny. Milton, it appears,

12. Hunter, *Paradise Lost*, 170.

either cannot make up his mind, or he simply sees no inconsistency; Eve is both derivative *and* equal. While this may be problematic to our way of thinking, Milton suggests, throughout his poem, that paradox is simply sewn into the fabric of life. Even so, Book 7 presses home some entirely *un*contradicted points: that humans, whether male or female, are made in God's image; that they are to be fruitful and multiply; that they have dominion over the rest of creation; that they are brought into the Garden after their creation, a point repeated at the poem's conclusion. It is undeniable that Adam and Eve are told that they will "die" if they eat of the forbidden fruit, though they are not told what death is, except that it is a penalty and that it will come on the very day of any violation (544–47). They are charged to govern their appetites in relation to the tree, which may mean that the apple symbolizes a limitation (see "fill / Of knowledge," 12.558–59), rather than presenting a strict prohibition. Adam and Eve may not be sufficiently informed to protect themselves against Satan, but there is no doubt that, however tempting it might be, the eating of the fruit of the tree is insistently prohibited, and that the prohibition is a lenient condition of their stay in Paradise.

No reader of *Paradise Lost* can miss how much celebrating goes on in Milton's celestial sphere. Milton's Sabbath is not in "silence holy kept" (7.594) as in some dull, Victorian Sunday. There is raucous celebration. Even so, in typical Miltonic complications, we are told that Heaven did not rest and the harp "Had work" (595). The line reuniting God and the Son after the Son's six days of work—"The Filial Power arrived and sat him down / With his great Father"—offers a slight touch of humor (587–88). Once again, before closing, the book affirms creating over destroying (which among other things de-emphasizes the War in Heaven), and makes it unclear whether the Garden is a place of reward or of trial. Adam and Eve are to "worship" God, but their designated occupation of ruling the rest of creation is a "reward" (628). Ruling is not seen here as work, but when did ruling (not to mention child-rearing!) not involve work, we might ask? Milton is again a little uncertain. The book closes with another problem: men, the angels sing, would be "thrice happy if they know / Their happiness" (631–32; see Dryden's *Aeneid* 11.240: "Thrice happy thou, dear Partner of my Bed"). Is this just a commonplace hyperbole, or does it suggest that Adam and Eve are not quite mentally equipped, as innocent beings, to know what they have in their possession? If that is the case, can they be said to be sufficient to stand? Can their Paradise exist only in a world in which they know what Paradise is, that is, in a fallen world?

Book 8 carries on the business of Book 7. When he converted *Paradise Lost* to a twelve book poem, Milton cut Book 7 at line 640, and added four transitional lines to Book 8. There is no real break, nor any "break" in the two enjambed lines that begin the book. Raphael has become quiet but Adam, enchanted, thinks he's still speaking. For the first time in the poem, Adam now becomes abstruse, pressing why there is an uneconomical disproportion between the small earth and the large heavens, and why the latter serves the former. Eve gets up to leave the men to their philosophizing, a troubling detail for those who would argue that Milton is generally a progressive author when it comes to the capacity of women. Is his treatment of Eve patronizing? Milton goes out of his way to address the question:

> Yet went she not, as not with such discourse
> Delighted, or not capable her ear
> Of what was high (8.48–50)

Eve is interested; she's not an airhead. Indeed, she asked the question about this apparent disproportion first (recall 4.657–58). She prefers Adam's discourse to Raphael's because it is mixed with flirtation and spousal affection. Milton tends to want to have it both ways. He wants Eve to be two-dimensional, and he wants to assert that kissing and astronomy can't be compartmentalized.

Since Adam eventually ends up earning Raphael's rebuke for excessive curiosity, we could see this passage as Milton's attempt to locate a golden mean between an absence of curiosity and too much of it. Milton could have said (or had Raphael or Adam or even God say) that Eve shouldn't trouble her pretty little head about astronomy. But he does not. What does he do? First, through Raphael, he addresses Adam's concern about disproportion by asserting that "great / Or bright infers not excellence" (8.90–91). The sun is not worthy in itself, but for its relational virtue: it nourishes the earth. This is also a moral claim about human beings that the poem will presently reinforce. Second, God put heavenly bodies out of human sight precisely so that the bewildering size of the universe will remind us of what we cannot know. Raphael's almost comically rapid-fire erudition in the next hundred lines about the universe's structure evades the question (even the Argument to Book 8 admits that Adam "is doubtfully answered"!), hastening to caution "Be lowly wise":

> joy thou
> In what he gives to thee, this Paradise
> And thy fair Eve. (8.170–72)

If knowledge is a solely male prerogative in *Paradise Lost*—and Milton a sexist author, as some readers claim—then it would make more sense for Raphael or Adam to inform Eve of as much at this juncture. Yet by leaving, Eve eventually looks wiser than Adam. This can hardly be a patronizing treatment of her. True, it will become clear that Milton, for narrative purposes, must, so to speak, "get rid of" Eve now, so that Adam might tell his creation story, but Milton did not have to make us wonder about Eve and astronomy. He insists that practical knowledge—"That which before us lies in daily life" (8.193)—is superior to abstruse knowledge. And Eve grasps this better than Adam.

Yet some abstruse knowledge does have its place, and Eve is not forbidden to share in it. If she prefers it interspersed with kissing, does this make Milton's treatment of her patronizing? I don't think so, but others may think it does. With respect to Milton's attitudes toward women, many scholars have made a vigorous case for Milton as a progressive writer relative to his era. In *Feminist Milton*, Wittreich reports that Milton was seen in the eighteenth and nineteenth centuries as a champion of progressive causes as they relate to women.[13] Gilbert and Gubar survey a long arc of female writers influenced by Milton's precedent:

A minimal list of such figures would include Margaret Cavendish, Anne Finch, Mary Shelley, Charlotte and Emily Brontë, Emily Dickinson, Elizabeth Barrett Browning, George Eliot, Christina Rossetti, H. D., and Sylvia Plath, as well as Stein, Nin, and Woolf herself.[14]

Eliot wrote of Milton as "my demigod";[15] Woolf conveyed more ambivalence, calling him "the first masculinist," yet then marveling at his "inexpressible fineness of the style."[16] Leonard has argued forcefully that Wittreich and others overstate their case on behalf of Milton, and that some feminists, such as Mary Wollstonecraft, had serious reservations about Milton's inability to rid his own thinking of the idea that women are sexual beings even while making a case for equality.[17] Though Leonard faults the present-day tendency to find Milton contradictory, he concludes that Milton "is capable of having a divided mind."[18]

Adam presses Raphael to hear the story of his creation. Milton's contrivance here doesn't do him credit: Raphael doesn't know the story of Adam's creation, he says, because on that day he was on an errand from God to check whether Hell's gates were fast shut. Of course, Satan could not escape from Hell without God's permission, and so Raphael is obliged to recognize that God sends his angels on such needless tasks "to inure / Our prompt obedience" (239–40). This may help explain what was going on in Book 6's futile war, but it doesn't speak well of Milton's narrative art.

13. Joseph Wittreich, *Feminist Milton* (Ithaca, N.Y.: Cornell University Press, 1987).

14. Sandra M. Gilbert, and Susan Gubar, "How Are We Fal'n? Milton's Daughters," in *The Madwoman in the Attic: The Woman Writer and the Nineteenth-Century Literary Imagination* (New Haven, Conn.: Yale University Press, 1979), 189.

15. *The George Eliot Letters*, vol. 5, *1869–1873*, ed. Gordon S. Haight (New Haven, Conn.: Yale University Press, 1955), 238.

16. *The Diary of Virginia Woolf*, vol. 1, *1915–1919*, ed. Annie Oliver Bell (San Diego: Mariner Books, 1979), 193.

17. Leonard, *Faithful Labourers*, 1:650–68.

18. Ibid., 1:704.

Adam recounts his own genesis, and his contest with God over whether that is quite adequate (250–559). It takes in his creation, God's subsequent creation of Eve, Adam's temporary loss of Eve after that, and his relocating of her. It also takes in Adam's rhapsodic account of his sexual ardor, Raphael's chastising of Adam for his sensuality, and Adam's defense of himself. We are immediately charmed by Adam's story (250–559): by his waking on the "flow'ry herb" (254) and turning his eyes to Heaven, the "ample sky" above (258); by the "liquid lapse of murmuring streams" portending the Fall (263); by the "fragrance" Adam senses in his heart (266); by his running on his new rubbery legs; by his address to the sun and the light and the earth. In Milton's syntactically brilliant lines we notice Adam's immediate recognition of the necessary existence of a superior power:

Tell me, how may I know him, how adore,
From whom I have that thus I move and live,
And feel that I am happier than I know. (8.280–82)

Receiving no answer from Creation, Adam lies down for a nap. When God himself appears to Adam, only a few lines later, we notice the arresting "When suddenly stood at my head a dream" (292), in which "dream," with its long vowel and the pause that follows, makes the appearance of God seem uncertain, perhaps even provocative. "Stood," which half-rhymes with "head," rightly comes before "dream" because Adam notices the standing before he notices *what* is standing.

God leads Adam (still dreaming) to Paradise, and sets out the rule of life there. He makes it clear that the Tree of Prohibition has no magical quality; it is a "pledge of thy obedience" (325). If he eats, Adam will be expelled into a "world / Of woe and sorrow" (332–33). Milton's language is characteristically mixed here. Adam is "Submiss" (316), but God makes him and Eve "lords" (339), and before we know it Adam names the animals, and then presumes further by registering an objection. Do we not hear the perpetually dissatisfied John Milton in Adam? The scene between God and Adam should, I believe, be taken as partly humorous, but it makes a serious Miltonic point: that

Adam (and by extension, Eve) are beings rightly capable of contention, and even discontent. It is remarkable that they should be given these powers and inclinations, and that God should put Adam on trial to name what he wants in a partner—or that he wants a partner at all. (Eve, however, is not given the power to choose her mate.) It is remarkable that in God's presence Adam should say "In solitude / What happiness?" (364–65). Even more remarkable is the fact that Adam says, with Milton's approval, a partner is needed to "solace" his "defects" (419). Isn't this the man who was just created perfect? It appears that man alone is only *relatively* perfect. He must have a partner to fulfill him, offering "Collateral love, and dearest amity" (426). Milton made the same case about marriage in his divorce tracts, twenty years earlier. It's not enough for marriage to be sexual and procreative; it must be companionate. Spouses need each other. None of these things can be found in Genesis, where Adam takes what God gives him. There is no negotiation.

God now puts Adam into a trance. There is nothing squeamish about the birth of Eve that follows: God

> took
> From thence a rib, with cordial spirits warm,
> And life-blood streaming fresh; wide was the wound,
> But suddenly with flesh filled up and healed. (8.465–68)

For the appreciative Adam, Eve becomes the sum of all beauty, infusing, as Adam says, "Sweetness into my heart unfelt before" (475). But when Adam wakes, Eve has disappeared and, as Adam puts it, "left me dark" (478). In a scene that reminds us of Milton's Sonnet 23, where the image of the poet's dead wife disappears as he wakes from a dream, Adam falls into despair. It turns out to be temporary, but it reveals a vulnerability to female attraction that gives the lie to Johnson's judgment of Milton, that he had "a Turkish contempt of females."[19] When God brings Eve to him (who has, ironically, been gazing at herself in

19. Johnson, *Lives of the Poets*, 171.

the pool), Adam celebrates their union with unusual fervor. Eve is not merely a spouse, but

> Bone of my bone, flesh of my flesh, my self
> Before me; woman is her name, of man
> Extracted; for this cause he shall forgo
> Father and mother, and to his wife adhere,
> And they shall be one flesh, one heart, one soul. (8.495–99)

This is a powerful speech, spoken to God, who, one presumes, is satisfied with it, even though it almost elevates Eve into a god herself. But lest we think Adam is only spiritually attached to Eve, the poet shows us Adam leading her straight to the bower and to what he calls "the sum of earthly bliss" (522). All's going well so far. Eve and Adam are not presented as spiritual beings. Much in their union from the outset is sensuous (a word Milton seems to have coined in 1641); recall the celebration of sex in Book 4. Milton emphatically did not believe, with Augustine and with generations of church fathers, that Adam and Eve were chaste until they fell.

Adam addresses Raphael again, launching into extravagant praise of sensual love that alarms the angel. Adam speaks of being "transported" when he has sex with Eve (530–31), "weak / Against the charm of beauty's powerful glance" (532–33). He claims he knows that Eve is his intellectual inferior, but when he's around her, "so absolute she *seems*" (547), "complete" (548), and "*Seems* wisest, virtuousest, discreetest, best" (550), to such a degree that she becomes more desirable than God. (Note the hesitancy in the repeated *seems*.) She becomes an idol, in whom "All higher knowledge ... falls / Degraded" (551–52). This is strange. Adam has not spoken of Eve in this way before; he has not idolized her. He has revered her: there's a difference. As for sexuality, it has already received the narrator's blessing and God's as well. For his part, Raphael responds harshly. He refers to Eve's beauty as merely an "outside" (568). He says that this outside is worthy of Adam's love, but then, scarcely a few lines later, he refers to Eve's "shows" (575). If in Book 4 sex was "Hail"ed as "wedded love" (4.750), here Raphael puts sex on a bestial level: he explicitly condemns passion and being "sunk in carnal pleasure" (593). He sets that pleasure against heavenly love. It is an abstemious outburst on a par with St. Peter's outburst in *Lycidas* (113–31). Does Milton share Raphael's opinion? Maybe his own view of sexuality is conflicted, as Leonard, citing Wollstonecraft as an ally, also contends.[20] This is the opinion of James Turner writing about the divorce tracts: for all of his liberated views, Milton harbored a reactionary attitude at times toward women.[21] If that is so, it comes out here—awkwardly so, because it is inconsistent with much of the rest of the poem. But Milton repairs the damage.

The narrator has Adam, only "half-abashed" (595), retort that he thinks higher of the wedding bed than Raphael, and that he appreciates Eve's graceful gestures and words as well as her body. In short, Adam stands up to Raphael. This would suggest that the narrator wants to put Adam on a nearly even footing with Raphael, just as he did with Adam and God in the previous scene. Adam goes on to say that the weakness he experiences in love-making is only what he experiences, not what he reveals to Eve. But he backs off from his position, and Raphael, in saying "without love no happiness" (621), backs off too from his angry prudishness. The dispute is unsettled— perhaps more debates will clarify it! The topic is quickly abandoned when Adam, wishing to change the subject, asks about angelic sex, and Raphael boasts that it's better than human sex because it is more spiritual, not impeded by bodies. The book closes quietly. The quarrel is put aside. The prospect of future angelic visits is entertained by Adam: he tells Raphael, "thou to mankind / Be good and friendly still, and oft return" (650–51). It is an invitation. Had Adam and Eve not fallen, their future would presumably have been full of afternoons of conversations, including arguments, with angels.

20. Leonard, *Faithful Labourers*, 1:650–68; and Mary Wollstonecraft, *A Vindication of the Rights of Women*, 1792 (repr. New York: W. W. Norton, 1967).

21. James Turner, *One Flesh: Paradisal Marriage and Sexual Relations in the Age of Milton* (Oxford: Clarendon, 1987).

8

The Fall

(BOOK 9)

Book 9 is the central book of *Paradise Lost*. In it, the narrator tells us for a second time, and definitively, what his purpose is in writing the poem. Satan, frightened out of Paradise, returns to the Garden and expounds on his own purpose. Eve proposes a separation from Adam, which Adam refuses, then grants. Eve, now separated, is tempted by Satan, and falls. Adam is then tempted by Eve, and falls as well. The book closes with a bitter quarrel between our first parents. But the special attraction of Book 9 isn't its bare events or even their cumulative effect. It is rather what Milton brings out of himself and his store of experience to the sparse biblical account he inherited that has the effect of making us think, almost heretically, that the biblical account of Genesis is inadequate to our humanity. It awaited Milton's complex re-telling, his humanistic understanding, his bold appropriation. In this respect, the retelling of Genesis in *Paradise Lost* isn't a mere derivation, but Milton's own story.

Or actually, it is both. When we reach the conclusion of Book 9, we say "yes, that is the way, of course, that Milton would do it, and that is the way it probably really happened if it happened at all." Set free by the lack of specificity in Genesis, Milton's poem can be his own literary property. And yet he does not want us to regard it solely as such. It is, as he would have it be, the story of stories, in somewhat the way that Leopold Bloom's story in *Ulysses* is the master story of all stories. Book 9's reconsideration of every facet of every issue in the poem thus far, its carefully chosen words, its attention to the nuances of the speaking voice, its fraught assessment of motives, even its perplexity and inconclusiveness, are deeply satisfying. It does more than simply relate the Fall. It steals from us our glib opinions; it makes us take on its mystery. Moreover, it deals without strain with issues that are at the core of Milton's work: issues that are as inevitable as they are ultimately unsolvable. Book 9 tests us and tempts us; it forces us to ask what marriage is; it compels us to decide between the claims of spouse and of God; to wonder if virtue can coexist with innocence; to ask whether the state of innocence is sustainable or even desirable; to ask if God is justifiable, given the strength of human loyalties. It is the encompassing ambition of Book 9, even exceeding that of the first two books, that makes us gravitate to it to find the poem's heart, and Milton's.

The book begins with a personal passage, the fourth and last proem of the poem, the others having come in Books 1, 3, and 7. The first forty-seven lines set forth the poet's task, alluding to anxieties that are so far not explicit in the poem. "No more of talk" is blunt (1): while the narrator will not "talk" (or, rather, *write*) further of the good times between our parents and the angel, it also means that the literal "talk" (*conversation*) that went on in the Garden is now, or will soon become, out-of-date in the new dispensation. There is a suggestion in both meanings that the Fall's true subject is transience. The narrator "must *change* / Those notes to tragic" (5–6, my italics). He also refers to his poem as "heroic song" (25), that is, epic—a word that he doesn't ever say. We know that Milton sees epic as a capacious genre, large enough for the pastoral, the lyrical, the tragic, and the martial. Now the pastoral and martial are over. A plainer style again makes an impression on us in the lines "That brought into this world a world of woe" (11), or "Not hers who brings it nightly to my ear" (47). But the predominant tone of lines 1–47 is rather elevated, even when it is sneering, such as when Milton rakes over the heroic tradition and all its trappings before dismissing it in favor of a new one in which "the better fortitude / Of patience and heroic martyrdom" is celebrated (31–32). Neither the lofty gestures of ancient epic nor the fripperies of medieval and Renaissance romance will lure him (see 33–40). He will sing an *anti*-military song, and sing it in (he implies) unadorned imagery, even though it will remain an epic. Milton sets forth a program here, but we don't know yet who the new hero will be (surely, we think, it won't be Adam or Eve!), or how it will be reflected in an event. Up until now, in the passages involving the Son and Abdiel, we have a hint; but Adam and Eve are, after the Fall anyway, sinners. Who can be Milton's hero of patience and heroic martyrdom? We are not surprised that the passage ends on a defensive, vulnerable note. The poet has exposed himself to the possibility of failure: his new epic, celebrating patience, may not satisfy expectations.

Milton's conception of the epic style, inherited from Torquato Tasso, encouraged a playfulness of words, even in solemn passages. We notice the punning on "part" (7–8), meaning both *agency* and a *role* in a tragic play. We notice all the "dis" words (further suggesting apartness) in the opening twenty lines, culminating in the "distance and distaste" predicted to be God's response to the Fall (9). Hereafter, God will love us, but he will not like us. With "distaste" begins a series of eating and fruit puns carried to the last lines of the book. We notice that God's judgment brings "into this world a world of woe" (11), a line with bitter humor. Misery as "Death's harbinger" is a powerful conceit (13). Next to this ironic humor, Satan's pathetic longing comes as a shock. He loves Paradise! It's better than Heaven! It's a seat "worthier of gods" (100)! He can appreciate the way God's virtue is generously given to Paradise rather than hoarded in Heaven. Satan is—and we are sympathetic—profoundly affected, if only temporarily so (50). "With WHAT deLIGHT could I have WALKED thee ROUND" (114), he utters in perfect rising meter, so affectingly that we forget that Paradise was built *because* of his revolt. But soon enough, Satan recognizes that "all good to me becomes / Bane" (122–23)—a capsule definition of envy. Satan reveals that action and lying are the drugs that keep at bay his "relentless thoughts" (130).

Satan has returned after seven days (he had been circling the earth in the meantime). He arrives on the thirteenth day after the Creation. Milton, we recognize, has given Adam and Eve time to grow as a couple. Why? Genesis gave Milton no direction here. Milton could have had Adam and Eve tempted right after their creation. But that would have made their fall too easy. He didn't have to create a Miltonic dispute between Adam and Eve. He could have had them separate unintentionally, absorbed as they are by the work in the garden. As it is, the Separation Scene isn't just an accidental incident, but a carefully calculated and organized adult drama (205–384), a clash of ideas and personalities that would be satisfying in itself, but that also connects closely to the meaning of the Fall. It will be easy to see from what follows that I reject entirely Johnson's judgment that Adam and Eve are not human enough to sustain our interest as characters in a drama.[1]

The drama starts so innocently amid the scent of morning flowers that we don't notice Adam and Eve are called "the human pair" (197), and not "Our first parents," nor do we flinch when Eve calls her husband, directly, "Adam." The language is becoming more grown up. It turns out Eve thinks she and Adam can get more done if they waste less time on talk and affection. Therefore, they should work apart. Superficially, Eve seeks Adam's instruction about the growing size of the garden. What she really wants is to increase her authority in the relationship. Milton faults Eve here for being too interested in work; Eve has "forgotten that happiness and love are primary."[2] She is concerned lest the hour of supper come unearned. She speaks of "divid[ing] our labours" (214). Is this Eden? We may think that Eve is

1. Johnson, *Lives of the Poets*, 193–94.
2. Summers, *The Muse's Method*, 170–71.

wrong, because we have already been told that Adam and Eve can't do anything that God needs. But is *Paradise Lost* consistent in the matter of what Adam and Eve must do for work? If God didn't want the garden tended, he wouldn't have made it so fecund. We are invited to ask what Adam and Eve will do with their days to come. Isn't some of their work tending children, and isn't an orderly garden a proper place for children? And apart from utilitarian reasons, isn't Adam right to praise serious intentions in Eve, and doesn't that make her request to separate more compelling?

But Milton doesn't make it easy for us. Eve puts us off, if only slightly, with her apparent dismissal of love's pleasures and her utilitarianism. For his part, Adam starts a tactful, even elegant, disagreement in the "old language" of the poem—"Sole Eve, associate sole, to me beyond / Compare above all living creatures dear" (227–28), but soon he's patronizing Eve with "nothing lovelier can be found / In woman than to study household good" (232–33). *In woman*? Such clumsy phrasing doesn't make Adam wrong, per se, though it does make him—for a moment—insufferable. But he recovers: Eden is not a workhouse, he insists; there is much to be said for love's diversions, and God made us for delight, after all. Then Adam gets to the heart of the matter. His speech in lines 253–65, on Satan's motivations (envy, especially of conjugal love) in addition to Satan's proximity and his slyness, is all right and relevant. But just when we think Adam has gained the upper hand, he stumbles again with his pedantic and insulting

> The wife, where danger or dishonor lurks,
> Safest and seemliest by her husband stays (9.267–68)

The wife? Not surprisingly, Eve is upset. And she should be. She is not merely a wife, but the mother of mankind. Does Adam love her, or is he playing a role, and expecting her to play one as well? I may be exaggerating the wound to Eve's vanity here, but one notices that she drops for good her idea of efficiency and turns her attention toward what she sees is a mistrust of her "firmness" (279).

There is some dispute among Milton's readers as to what Eve desires. Does she want efficiency? affection? Does she want her ego stroked, as some traditionalists contend? Does she seek independence and selfhood, as some feminist critics argue?[3] Herman posits that what Eve desires more than anything is knowledge and equality, something that was planted in her dream temptation; he concludes that Milton takes Eve's side against misogyny and inequality.[4] Whatever one thinks, Eve never argues for efficiency again. Is that because she's not really interested in it? The reader notices in her next lines the deliberate twisting of syntax and self-interruption:

> Thoughts, which how found they harbor in thy breast
> Adam, misthought of her to thee so dear? (9.288–89)

Eve's words are brilliantly tart; they suggest a lover's injury. Adam sees this injury and attempts damage control, arguing that he doesn't want to see Eve, whatever her ability to stand, exposed to temptation. This smacks of false gallantry, and isn't wholly convincing, but then Adam shrewdly points out just how smart Satan is (namely, he can corrupt angels!), and adds that when temptation comes he, Adam, will be stronger with Eve at his side. Together they make up, after all, a companionate marriage—as Milton extolled in the divorce tracts and as Adam argues to God (8.416–26). Adam's argument is sound, but Eve now deploys her heaviest artillery: she argues the position of *Areopagitica*. If she can't go it alone, then Paradise becomes a "narrow circuit" where Adam and Eve are "still in fear of harm" (9.323, 326). To face and resist temptation is to earn the honor of Heaven. We are prepared to resist, Eve says; why should we fear? Did God make us imperfect? To fear temptation, Eve all but says, is to settle for "a fugitive and cloistered virtue," in the language of *Areopagitica*.[5]

Adam's right-headed reply to the *Areopagitica* argument ought to be decisive: man can be good but err by being deceived. Man's reason,

3. Froula, "When Eve Reads Milton," 327–29.
4. Herman, *Destabilizing Milton*, 127.
5. *Areopagitica, CPEP*, 939

given the wrong information, can be misled to counsel what a man (or woman) really doesn't want to do. We have free will and capability, but our enemy is strong and we are fragile. No, I don't mistrust you. I love you. Why court danger? It will come on its own. Considering the danger Adam and Eve are in, we may think that Adam is right, even if we sympathize—surely Milton wants us to be sympathetic—with Eve's desire for autonomy. But before his argument has the chance to sink in, Adam, who fears the company of a pouting Eve all morning, caves: "Go; for thy stay, not free, absents thee more" (372). At least momentarily, Milton takes sides—a conservative side—as is revealed in the scathing "So spake the patriarch of mankind" (376). Adam has abdicated his authority, underlined by Eve's reminder that she leaves "With thy permission" (378). That Eve's position is viewed as at least partially flawed is revealed in Eve's conviction that Satan, being proud, will not tempt "the weaker" first (383). Of course he will!

It is a tremendous encounter, rich as life itself, richer than a political program. It won't do to say that Adam is right and Eve wrong, or vice versa. They are both right, both wrong. There is no place in the poem where Milton writes so richly, so inconclusively. He seeks not to find heroes and villains, but to set forth our first parents in their fullest capacities. The separation scene harkens back to "L'Allegro" and "Il Penseroso," where again the reader is presented with two evenly matched choices. Frustrated by such apparent indeterminacy, we may embrace Diane McColley's insistence that Adam and Eve are innocent until the actual fall, and that what we look upon here as wrongful behavior on their part is only what happens when innocence grows up and must face real-world problems of governance.[6] Looked at this way, Adam and Eve represent innocence as it is lived or could be lived in our world: their union is one that would involve negotiations, even argument. What we see here, says McColley, are the equally demanding claims of personal liberty (Eve) and of security (Adam). What

6. Diane McColley, *A Gust for Paradise: Milton's Eden and the Visual Arts* (Urbana: University of Illinois Press, 1993), 31–34.

McColley would reject here is the traditional dividing line between innocence and experience. She argues that conflict is inevitable and desirable. Even as they experience their first argument, Adam and Eve are unfallen.

The separation of Adam and Eve—"Thus saying, from her husband's hand her hand / Soft she withdrew" (385–86)—is heartbreaking. The narrator himself is caught up in the pathos of Eve as a "fairest unsupported flow'r," though he tries to remain objective (432). Satan for his part expects to find the two of them together, and is astonished to find Eve alone. Her heavenly/earthly beauty stuns him; it is, in a typical Miltonic paradox, a "rapine sweet" (461), which leaves Satan "stupidly good" (465)—dumbstruck, as in both *mute* and *mindless*. In a reverse of the Fall, Eve seduces Satan. A passage of great sensual power here reveals Satan's lust and malevolence as he comes on to Eve:

> on his rear,
> Circular base of rising folds, that tow'red
> Fold above fold, a surging maze, his head
> Crested aloft, and carbuncle his eyes;
> With burnished neck of verdant gold, erect
> Amidst his circling spires (9.497–502)

Speaking and (ostensibly) reasoning, Satan is hardly to be resisted. He is overwhelming. (The wary reader, however, ought to notice the acrostic

> S
> A
> T
> A
> N

at lines 510–14, as if the poem were flashing a D-A-N-G-E-R sign.)[7] Satan opens with a tacky compliment, addressing Eve as "sov'reign

---

7. Jane Partner, "Satanic Vision and Acrostics in *Paradise Lost*," *Essays in Criticism* 57, no. 2 (January 2007): 129–46.

mistress" and "sole wonder" (532–33). He then goes on to call her closest to God in looks, a "celestial beauty" (540), too good for the beasts around her, a goddess to be served by the angels, and more glozing. Does the flattery work? Milton doesn't say explicitly, but "INto the HEART of EVE *HIS WORDS MADE WAY,*" with its heavy final stresses (550, my italics), makes it look like a fatal blow, whatever is to follow. There is much more to this multifold temptation. Satan tells a story of how he became a speaking serpent, a story that might be appealing to someone who has been told (in Book 5) by an angel that she might become a semidivine being in time. Other beasts, Satan says, envied him his daring. He says he became elevated after eating the fruit, transformed into an intellectual who could look into the universe, into all that is fair and good … but, Ah! All that is fair and good is summed up in Eve! Eve is certainly smart enough to see that the serpent is "overpraising" (615), but when she agrees to follow the serpent to the tree, the phrase "our credulous mother" conveys typically mixed emotions (644). She has been taken in. How could she have withstood?

Eve does resist, at least initially: when she arrives at the fatal tree, she says "Fruitless to me, though fruit be here to excess" (648). She's still poised enough to be witty. Her declaration that there is only one law in Eden appears solid, as does her Miltonic perception, "we live / Law to ourselves, our reason is our law" (653–54). It puts her into the right: Eden is Paradise because reason in almost every case suffices. Hearing this resistance, Satan directs all of his weaponry at Eve. He acts like the outraged friend of mankind. He turns the prohibition into a great cause. He describes the fruit as if it were an idol, something that isn't lost upon Eve, who later idolizes the fruit. As he calls Eve the "Queen of this universe" (684), he also denigrates God as a mere "threat'ner" (687), who is more generous to beasts than to people. And after all, Satan argues, is not knowledge of good and evil a desirable thing? Better informed, you can better shun what you understand—a most Miltonic position. To forbid access to the tree is to make Adam and Eve "low and ignorant" (704). Eating the fruit would make them "gods" (708). (We notice the plural. Satan is now a polytheist.) Is Eve paying attention? But what does it matter what Satan's key temptation is? He is throwing a handful of rocks at a stick in the hope that some will hit the target, sheer plentitude being a favorite device of specious arguers: "These," he says, "these and many more / Causes import your need of this fair fruit" (730–31). What's more, it's noon; Eve must be getting hungry.

Satan has hit her with many arguments. He has spoken to an ambitious side of her nature that wants to be equal with Adam now that she is growing up. Above all, he has worked a miracle in Eve's presence. The bottom line is that *a serpent has spoken*. Could anyone resist this? A grown person, conceivably, but remember that Eve is young; the hand that eats the apple is "rash" (780). It is an "evil hour," but a "rash hand"—not an evil one. She's just had an argument with Adam. She's out to prove something. What leads up to the eating of the apple is attributable to youth. A more experienced Eve would have consulted Adam. A more experienced Eve would not even have listened to Satan, knowing that obedience is a matter of willpower, not reason. But up until the eating, Eve is innocent. After the eating, Eve's thinking becomes cloudy and intoxicated, then envious, deceitful, sinister. She contemplates not telling Adam of the eating of the fruit, so as to shut him off from her new source of power. She worries that Adam will be awarded a replacement wife, a thought so fearful to her that she resolves to "share" her fall with Adam (831). She prepares a face to greet Adam. She prepares a lying, theatrical speech, with protestations of missing Adam, and a testimonial to the benign power of the fruit, though one senses that she doesn't really believe it. Then she threatens Adam by telling him that if he doesn't eat soon, she may be constrained to renounce him, owing to her newly acquired divine being. Her speech is phony, evidently, for in her face "distemper flushing glowed" (887), while Adam's full recognition is emphasized in the harsh consonantal sound describing him: "amazed / Astonied stood and blank" (889–90). This, and not the Separation Scene (which can earn Eve our regard), shows Eve at her worst in the poem.

Adam's response is "inward" (895). Milton may want the reader to speculate on *why* Adam speaks to himself here. Is he emphasizing the first break from the communal life? Most simply, Adam's thoughts show us he is not deceived. Milton wants that to be clear. Adam keeps these thoughts to himself because he thinks they are ignoble: he too is practicing self-deception, like Satan on Niphates. For Eve's sake, he might be putting the best construction on things. His inward speech is as rash as Eve's behavior. Adam is a desperate boy now. Within a minute of hearing Eve's plea, he says "Certain my resolution is to die" (907). He cannot imagine another Eve if this Eve were taken away:

> I feel
> The link of nature draw me: flesh of flesh,
> Bone of my bone thou art, and from thy state
> Mine never shall be parted (9.913–16)

It is turbulent, desperate language, but we are inclined to take Adam's side. Awash in that fellow feeling, we can easily forget the lines that follow, and that lead into what he actually says to Eve:

> So having said, as one from sad dismay
> Recomforted, and after thoughts disturbed
> Submitting to what remediless,
> Thus in calm mood (9.917–20)

Here is a Miltonic complication indeed. We are attuned with Adam's loyal resolve, but we are told that Adam is seeking comfort and a calm heart, not some generous heroic martyrdom. In that self-indulgent frame of mind he rationalizes Eve's deed (925–52)—and then, after all the rationalizing, simply gives up on his situation and declares:

> However I with thee have fixed my lot,
> Certain to undergo like doom; if death
> Consort with thee, death is to me as life;
> So forcible within my heart I feel

The bond of nature draw me to my own,
My own in thee, for what thou art is mine;
Our state cannot be severed, we are one,
One flesh; to lose thee were to lose myself. (9.952–59)

Is this laudable, even heroic? Some readers might say nothing so full
of Satanic despair and selfishness and obsessive fixity could be laud-
able. Read with certain emphases on all the occurrences of "my," "me,"
"mine," and "myself," the speech comes across as *self*-centered, a coun-
terpart to Eve's vanity at the temptation. Adam acts like he's taking a
hard way out, but actually he alleviates his agony of decision making
and avoids the issue. Unlike Milton in his best sonnets, Adam does
not take the time to work through his impulses. Those who find Adam
at fault here note the narrator's line that Adam was "submitting to
what *seemed* remediless" (919). (That *seems* again; is it truly remedi-
less?) He submits when he should draw upon his mental resources.
He could have interceded with God, as the Son does with man. But
whatever he should have done, he should not have succumbed, in
Fish's phrase, to the "temptation to action."[8] After Adam announces
his decision to eat, Eve lauds his "trial" (861, 975), but there has been
no trial. Eve's effusive compliment comes off as a jeer.

Milton insists that Adam isn't deceived, but "fondly overcome
with female charm" (999). "Female" here is a frosty word, as the narra-
tor seeks to salvage Adam's superior mind, and "fondly" would appear
to mean "affectionately." Yet in the scene that ensues, with Adam and
Eve acting like drunken fools, it is hard to find Adam at all rational.
Milton does not treat him like a man who has done something right;
perhaps "fondly" is also to be heard as "foolishly." Yet it is the irratio-
nality of Adam, fighting against an invisible God to hold on to his
visible and tactile wife that, in the eyes of many readers, makes Adam
defensible here and even appealing. Adam gives up his life and accepts
death ("whatever thing death be," 695) for Eve. We find it hard to
condemn him, even as we are conscious of his faults, and hence we

8. Fish, "The Temptation to Action in Milton's Poetry."

suspect that Milton is also secretly on his side, in spite of all the harsh things he says about Adam's weakness. Waldock, one of many following Blake, sees this as a crucial passage in the entire poem. Milton, defending God, wants us to join him in justifying God and hence in condemning Adam. But because of the commitment in Adam's love, we simply cannot be so harsh. We must take Adam's side if we are to obey our full humanity. This for Waldock means that the poem's rationale, the defense of God, must of necessity fail.[9] Surely Milton would not himself have forsaken Eve. We re-read Milton's sonnet to his dead wife, written not long before he wrote *Paradise Lost*, and we feel confirmed in supporting Adam here. But in so doing, are we simply ratifying Adam's sin, sending him on his way with a slap on the wrist? Milton called this fall "tragic" (6); why not take him at his word?

The argument is more complex, as we know. Even as we subversively approve of Adam, we're aware that Adam is not selfless at all, and is certainly impetuous. He gave up on God too quickly, and he doesn't take the full measure of Eve's disobedience and her possible post-Fall motive, jealousy. On top of that, he is, by God's rules, guilty of negligence in letting Eve go. If that is the case, isn't he trying to mitigate his first crime by committing another? But even if we censure Adam and Eve both, we are drawn to them. As for Eve, and our judgment of her, remember how inexperienced she is, and how unfairly stacked the odds are against her resisting Satan, with all his experience. That apt oxymoron, "Eve, our credulous mother" (644) says it all: "credulous" is spit out with contempt. "Mother" is reverent. Milton is not making it easy for us. A portion of Milton's theology in *Paradise Lost* is at odds with his values, but Milton must have been aware of several of the various dilemmas he causes his readers to experience. Surely he had a sense of his overside (so to speak) that condemns Adam and Eve, but he also listens to his underside that embraces them. His poems seduce us into embracing his underside, only to slap us in the face, to correct

9. Waldock, *"Paradise Lost" and Its Critics*, 54–57.

us with unshakable orthodoxy. The "guerrilla" Miltonists tend to give Milton less credit for conscious technique.[10] They look at him as a man tragically divided by his experience in the English Revolution, one who can't be counted on to make up his mind; they regard *Paradise Lost* almost as if it were a book of confessions. Whatever position one takes, one has to decide how Adam and Eve are used by the narrator. The ability to fall must be built into their hardwiring, but not *so* built in that they must act in a certain way. God's purpose was to make people who could be tempted and fall so that their resistance to temptation would mean something. Making our parents weak and capable of falling doesn't mean willing them to fall. Or does it? That problem takes us back to Book 3 and its imponderable predicament having to do with foreknowledge and foreordination. It also takes us back to Book 5, which makes innocence and imperfection somewhat compatible.

The rest of Book 9 describes the aftermath. The diction in this passage urges us to remember Adam and Eve's more blessed eroticism as summoned up in Book 4. Now, after the Fall, Adam and Eve are "intoxicated" (9.1008). Adam offers flirtatious glances. They "swim in mirth" (1009). Vainly they sense "divinity" within them (1010). Eve casts "lascivious eyes" on Adam (1014), like a voyeur, and they engage in "dalliance" (1016)—a poisonous word, at odds with the heartfelt love of Book 4. Eve for Adam has "purveyed" much pleasure (1021). Adam now celebrates that pleasure, not intimacy. He proposes that guilt is not the destroyer but the spice of fallen love. This part of the book is full of words and phrases like "play" (1027), "inflame" (1031), "enjoy" (1032), "their fill of love and love's disport" (1042), and "contagious fire" (1036). Adam and Eve head to a "shady bank" to practice shady amours (1037). When they wake up they have an argument. Clearly, they are not quite who they were before. But how different are they? They experienced passionate sex in the state of innocence (love "reigns here and revels," 4.765) as well as now, though this later-stage

10. Herman, *Destabilizing Milton*, 20.

sex has an element of the prurient. Sex is now the "solace" of their sin (9.1044). That sounds bad, but Adam in Book 8 argued that Eve would "solace" his defects (8.419). Ironically, defects are part of their perfection; defects bring them together. There are other suggestions of the comparability of the unfallen and fallen states. When Adam exercised authority in Book 4, his gentle hand "seized" Eve's hand (4.489). But he "seizes" her hand here too (9.1037). The love they share in Book 4 is called "dalliance" (4.336), as it is here (9.1016)—as was Solomon and his "fair Egyptian spouse" (9.443), or even more audaciously, between Satan and Sin (2.819)! We're told that there was no guilty shame in the Garden before the Fall, yet Eve comes to him "blushing like the morn" (8.511). Eve is not free in her behavior before the Fall, as she is after—or is she? Adam and Eve argue after the Fall, but they also argue before the Fall.

Again, the difference between innocence and fallenness may be one of degree rather than kind, like that scale of being that Raphael articulates in Book 5. Yes, Milton says otherwise, and often treats the Fall as a precipitous change. But when we read his poem, innocence and experience are not such opposite states. Rather, one grows out from another. "Grow" is the crucial word. Surely we can't imagine Eve and Adam changeless, addressing each other forever in stately phrases such as "my author and disposer" (4.635). Nor could we imagine a life without disagreements, considering that, in Adam's account, men and women, perfect beings and approved by God as such, need the help of each other. On account of the sheer profusion of *growth* in the garden, something resembling work has got to be done. Splitting up is inevitable. The profusion itself is an emblem of necessary change, just like that cycle of the day Adam and Eve celebrate in Book 5. McColley is right: in an innocent world, there would inevitably arise conflicting yet equally correct claims.[11] Therefore, Adam and Eve must argue. Why else would Raphael depict a life of trial where Adam and Eve might improve themselves over "tract of time" (5.498)? In such a

11. McColley, *A Gust for Paradise.*

world, falling is as unavoidable as rising. When Raphael tells Adam and the Eve on the same day to aspire and, at the same time, to be happy with what they have, he is practicing the double, "inclusive," vision of *Paradise Lost*. It's everywhere in the language of the poem. Adam and Eve are both right about work; they are both right about the question of working apart. Eve speaks of Adam's "dear side" (9.965), the side from which she was sprung. That "dear" can mean *precious*, but it can also mean *dire*. Eve innocently comes from Adam's rib, but earlier, in Book 1, we were troubled to read that the devils dig "ribs of gold" out of Hell's ground (1.690). When Eve celebrates Adam's "glorious trial of exceeding love" (9.961) in eating the fruit, she means to praise him. The reader sees all the negative meanings of "exceeding," and cannot help but be reminded that what Adam does is to a degree self-sacrificial, "glorious" like the Son, and unlike Satan. Adam's apologetic "link of nature" that connects him with Eve is a rationalization to be sure (9.914), but there *is* a link of nature, sanctioned by the author/God, who made the entire world out of himself. This is not confusion. It is Milton's profusion, which comes out of his determination to encompass the entire world's abundance in "the copious matter of my song" (3.413).

The quarrel that closes Book 9 is preceded by Adam's powerful dramatic utterance that reminds us (how could it otherwise?) of the narrator's "fall" from sight (3.22–55). Here is Adam:

> How shall I behold the face
> Henceforth of God or angel, erst with joy
> And rapture so oft beheld? Those heavenly shapes
> Will dazzle now this earthly, with their blaze
> Insufferably bright ... cover me, ye pines,
> Ye cedars, with innumerable boughs
> Hide me, where I may never see them more. (9.1080–84, 1088–90)

It is a confession of shame bordering on despair, but it gives a tragic dignity to Adam to have plumbed the magnitude of his crime. (Contrast Satan's unrepentant speech on Niphates.) Now, we are told,

Adam and Eve are assailed by tears and winds of passion and "anger, hate, / Mistrust, suspicion, discord" (1123–24). Their argument itself is bitter and banal at the same time. It is their second argument, but unlike the first, in which they argued to articulate the truth of their emotions, and held hands doing so, Adam and Eve here argue to score points. Adam cites Eve's willful desire to separate, not acknowledging that he let her go. If he takes no blame, Eve likewise takes none, accusing him at once of being a tyrant (you should have let me go) and a wimp (you shouldn't have). In response, Adam flat out lies, arguing that he ate the apple because he chose to die with Eve, not because he was afraid of living without her, and that his real fault was in overestimating Eve. In this last scene, Eve's accusations are irresponsible and Adam's are self-serving. What is missing from the argument, Milton underlines, is that neither is "self-condemning" (1188); that comes in the next books.

9

Recovery

(BOOK 10)

Book 10 starts by depicting an action that isn't completed in Book 9, the fall and punishment of Adam and Eve, but it gives the impression of beginning a downward motion in the poem, and it should. Here, we gather, *Paradise Lost* is starting to conclude. The central action of the poem is over, and there's nothing left to make us feel the sense of anticipation that we get from Books 1–9. Yet the poem begins to rise as well: it rises from Adam and Eve's wretchedness to their resolve, from their disorientation to their purposeful departure. It takes us through what they learn about living in a fallen world, a process that ends with the exchange of speeches between Michael and Adam at the close of Book 12. In this sense, then, the last three books of *Paradise Lost* paradoxically offer a rising action as well as a falling one. But the poem suggests in a few, critical places that rising and falling are not mutually exclusive.

We are surprised in the first fifty or so lines of Book 10 to see the narrator reveal that he's not condemnatory—not entirely. He opens by emphasizing that the Fall was Satan's act, that "He" perverted "Eve" and "Her husband she" (3–4). The rhyme links Satan and Eve, letting Adam off the hook. But, remembering his task of justification, Milton quickly argues that Adam and Eve were both equipped to resist Satan, and that they should have resisted (8–11). Nevertheless, the narrator is not certain of his own argument, for he makes God appear and present his own case (as God did in Book 3), arguing that his foreknowledge didn't necessitate Adam's fall (10.34–62). *Adam was free*, God argues. But, as if God doesn't think much of his own argument, he quickly puts the matter behind him: "But fall'n he is …" and now the task of the punishment remains (47), which God delegates to the Son as a gesture of mercy. The Son is "Man's friend" as well as his redeemer (60).

The Son arrives almost immediately. The tenor becomes more austere. No description of the Son's flight, as of Raphael's in Book 4, is offered. The time and temperature of the day ("evening cool," 95) is emblematic of the abating of God's wrath, but also the dampening of Heaven's once-friendly manner. Raphael is gone. Yet the passage describing the appearance of the Son (heard, not yet seen) is lenitive and beautiful (92–102), with several repetitions and a steady beat. The Son's address to Adam is mild, if slightly ironic in pretending that he doesn't know why Adam is not present. The pauses in lines 108–15 render Adam and Eve's hesitancy perfectly. The string of "ands" in 113–14—"And shame, and perturbation, and despair / Anger, and obstinacy, and hate, and guile"—is powerful, reminding us that Milton believed that the Fall comprehended all the human sins, and reminding us as well, and not accidentally, of Satan's plight in the first two books (recall 1.558). When the Son asks Adam if he has eaten of the tree, Adam's answer, following Genesis, is awful: evasive, buck-passing, accusatory, prevaricating and impudent (10.124–43). It blames God for the gift of Eve, and makes his own eating of the fruit an afterthought of the crime. Adam's self-exoneration earns the sarcasm of the Son.

Adam's passage is wordy, and in that respect it calls attention to Eve's answer to the Son's subsequent brutal question, "Say, woman, what is this which thou hast done?" (158). Milton's rendering of Eve's response to the charge opens a new chapter in *Paradise Lost*:

To whom sad Eve with shame nigh overwhelmed,
Confessing soon, yet not before her judge
Bold or loquacious, thus abashed replied.
"The serpent me beguiled and I did eat." (10.159–62)

These four lines reveal why Milton is prized for his command of syntax. The first three lines accumulate information, with adjectives and participles, but postpone resolution until Eve speaks directly. The speech then becomes a simple action, and explodes. Eve's directness makes Adam look self-excusingly Satanic by comparison. This comparison isn't outrageous if we consider that Adam and Eve have "fallen" like Satan from a blessed state, but whereas Adam was "bold and loquacious" as was Satan in Hell, Eve here is not. Some readers begin to develop suspicions about Satan here—if they were swept off their feet by him earlier—and to conceive a sense of heroism that is associated with modest truthfulness, not defiant chest-beating. Eve demonstrates more heroic virtues than Adam, leading many critics and even a screenwriter to see her as "the true hero ... who does the essential thing."[1]

The Son passes sentence on the serpent (and, indirectly, on Satan) and on Adam and Eve. His condemnation refers to Eve's seed (that is, mankind), which will bruise the head of the serpent, an indication that Eve will eventually produce the Redeemer who is also the destroyer of Satan. Eve will hereafter bring her children forth in sorrow, meaning both the pang of childbirth and the sorrow of post-lapsarian mortality. She will have to submit to Adam's will—a passage that suggests that Adam and Eve were originally made equal. Despite what the poem declares in Books 4 and 8 about Adam and Eve's inequality, the Son is equally harsh with Adam as with Eve, for both are equally sinful. Adam will return to dust (die) and, while living, "In the sweat of thy face shalt thou eat bread" (10.205). The Son then, in a tender moment, like a servant, "As father of his family" (216), clothes his chil-

1. John Collier, *Milton's "Paradise Lost": Screenplay for Cinema of the Mind* (New York: Knopf, 1973), 16. See also Barbara K. Lewalski, "Milton on Women—Yet Once More," *Milton Studies* 6 (1974): 3–20; and Raymond B. Waddington, *Looking into Providences: Designs and Trials in "Paradise Lost"* (Toronto: University of Toronto Press, 2012).

dren literally, and then clothes them with his "robe of righteousness" (222). He departs quickly and without ceremony, just as he arrived. Again, austerity is the order of the day.

A long middle section resumes the story of Sin and Death, now waiting at the Gates of Hell (229–409). Satan's success on Earth gives Sin "new strength" (243), and in this frame of mind she affirms her union with her son Death, who in turn affirms his willingness to follow her wherever she goes. In time and with a shock one realizes that their union is like Adam and Eve's. They plight their troth; they lend each other succor and aid; they go hand in hand. Death (Eve) follows Sin (Adam) as they move toward their destiny. Through the power of their intuition, they build a causeway from Hell to Earth, a creation to rival God's, a masterpiece of convenience for the soon-damned traveler who may book passage "Smooth, easy, inoffensive down to hell" (305). This is all a grisly business, but this section may be Milton's most droll; it is the humor of revulsion and contempt. He calls the bridge a "pontifice" (348), which is a literal reference to a bridge (Latin *pons*), but which slyly incriminates the pope as the architect of damnation.

Satan soon joins them, having fled Eden in fear before the Judgment (though he witnessed Adam's fall). Sin tells him that he is the "prime architect" of the bridge (356), and that she and Death were mere builders, having divined the purpose of their father. Parallels abound here: Sin and Death are to Satan as the Son is to God. We must recall that God refers to the Son as "My word, my wisdom, and effectual might" (3.170)—and that the Son does God's work in the Creation. Sin's affirmation that Satan, in his wisdom and successful revenge, has gained back what he lost in war, takes us back to the problems posed by the fallen angels in Book 1. Satan gives Sin and Death, his children, the rule of the earth, which is earned by their obedience. This obedience is in direct contrast to the disobedience of Adam and Eve, who proceed to lose Eden. Satan's charge to Sin and Death is like God's to Adam and Eve:

All yours, right down to Paradise descend;
There dwell and reign in bliss; thence on the Earth
Dominion exercise and in the air,
Chiefly on man, sole lord of all declared,
Him first make sure your thrall, and lastly kill.
My substitutes I send ye, and create
Plenipotent on Earth (10.398–404)

Satan concludes by telling his children to "be strong" (409)—precisely what Raphael told Adam (8.633)! They have been tested like so many other beings in this poem, and they have passed. One could go on citing parallels. Some of them couldn't in any way be considered humorous by our standards, but Milton was stronger-minded than we are, and he probably did regard them as such. Almost certainly as well he thought that these parallels were a positive affirmation of the unity of God's creation, of the eternal monism, the inescapable converging of opposites.

Satan returns to Hell, like a Roman general from battle, carrying on his face either "permissive glory" or "false glitter" (10.451–52). He makes his entrance and tells the story of his conquest of Eden, most of it true, except his assertion that God

> hath giv'n up
> Both his beloved man and all his world,
> To Sin and Death a prey. (10.488–90)

This segment is remarkable for the most grotesque passage in the poem, the Ovidian-Dantean metamorphosis of the fallen angels, writhing as if coiled in a snake pit:

> for now were all transformed
> Alike, to serpents all as accessories
> To his bold riot: dreadful was the din
> Of hissing through the hall, thick swarming now
> With complicated monsters head and tail,
> Scorpion and asp, and amphisbaena dire,
> Cerastes horned, hydrus, and ellops drear (10.519–25)

Desperate for relief from their thirst, the serpents make their way to a grove, in which God has made grow apples that turn to ashes in their mouths, and the serpents "With hatefulest disrelish writhed their jaws" (569). Even readers who are dubious of imitative sound cannot fail to hear the mastication in that thick-woven line, just as we heard the sibilance in "dismal universal hiss" (508). It is an awful punishment, yet Milton takes something off of it, which marks a difference from Dante. The angels don't undergo this punishment perpetually, nor will they. It is a "yearly" humiliation, just as the sight of the gorgons and other monsters of Hell (as we learn in Book 2) are brought to these sights "by certain revolutions" (2.597). They do not dwell in them perpetually, as Dante would have made them do. This is a peculiarity. Milton is simply not fascinated by physical punishment. It is the apprehension and the indignity of punishment that punishes.

Having made their way to Paradise, Sin and Death face their new world like Adam and Eve. When Sin asks what Death thinks of this new empire, Death answers in the terms resonant from Book 1: "To me, who with eternal famine pine / Alike is Hell, or Paradise, or Heaven" (10.597–98). What places impress upon us depends on the frame of mind we bring to them. Satan says "The mind is its own place" (1.254), whereas Death says, in effect, "the mouth is its own place." When Death complains to his mother that there isn't enough yet to "stuff this maw" in Paradise (10.601), in a humorous (if grim) rejoinder Sin promises a long term feast, starting now with "herbs, and fruits, and flow'rs" (the salad course), then working up to a fish and poultry course (603–4), until, Sin having infected the human beings, they will become Death's "last and sweetest prey" (609), the *pièce de résistance*. But God's plan, as revealed next, has Sin and Death as his garbage men:

> I called and drew them thither,
> My Hell-hounds, to lick up the draff and filth
> Which man's polluting sin with taint hath shed (10.629–31)

When they are done serving God's ecology, they will be thrown to Hell, where they will obstruct the mouth of Hell forever. That is the terminus of Milton's story. It is a long way off.

The next fifty or so lines detail the changes in the earth after the Fall. They are—at least in the estimate of this reader—somewhat parenthetical. Milton relegates them to only a few lines, and the verse, though not vague and detached, is rote and dull:

> some say the sun
> Was bid turn reins from th' equinoctial road
> Like distant breadth to Taurus with the sev'n
> Atlantic Sisters, and the Spartan Twins
> Up to the Tropic Crab; thence down amain
> By Leo and the Virgin and the Scales (10.671–76)

And so on. One can only wonder what happened to the boy at St. Paul's who thrilled to the lines of Du Bartas! Remembering Book 7, or 3, or elsewhere where Milton conveyed excitement about the universe, we might surmise that Milton didn't want the "changes in the earth" passages to compete with, and possibly take something away from, Book 7. It's more likely that the subject quickly exhausted his interest, and that he was eager to get back to Adam and Eve. Certainly, if there were any need to prove Milton a humanist, it would be the disproportionate difference between these two subjects in Book 10. When we return to Adam, it is if Milton comes alive again, and we remember that one of his ambitions was to write a biblical drama.

The last section of Book 10 (719–1104), while being a drama and therefore intensely concentrated upon itself, also revisits the entire poem. When we meet Adam at the outset, he is truly in the Satanic predicament that we witnessed in Books 1 and 2:

> O miserable of happy! Is this the end
> Of this new glorious world, and me so late
> The glory of that glory? Who now become
> Accursed of blessed; hide me from the face
> Of God, whom to behold was then my highth
> Of happiness (10.720–25)

This is the nadir of the post-lapsarian drama, low in the sense that Adam is depressed in fortune, and nearly damned like Satan. He is morally weak: full of regret, mendacious, self-pitying, and theatrical in the worst sense. But there is something else that emerges, which is Adam's sense that he will bear the weight of his sin through the ages. Like Satan, he will lead others into sin, but Adam realizes that fact with a laudable tragic attitude rather than with self-promotion or evasiveness. When he carps, "Did I request thee, Maker, from my clay / To mold me man" (743–44, and the epigraph to *Frankenstein*), we see a childish streak in him, just as we do when he too late claims that God's terms were too hard. Even so, Adam concedes, he himself accepted the terms; he made a deal with God, one he is obliged to keep. Generally we may say the lines below summarize Adam's development:

> Him after all disputes
> Forced I absolve: all my evasions vain,
> And reasonings, though through mazes, lead me still
> But to my own conviction: first and last
> On me, me only, as the source and spring
> Of all corruption, all the blame lights due (10.828–34)

Adam's nocturnal agonies typically go from an accusation of God to an exoneration of God, so that, like the narrator, he too becomes God's advocate. Yet it is hard to tell whether what we hear from Adam is truly responsibility or self-pity. In this respect, Adam's psychology is like our own in comparable situations—or, again, like Satan's in Books 1 and 4. We might at times judge Adam harshly in this passage, but also—as with Satan—we find his agony affecting, such as when he expresses a desire to "lay me down / As in my mother's lap" (10.777–78). Adam has no mother!

When Eve approaches, Adam unleashes invective that, were it excerpted (867–908), could prove many times over Milton's misogyny, especially when juxtaposed with similar invective in the divorce tracts. The speech, however, taken on its own, is so full of overkill and mistaken accusations that we must be wary of attributing its thoughts to Milton. For Adam certainly lies, and the narrator knows he does, when he says he would have "persisted happy" without Eve (874). He claims that he imagined Eve wise, and that's why he let her go. But in fact he was afraid of Eve's vulnerability, and he let her go because he didn't want to offend her with his doubts. He slanders Eve by saying that she's a "show," a mere "rib," but that is all the more reason (if it were true) not to let her go (883, 884). Adam paints himself as a victim of Eve, and he questions God's wisdom in making her, forgetting that he was the one who asked that she be made. The final part of his speech exceeds all bounds, finding women a flaw in all creation, and expounding a future of catastrophes of dating and courtship that becomes quite contemporary-sounding.

As Adam dismisses Eve, here as in the Separation Scene, Eve, though gentle and contrite, does not essentially give ground. I am your wife, she says: you cannot leave me; I cannot live without you. Her speech, beginning "Forsake me not thus" (914–46) is one of *Paradise Lost*'s most moving passages. Constant recitation of it will neither palliate its strength nor wear away its subtle art. It works mainly by its sophisticated simplicity and plangent repetition—of sounds, words, phrases and grammatical figurations. These lines serve to illustrate:

> Forsake me not thus, Adam, witness Heav'n
> What love sincere, and reverence in my heart
> I bear thee, and unweeting have offended,
> Unhappily deceived; thy suppliant
> I beg, and clasp thy knees; bereave me not,
> Whereon I live, thy gentle looks, thy aid,
> Thy counsel in this uttermost distress,
> My only strength and stay; forlorn of thee,
> Whither shall I betake me, where subsist? (10.914–22)

There is the repetition of "me" and "thy" and the matching of the pronoun-noun units: thy looks, thy aid, thy counsel. But beside that parallelism, there is a virtuoso playing off of short and long phrases: two short, then one long, a quality more noticeable when rearranged:

Thy gentle looks
Thy aid
Thy counsel in this uttermost distress (10.919–20)

Milton poignantly remembers his poem's past. Here Eve reaches back and picks up the facile "He for God only, she for God in him" (4.299), varying it with "both have sinned, but thou / Against God only, I against God and thee" (10.930–31), which is not facile at all. What might be taken here as the reestablishment of the subordination of women in fact is not so. Eve looks not only contrite, but generous, even masterful. She takes command of the situation she has put herself and Adam into. This constitutes her maturity, her abandonment of narcissism. Her closing lines—"On me, sole cause to thee of all this woe, / Me, me only, just object of his ire"—come across forcefully (935–36). These lines echo the earlier words of the Son:

Behold me, then, me for him, life for life
I offer, on me let thine anger fall;
Account me man (3.236–38)

As the Son's lines are considered heroic, so must also Eve's be. While Adam will become the person to whom the phrase "heroic martyr-dom" applies (9.32), Eve is more heroic than Adam, as she leads the way from resentment and despair to regeneration. We might be inclined to say, suspecting a traditional division of labor at work in the poem, "ah yes, it is the woman who offers prayer and contrition." But contrition is not to be considered a feminine virtue alone.

Adam is "disarmed" by Eve's words (10.945). Only when he is so, paradoxically, can he be a Miltonic epic hero—like Milton's narrator, who has striven over the writing of *Paradise Lost* to "disarm" his verse, to write of inner rather than merely of outer things. It is Eve who quietly and humbly makes Adam start to become a man. Adam begins to recover only when he proposes that they pray together (952–57). However, at this point his prayers would be conditional, and not disinterested. "If prayers / Could alter high decrees," he says, revealing that prayer for him is a contractual thing (952–53). But, again, inspired by Eve, he proposes that they

> strive
> In offices of love, how we may light'n
> Each other's burden in our share of woe (10.959–61)[2]

It is striking that what was love waving "his purple wings" (4.762) has now become strictness of conscience, the work of relationships. This work is not quite what Eve had in mind at the Separation.

Eve shows resourcefulness and courage in suggesting two solutions: abstinence or suicide. Adam shrewdly and wisely rejects them both as indices of despair rather than of self-sacrifice. He rejects them as rejections of the terms of life itself. This affirmation of life, and even pleasure, even after original sin, is altogether Miltonic, and we can see it as a refutation of Raphael's monkish distrust of the body's needs. Now, out of what could be despair, the despair of Satan in the early books, Adam forges a belief, discarding "Rancor and pride, impatience and despite," instead embracing "hope" and God's "just yoke" (1044–45), and labor: "Idleness had been worse" (1055). He will kindle fire to fight the cold that is on its way, and pray to God for instruction. Instead of speculating on God, he affirms faith: "Undoubtedly he will relent" (1093). The book ends with Adam and Eve "watering the ground" with their tears (1071, 1083).

2. Adam's phrase about love's "offices" might well have influenced Robert Hayden's great poem "Those Winter Sundays," where knowledge of those difficult "offices" of love is associated with genuine adulthood: "What did I know, what did I know / of love's austere and lonely offices?" In *Collected Poems*, ed. Frederick Glaysher (New York: Liveright Publishing, 1985), 41.

10

A Meeting of Epic & History

(BOOKS 11–12)

Books 11 and 12 have their poetic moments, especially in the waning lines of 12. But what Samuel Johnson controversially said about *Paradise Lost* as a whole, that "none ever wished it longer than it is," is indisputably true, with some exceptions, of these last two books.[1] Even the books' defenders would concede this. There are several quotable passages in Books 11 and 12, but little of the soaring majesty of the early books, or the middle ones. Lewis calls Books 11 and 12 "inartistic," the result of Milton's hasty desire to end his long task.[2] He chastises Milton for presenting a long history lesson, which he characterizes as "an undigested lump of futurity."[3] Over two centuries earlier, Joseph Addison felt that Milton in these two books "neglected his poetry."[4] Milton's eighteenth-century editor, Thomas Newton, puts Books 11 and 12 below what came before it: "It is the same sun, but not in its full blaze of meridian glory; it now shines with a gentler ray as it is setting."[5] Newton's view may be condescending, but it does offer a

---

1. Johnson, *The Lives of the Poets*, 196.
2. Lewis, *A Preface to "Paradise Lost,"* 129–30.
3. Ibid., 129.
4. Addison's Papers on *Paradise Lost*, 217.
5. Thomas Newton, ed., *Paradise Lost*, by John Milton, vol. 2 (London, 1790), 446–47.

way out of the conclusion that Milton fails as an artist. Books 11 and 12 of *Paradise Lost* are not "inartistic," but appropriate to what they are called upon to do, namely, tell a history. And in that task, there are still many "ornaments and graces of poetry" to enjoy, howsoever chastened the style.

Newton's position is fleshed out at length in Michael Hollington and Lawrence Wilkinson's indispensable short study of the final books, which they argue are not "immediately powerful"; they "demand patience."[6] They form part of the inclusive vision that is *Paradise Lost*, and it is this organized and careful articulation of the whole that we see especially on display. In these two books, Milton, fearless of the demands of epic that call for a splendid style, laboriously works brick by brick to articulate his theme. Is this artistic, they ask? Yes, there are constant, careful linkages in these books: echoes of words or sounds whose purpose is to give Milton's history coherence. The reader should see a careful pattern of words having to do with falling and rising, as Adam and Eve and other biblical characters fall and eventually rise.[7] The reader should see a journey motif comprising "leaving home, wandering and eventual return," and involving people as diverse as Adam and Eve, Abraham, Solomon, Christ, and the Apostles.[8] The repetitions manifest *Paradise Lost*'s typology, which is the Christian idea—worked out in the narrative—that the Old Testament prefigures the New, that history doesn't move forward but contains a perpetual reenactment.

This is why *Paradise Lost* can be said to be about the biblical successors of Adam and Eve, and ultimately about all of us. That is why Milton works at a low heat in Books 11 and 12: he has set out to find and *teach* the Grand Scheme, at any expense. That does not mean there is no art in these last two books. The usual habits of Milton's poetry appear here: meter, repetition of words, grammatical parallels,

---

6. Michael Hollington and Lawrence Wilkinson, eds., *Paradise Lost, Books XI–XII*, by John Milton (Cambridge: Cambridge University Press, 1976), 9.

7. Ibid., 16.

8. Ibid., 18.

repeated vowels and consonants that give the effect of coherence and lend the verse authority, if not color. But the art doesn't call attention to itself; it strives not to be exciting. Here are just so many repetitions as to give the verse a knitted effect, but not so many as to make it too stylized:

> With glory and power to judge both quick and dead,
> To judge th' unfaithful dead, but to reward
> His faithful, and receive them into bliss,
> Whether in Heav'n or Earth, for then the Earth
> Shall all be Paradise, far happier place
> Than this of Eden, and far happier days. (12.460–65)

This repetitiveness, which enforces the idea that history is repetitive, helps give the final books a strangely consoling quality in spite of their pessimism: the poem insists that nothing can be done about history, which goes predictably on its way. But this consolation may come at a price. Books 11 and 12 sometimes appear to be an exercise in rationalizing. One can hear beneath their bland assurances or weary predictions the stricken thoughts of the defeated revolutionary. The early style of *Paradise Lost* is revolutionary, while the last books—again with some exceptions—are orthodox, schoolmasterly. As such, the style of the last two books is essential to the final meaning, but not the whole experience of *Paradise Lost*.

Even Milton's most fervent advocates struggle to defend these books beyond offering an explanation as to why their low-key rational approach exists. Summers evades consideration of style altogether, and attends to the books' subject, the consequences of the Fall in history.[9] Fish argues that Milton is trying a neutral, emotionless, "non"-style,[10] as if Milton were fundamentally distrustful of style (and its association with Satan), and were distancing his post-Fall narrative from the extravagance of traditional epic poetry—an extravagance that Milton himself exulted in! Some readers, following the lead of Robert

9. Summers, *The Muse's Method*.
10. Fish, *Surprised by Sin*, 291, 300–303.

McMahon, would go even further, and regard the story of *Paradise Lost* as being that of two narrators.[11] One is the "Bard," who writes the early books, and who gives Satan a great deal of adulation. The second is Milton himself, who has escaped the false values of Narrator One, and who shows his eventual emergence as the wise, true, and sober narrator (much as a new narrator emerges at the close of *Lycidas*). This narrator emerges most fully in the last two books. In one way or another, *Paradise Lost* subverts the epic excitement of the early books, replacing it with the composed, didactic verse of the last two books. This, they hold, is a style that reflects true Christian humility.

I used to believe this argument, and even wrote an article defending the muted approach of the final books.[12] But I changed my mind when I realized that as a reader I would gladly trade the last two books for the poem's final hundred or so lines, with their sudden recovery of imagination at the close. (Kingsley Amis esteemed lines 12.624–26 "the most poignant moment in all our literature"—good enough to cure a hangover!)[13] We should remember our Coleridge: "not that poem we have *read* but that to which we *return*, with the greatest pleasure, possesses the genuine power, and claims the name of *essential poetry*."[14] The poetry of Books 11 and 12 is "artistic," finely crafted and organized, as is most all of *Paradise Lost*. But if we wish the "essential poetry" of Coleridge, we must return to the other books to find verse that shakes up and reorganizes the world that we thought we knew.

Most of those readers who disdain Milton's poetic efforts in Books 11 and 12 would acknowledge, however, that there is a reason for them. These verses are in this respect like Milton's God: even if you don't like him, you know he is needed. Milton as well must have

11. Robert McMahon, *The Two Poets of "Paradise Lost"* (Baton Rouge: Louisiana State University Press, 1998).

12. Michael Cavanagh, "A Meeting of Epic and History: Books XI and XII of *Paradise Lost*," *English Literary History* 38, no. 2 (June 1971): 206–22.

13. Kingsley Amis, "The Hangover," in *Everyday Drinking: The Distilled Kingsley Amis* (London: Bloomsbury, 2010), 85.

14. Samuel Taylor Coleridge, *Biographia Literaria*, 1817, repr. in *Collected Works of Samuel Taylor Coleridge*, vol. 7, ed. James Engell and W. Jackson Bate (London: Routledge, 1983), 23.

thought much of the blandness of Books 11 and 12 justifiable in light of the purpose it serves. We must remember that Milton not only wrote history; he made it. *Paradise Lost* itself is a work of history, the history of an episode that determines subsequent history. It was the fall of man that foredoomed the English Revolution, the failure of which nearly crushed Milton, who went from predicting a free Republican England to having to accept the restoration of a despised monarchy and prelatic authority. Though we don't know what lay in store for Adam and Eve had they not fallen (presumably increasing farm work and the raising of children), their fall causes history to change its course. And therefore a poem about them must also be a poem about history.

But there's more: in Milton's view, Adam must be *witness* to the history gone bad, from the time of the Fall to Milton's own age. Adam must not only witness history, he must *own* it, and he must be tutored in this task by an angel who is less "affable" (7.41 and 8.648) and voluble than Raphael. There will be no smiles, and few similes. In some ways, Milton's Adam is like Aeneas, who in Book 8 of the *Aeneid* bears a shield telling the future history of Rome, a future that comes out of the fall of Troy. Aeneas doesn't understand that history, but it is paradoxically his responsibility. In Milton's case, Adam must come to understand that future history before he leaves Eden. He will, so to speak, bear that history on his shoulder. He will be tried or tempted by it. As we have seen, every character in *Paradise Lost*, even God, is put on trial. In Books 11 and 12, the trial is a threefold temptation. Adam is tempted to resist seeing his part in history; he wants to blame history on his successors. He is tempted, once having accepted his part in history, to despair, that is, to believe history is without meaning. Finally, he is tempted to repeat his own errors as he watches the tableaux that Michael presents to him. Overall, "each vision is primarily necessary in order to correct the partial conclusions which Adam has derived from the previous one," and so in the time taken for Michael's show, we are to understand a metaphorical lifetime that Adam leads.[15]

15. Summers, *The Muse's Method*, 193.

He will become mature. Even for a poet as deft as Milton, this is a challenging format. Adam must be taught everything.

He must be taught, as was Milton, that history will not produce ideal commonwealths. The best that history can produce are virtuous resisters of history's corruptions: Noah and Enoch for example, and the author of *Paradise Lost*, are people who see beyond the confines of history, and who are connected to a higher world, though they do not prosper in this world. Adam must discern parallels in the biblical stories told by Michael. He must see how the tableau of war (11.638–73) is connected to the war in Heaven; how his and Eve's story prefigures the story of the Sethites (573–97); that Abdiel is the prototype of Noah and Enoch; that Cain's envy, like Satan's, is fatally destructive. When Michael comes to teach Adam, Adam knows a few things, including the demands of humility. But he has a long way to go if he is to be a hero, which he is destined to be.

Another theme is developed: the conflict of Paradise as a place and as a state of mind. When Michael tells Eve they are to be dismissed from the Garden (11.259–62), Eve becomes more emotional than at any other time in the poem. Her outburst (268–85) is not only impressive in itself but, with all its references to flowers, buds, growing and breeding, and to the native soil of Eden and "flow'rs / That never will in other climate grow" (273–74), it gathers back the pastoral into the poem. (It was this line that made Emily Dickinson wryly dub Milton "the great florist.")[16] But Adam's melancholy speech that follows it (296–333) weaves the pastoral with something larger: the idea of place, and the senses that connect us to place. Adam is lamenting more than the loss of a garden; he is lamenting the loss of the visible manifestation of God in the world, something with which Milton concerned himself as early as the Fifth Elegy, and that is close to the narrator's problem too. From here onward, Adam may feel God's presence, but he cannot *sense* him, as was depicted in Book 8. Adam must

16. Emily Dickinson, *The Letters of Emily Dickinson, 1845–1886*, ed. Mabel Loomis Todd (Boston: Little, Brown, 1906), 187.

be weaned away from the Garden—from a sense of place altogether. He must appreciate the unseen; he must be put into the position of the narrator. He must recognize that salvation lies outside of history, and that it can be recuperated only from within. Because this salvation can be felt within, Michael can tell Adam and Eve that the land they will live on outside of Eden is "fitter soil" (262), for Paradise is a state of mind, and is achievable in the dust and heat of a fallen world. Several passages in the final books bear this idea out. One is the Son's declaration (22–30) that Adam and Eve's tearful prayers at the close of Book 10 are sweeter to God than any benefits they might have produced in the Garden by working the soil. Even if this does not mean the Fall was a good thing, it does suggest that misery can be potentially ennobling and redemptive. We are told that Adam and Eve can make God "placable and mild" when they seek sincerely to appease him (151). Though the revelation of the destruction of Eden is horrible (the Flood, as depicted in 823–35 is among the best passages in the final books), it demonstrates that God attaches "to place / No sanctity" (836–37). This can be a consoling thought.

Some readers simply can't make Milton a consistent poet, for in these last books he drifts from the monism (both nature- and God-affirming) that he has invoked and sometimes argued. Later invoking the Sethites as an example, Michael delivers a sermon on the proper upbringing of women, which is harshly puritanical in the modern sense of that word. The story of Cain and Abel finds its resolution only in an invisible God whose justice is far off. Abraham is celebrated for believing in a God who leads him to an unknown place. Paradise, destroyed in the Flood, becomes a de-sanctified place: God is not there any longer. It becomes thereafter only "The haunt of seals and orcs and sea-mews' clang" (835). God created Paradise, but he's an absentee landlord now. As John Rogers points out, there is little of Milton's wonted *copia* in these last books.[17] The world is no longer

17. John Rogers, "ENGL 220: Milton. Lecture 20—*Paradise Lost*, Books XI–XII," Open Yale Courses video, 45:43, recorded Fall 2007, available at https://oyc.yale.edu/english/engl-220/lecture-20.

charged with the grandeur of God, and Milton's language, while it is organized and careful, is no longer charged with enthusiasm and excess. The punning and extravagance and sly humor of the earlier books give way to the utilitarian. Imagine a "pontifical" bridge or a Paradise of Fools here! The poem becomes dualistic, positing a barely tolerable "here" of this world, and an out-of-reach "there" of the next. According to Michael, nothing much can be done to make the "here" of our lives any better than it is. There is no use in replacing bad leaders; they will only be replaced by others as bad or worse. An odd political quietism settles over the last books. What happened to the Milton who wanted more, who wanted to be divine and sensual, who wanted to be lover and singer, who wanted it both ways at once?

But something transpires at the very end of *Paradise Lost* that reaches back and integrates an earlier Milton. Adam, his spirits greatly lifted, speaks of the "goodness infinite" of God (12.469), a goodness that God will bring out of the Fall. This goodness is even greater than the Creation, Adam says (471–73). He wonders if he should rejoice rather than repent (474–75). When Michael, in response, begins to speak of the "inward consolations" of those who suffer for good causes (495), we sense the poem is trying to turn. It still presents the worst case, that "so shall the world go on / To good malignant, to bad men benign" (537–38), but it also yearns to bring a hint of paradisal happiness back into play. Adam in his last speech (553–73) rises into a verbal ecstasy. There is both humility *and* grandeur in his assessment of our possibilities. He will serve God and be meek and suffer for truth's sake, but he sees himself as able to gain both "peace of thought" *and* "fortitude to highest victory" (558, 570). He will "love with fear" his newly understood God (562). His acceptance of Christ as his redeemer is both an act of self-abnegation and a boast at his having endured the vision of Michael and seen all of the awfulness of human history ahead of him.

What Adam proposes for himself, and what Michael sanctions, is, again, the convergence of two worlds: the practice of otherworldly virtue in this one. We notice here how Adam and Michael become "in tune" with each other, as do Adam and Eve in the last lines. Such amalgamation may be found in Michael's last speech (575–605), where Michael "picks up the accumulated weight of the poem," and the epic acquires, unexpectedly, some lightness of being.[18] Though the gist of Michael's speech is that knowledge of the Redeemer is worth all the other kinds of knowledge ("all the stars" … "all th' ethereal powers, / All secrets of the deep, all nature's works" … "all the riches" … "all the rule" … "only add" … "add faith, / Add virtue, patience, temperance, add love," 576–83), the various uses of "all" and "add" in these lines have the effect of a celebratory symphonic finale. Adam shall lose Paradise, but also regain it; Eve is punished, but she will be the bearer of the seed of man's delivery. Adam and Eve are banished, but, as Belsey succinctly puts it, they have Providence, and they have each other.[19] This merging of a blessing and a curse was too much for Richard Bentley, who in his 1732 edition had the audacity to change Milton's final two lines as follows:

> They hand in hand with wand'ring steps and slow
> Through Eden took their solitary way. (Milton)

> Then hand in hand with social steps their way
> Through Eden took with Heavn'ly comfort cheered. (Bentley)

Seeking to make Milton more consistent, Bentley ended up making him trivial. The ending of *Paradise Lost* beautifully revisits many of the poem's themes and motifs.

Whereas in Book 4, Eve was the woman of "delay" (4.311), there is now in her "no delay" (12.615). Her exquisite declaration, recalling Ruth to Naomi—

> with thee to go
> Is to stay here; without thee here to stay
> Is to go hence unwilling (12.615–17)

18. Hunter, *Paradise Lost*, 110.
19. Belsey, *John Milton: Language, Gender, Power*, 84.

—touches upon almost every theme associated with her and Adam, especially her declaration that nothing is sweet in the Garden "without thee" (4.656). Her admission to the "willful crime" (12.619) repeats her submission speech in Book 10, "Forsake me not thus, Adam ..." (10.914–36). Her "By me the promised Seed shall all restore" (12.623) has that key word *seed*—"So small, so intimate, so definite, is the word that the line becomes breathless with it and with the hope of it," as Charles Williams effused[20]—which harkens back to "the blissful seat" (1.5) of Paradise's restoration, and so connects Eve to the Son. But it also connects her, ironically, to the recent hateful Restoration of the House of Stuart. That Milton would make his meaning so ambiguous here (we think again of the "ribs of gold" taken out of the ground in Hell [1.690], and that passage's connection to Eve's creation [8.466–69]) is astonishing. Her reconciliation with Adam (12.617–18) reverses her narcissistic waking after birth. Those readers who cannot give Milton credit for being more than a run-of-the-mill misogynist of his time must face here a final instance of Eve's accomplishments, as she gets the poem's last word, in a fourteen-line quasi-sonnet (610–23).

Geoff Dyer finds the close of the poem "the most beautiful thing in all of literature; as Adam and Eve leave Eden, they are us."[21] Nothing in later English pastoral poetry—so imitative of Milton—matches the meeting of the otherworldly and the pastoral-mundane in these final lines (12.624–49). On the one hand, there are the descending cherubim and their "meteorous" figures gliding over the "marish" [marsh] (629–30). There is the "brandished sword of God" blazing "Fierce as a comet," and the "dreadful faces" and the "fiery arms" of the angels (633–34, 644). On the other hand, there is the innocent laborer (whom we remember from Book 1, returning home at evening [1.783]); there is the lingering of Adam and Eve on Eden's hill, the slow reluctant motion down the cliff, the hand-holding, the tears. Adam

20. Charles Williams, "An Introduction to Milton's Poems," 1940, in *Milton Criticism: Selections from Four Centuries*, ed. James Thorpe (London: Routledge and Kegan Paul, 1951), 262.
21. Geoff Dyer, "By the Book," *The New York Times Sunday Book Review*, July 2, 2016: 6.

and Eve are wandering, yet under the guidance of Providence. They must face death, but they also have promise for the future. As Belsey profoundly observes, "the final lines ... are the inscription of the end of a tragedy which is also the beginning of an adventure."[22] Adam and Eve are happy and sad. "Natural tears" cannot be wholly tragic tears (12.645). Unlike the laborer who is "Homeward returning" (632), Adam and Eve venture out into a strange land. But we remember (from 8.296–306) that Adam was born *outside* of Paradise, and was brought into it. So now, going into the fuller world, he is going home! Similarly, as we were in *Lycidas*, we are moved here from a theological space (the Garden) into the natural world, and consoled there, even if not fully. As in the "Nativity Ode," in *Lycidas*, and in Sonnet 18, Milton quiets things down, recognizing that his resolution must enact itself at the commonplace level. Whatever is worked out and resolved will be the product of Providence, nature, and time.

22. Belsey, *John Milton: Language, Gender, Power*, 83.

11

"The Finest Things"

MILTON'S STYLE

Here I essay some signal traits of Milton's style, suggesting how compelling choice passages can be when one returns to linger over them, determined to give free rein to the poem's "power and charm."[1] William Hazlitt rightly observed that Milton "strives hard to say the finest things in the world, and he does say them."[2] Centuries of readers have kept Milton close: Robert Burns carried a pocket Milton "perpetually about with me";[3] Phillis Wheatley refused to part with her gifted volume, even under financial duress;[4] Charles Darwin took a copy on every excursion from *The Beagle*;[5] John Muir packed it on his thousand-mile trek to the Gulf of Mexico.[6] For some, a

1. Matthew Arnold, "Milton," in *The Works of Matthew Arnold*, vol 4, ed. Thomas Burnett Smart (London: Macmillan, 1903), 49. See also Erik Gray, *Milton and the Victorians* (Ithaca, N.Y.: Cornell University Press, 2009).

2. William Hazlitt, *The Collected Works of William Hazlitt: Lectures on the English Poets and on the Dramatic Literature of the Age of Elizabeth*, vol. 5, ed. A. R. Waller and Arnold Glover (London: J. M. Dent, 1902), 58.

3. Robert Burns, Letter to William Nicol, June 18, 1787, in *The Letters of Robert Burns*, ed. G. Ross Roy, 2nd ed. (Oxford: Oxford University Press, 1985), I.123.

4. Paula Loscocco, *Phillis Wheatley's Miltonic Poetics* (New York: Palgrave Pivot, 2014).

5. Charles Darwin, *Charles Darwin: His Life Told in an Autobiographical Chapter, and in a Selected Series of His Published Letters*, ed. Francis Darwin (London: John Murray, 1892), 31.

6. John Muir, *A Thousand-Mile Walk to the Gulf*, ed. William Frederic Badé (Boston: Houghton Mifflin, 1916), 17–18.

childhood encounter proved transformative, as Vachel Lindsay: "Milton made me a poet and blessed me and cursed me at nine years of age";[7] Borges never regretted immersing himself in Milton's complete works instead of larking around Paris as a teen;[8] Zora Neale Hurston enjoyed a similar youthful epiphany:

In a pile of rubbish I found a complete copy of Milton's works ... I read *Paradise Lost* and luxuriated in Milton's syllables and rhythms without ever having heard that Milton was one of the greatest poets in the world. I read it because I liked it.[9]

Many have spoken of the pleasures of returning to the poem: John Clare said *Paradise Lost* was one of only two "books of poetry that I have regularly read through";[10] Zadie Smith revisits the poem "every summer as my patience for new things runs out";[11] Erica Dawson never goes "more than two weeks without reading some part of *Paradise Lost*."[12] And Milton can provide solace: translating *Paradise Lost* offered Czesław Miłosz "the key to survival" in post-war Poland;[13] Martin Amis would select *Paradise Lost* as his solitary "desert island" companion;[14] Emerson calmed himself during a transatlantic storm by reconstructing *Lycidas* from memory.[15] While many find Milton's style at first a "real barrier," his style is the very reason we ought to

7. Edgar Lee Masters, *Vachel Lindsay* (New York: Charles Scribner's Sons, 1935), 328.

8. Jorge Luis Borges, *Borges at Eighty: Conversations*, ed. Willis Barnstone (New York: New Directions, 1982), 100

9. Zora Neale Hurston, *Dust Tracks on a Road: An Autobiography* (Philadelphia: J. B. Lippincott, 1942), 135.

10. John Lucas, *John Clare* (Plymouth, U.K.: Northcote House, 1994), 15.

11. Zadie Smith, "Zadie Smith's Holiday Picks," *The Guardian*, June 21, 2001.

12. Erica Dawson, "Interview with Erica Dawson, Featured Poet," by Madison Jones, *Kudzu House*, December 13, 2015, http://kudzuhouse.org/interview-with-erica-dawson-featured-winter-solstice-poet/.

13. Andrzej Franaszek, *Miłosz: A Biography*, trans. Aleksandra and Michael Parker (Cambridge, Mass.: Harvard University Press, 2017), 233.

14. Martin Amis, interview by Sue Lawley, *Desert Island Discs*, BBC Radio 4, December 28, 1996.

15. Ralph Waldo Emerson, *The Journals and Miscellaneous Notebooks of Ralph Waldo Emerson, Volume IV: 1832–1834*, ed. Alfred R. Ferguson (Cambridge, Mass.: Harvard University Press, 1964), 102–3.

bother with him.[16] This insight has been neglected in recent decades, as scholarly studies of Milton's historical and intellectual circumstances, fruitful as they have often been, have overshadowed discussions of his poetic craft. Entire essay collections by distinguished Miltonists can proceed without once mentioning meter or rhythm. Hazlitt's observation stands as a reproach, making us wonder whether ambitious verse, no matter how well it is done, has fallen into disfavor.

This is a change. As recently as 1965, Robert Lowell could observe:

We have some impatience with prosaic, everyday things of life—I think those hurt us. That sort of whimsical patience that other countries may have—that's really painful to endure: to be minor. We leap for the sublime. You might almost say American literature and culture begins with *Paradise Lost*.[17]

Yet Lowell himself propelled a generational shift to "prosaic, everyday things," with a career that "started as epic and ended as personality."[18] The shift to the quotidian had commenced earlier, with the modernists; in 1926, Allen Tate was already

convinced that Milton himself could not write a *Paradise Lost* now. Minds are less important for literature than cultures; our minds are as good as they ever were, but our culture is dissolving.[19]

Much contemporary poetry feels off-hand, "our monotonous sublime" compared to even the earliest of Milton's verse.[20] What's sublime about the style of *Paradise Lost* is obvious because Milton flaunts it: a vaulting

16. Christian Wiman, "Milton in Guatemala," 1998, in *Ambition and Survival: Becoming a Poet* (Port Townsend, Wash.: Copper Canyon Press, 2007), 14.

17. A. Alvarez, "A Talk with Robert Lowell," 1965, in *Robert Lowell: Interviews and Memoirs*, ed. Jeffrey Meyers (Ann Arbor: University of Michigan Press, 1988), 104.

18. William Logan, "Milton in the Modern: The Invention of Personality," in *Green Thoughts, Green Shades: Essays by Contemporary Poets on the Early Modern Lyric*, ed. Jonathan Post (Berkeley: University of California Press, 2002), 173.

19. Allen Tate, letter to Donald Davidson, May 14, 1926, in *The Literary Correspondence of Donald Davidson and Allen Tate*, ed. John Tyree Fain and Thomas Daniel Young (Athens, Ga.: University of Georgia Press, 1974), 166.

20. Robert Lowell, "Waking Early Sunday Morning," in *Near the Ocean* (New York: Farrar, Straus and Giroux, 1967) 24.

ambition to achieve greatness; an ever-shifting chorus of voices, even reprehensible ones, as spokespersons; delight in ostentatious idiom and wordplay; long sentences with cascading enjambment; a sense of the propriety of formula; thought-halting similes that enhance events or characters; swelling epithets, such as referring to Satan as "th'apostate angel" (1.125); lists of proper names of people and places, reminding us that epics were supposed to be repositories of learning; grammatical inversions and suspensions that remove the language from the colloquial and give it what Tasso—Milton's chief model for the epic style—called *asprezza*: roughness, or difficulty.[21] Almost everywhere we are treated to what Alexander Pope termed an "exotic style," one that makes urgent the action at hand and aggrandizes the poet who has the temerity to relate it on paper.[22] To cite Lewis's favorite term for this quality, *Paradise Lost* is suffused with *solempne*, a Middle English word connoting festivity, stateliness, "calculated dignity."[23] Elsewhere, Milton praises poetry for being "more simple, sensuous, and passionate" than logic or rhetoric.[24]

Writing of Satan as "Him," the narrator of *Paradise Lost* recounts the brutal end of his rebellion in Heaven:

> Him the Almighty Power
> Hurled headlong flaming from th' ethereal sky
> With hideous ruin and combustion down
> To bottomless perdition, there to dwell
> In adamantine chains and penal fire,
> Who durst defy th' Omnipotent to arms. (1.44–49)

It is easy to see why Wordsworth celebrated this staggering passage as "one of the most wonderful sentences ever formed by the mind of man."[25] Richard Wilbur applauds its plummeting line endings as a

21. Torquato Tasso, *Discorsi del poema eroico*, 1594, Book 5, trans. in F. T. Prince, *The Italian Element in Milton's Verse* (Oxford: Oxford University Press, 1954), 39.

22. Joseph Spence, *Observations, Anecdotes, and Characters of Books and Men*, 1820, ed. J. M. Osborn (Oxford: Oxford University Press, 1966), I.197.

23. Lewis, *A Preface to "Paradise Lost,"* 17.

24. *Of Education, CPEP*, 977.

25. Cited in Leonard, *Faithful Labourers*, 1:83.

rebuke to the weakness of free verse, which has "no expectations to disappoint."[26] A first-time reader might not have thought that "Him" could appear at the beginning of a line of an English poem, that "combustion" could be in a poem at all (except ironically), or that a poem's lines could hurtle so heedlessly as these do, taking us from event to aftermath, from Heaven to Hell. The style encountered in *Paradise Lost* has an almost narcotic effect on the reader—not of sedation, but of *astonishment*, as Johnson insisted.[27] How far this is from much of contemporary poetry, with its laid-back, quirky, unassuming flavor. As Gary Snyder dismissed Milton in 1959:

> What use, Milton, a silly story
> Of our lost general parents,
>   eaters of fruit?[28]

The movement in English verse toward the colloquial and plain-spoken is usually associated with the Romantic poets of the early nineteenth century, or the twentieth-century rise of Modernism. But the objection to the language and sublimity of Milton began not long after he died, with people such as George Smith Green (1756), and John Wesley (1763), James Buchanan (1773), and Samuel Johnson (1779), who worried Milton's language made him "unintelligible" for the ordinary reader.[29]

Today, many potential audiences for Milton's poetry don't care about thoughts from a century ago by T. S. Eliot and Ezra Pound ("Milton is the worst sort of poison"),[30] and they certainly don't care

26. Richard Wilbur, "An Interview with Richard Wilbur," by David Curry, 1962, reprinted in *Conversations with Richard Wilbur*, ed. William Butts (Jackson: University Press of Mississippi, 1990), 5.

27. Johnson, *The Lives of the Poets*, 190.

28. Gary Snyder, "Milton by Firelight," 1959, in *Riprap and Cold Mountain Poems* (Berkeley, Calif.: Counterpoint, 2009), 9.

29. John Wesley, "To the Reader," in *An Extract from Milton's "Paradise Lost." With Notes* (London: 1763), 3.

30. Ezra Pound, "The Renaissance: I—The Palette," *Poetry* 5, no. 5 (February 1915): 231. See also T. S. Eliot, "Milton," *Proceedings of the British Academy* 33 (1947): 61–79.

about the Romantics, much less the Augustans. But they do infer a notion of poetry from what they read, and what they hear spoken at poetry readings. In these quarters, the news for *Paradise Lost* is not encouraging, as Randall Jarrell could see already in 1953:

> *Paradise Lost* is what it was; but the ordinary reader no longer makes the mistake of trying to read it—instead he glances at it, weighs it in his hand, shudders, and suddenly, his eyes shining, puts it on his list of the ten dullest books he has ever read.[31]

Mary Oliver outright dismisses the "intended formality" of "older" poetry, preferring instead "the natural and friendly intimacy" of today's authors, whose style is "neither elaborate, nor prepossessing, nor self-conscious, nor rhetorical."[32] The poet is not a grand teacher, but plays the role of unpretentious "fellow-citizen, neighbor, and friend." Ted Kooser's program for poetry is similarly anti-elitist; according to Kooser, poetry ought primarily to communicate with others and touch their hearts.[33] By his account, poetry is not a craft apprenticed on the slopes of Parnassus, but a skill for the betterment of daily life. "It takes a big mind," says Kooser, "like John Milton's ... to wrap up an idea and make a good poem, and most of us just aren't that smart."[34] For Kooser, poems should be "transparent," not too ostentatious, nor too "clever," too alliterative, too "musical" or too "noisy."[35] Vocabulary should be familiar. The language of poetry should not call attention to itself. *Asprezza* is precisely what he tries to avoid.

Kooser and Oliver's ideas about poetry are widespread. They are congruent with Garrison Keillor's notion that what we need are not more excellent or complex poems, but just "good poems";[36] or Stepha-

31. Randall Jarrell, "The Obscurity of the Poet," in *Poetry and the Age* (New York: Alfred A. Knopf, 1953), 3.

32. Mary Oliver, *A Poetry Handbook* (San Diego: Harcourt Brace, 1994), 77.

33. Ted Kooser, *The Poetry Home Repair Manual: Practical Advice for Beginning Poets* (Lincoln: University of Nebraska Press, 2005), xi.

34. Ibid., 14.

35. Ibid., 68, 71.

36. Garrison Keillor, ed., *Good Poems* (London: Penguin Books, 2002).

nie Burt's cloying anthology title, *The Poem Is You*.[37] (Though even Burt admits that "few contemporary poems merit that kind of attention" commanded by Milton.)[38] This ethos gets expressed in the way poets conduct themselves at readings: schmoozing with the audience, relating connections between their poems and their lives. In creative writing classes, one can usually find professors recommending cutting back; attending to everyday detail; keeping an intimate voice; and avoiding over-the-top language. Henri Cole expresses concern about the ways in which graduate programs in creative writing have enforced conformity:

And I would say that if the whole MFA thing has had a single effect on American poetry, it's been pushing it towards a kind of tepidness of utterance, in which extremity of emotion, anything *in extremis*, is regarded almost with suspicion, or as if it were some kind of mania.[39]

One can trace some of these ideas to Richard Hugo's widely influential (and excellent) *The Triggering Town*, where the beginner is enjoined to "think small": "If you can't think small," Hugo snarls, "try philosophy or social criticism."[40] Milton's style isn't a viable option for today's verse, which instead prefers the aesthetic of "home repair," the casual style.

"Greatness of mind" *(8.557)*

In 1983, Donald Hall charged that "contemporary American poetry is afflicted by modesty of ambition."[41] To Hall, contemporary poets won't make the investment in a long-enduring, difficult style, as Mil-

37. Stephanie Burt, *The Poem Is You: 60 Contemporary American Poems and How to Read Them* (Cambridge: Belknap Press, 2016).

38. Stephanie (Stephen) Burt, "In Defence of Minor Poets," *Partisan Magazine*, April 5, 2016, http://www.partisanmagazine.com/blog/2016/4/2/h71c3htrsnuiypwtunmmnsuokp5wvx.

39. Henri Cole, "John Berryman at 100, A Celebration: Panel 2 with April Bernard, Henri Cole, and A. Van Jordan," YouTube video, 47:10, The Poetry Society of America, along with Columbia School of the Arts, Barnard Women Poets, and Heyman Center for the Humanities, posted by SoF/Heyman, May 7, 2015, https://www.youtube.com/watch?v=saOKq1dPsyg.

40. Richard Hugo, *The Triggering Town: Lectures and Essays on Poetry and Writing* (New York: W. W. Norton, 1979), 7.

41. Donald Hall, *Breakfast Served Any Time All Day: Essays on Poetry New and Selected* (Ann Arbor: University of Michigan Press, 2003), 155.

ton did, forsaking immediate recognition for a hard-won poetry that will please in many readings. They don't do the homework of reading the ancients in the original language. They are too easily pleased with their work. They publish too quickly. One can hardly read Hall's essay without thinking of how Milton came to regard his whole life a preparation for *Paradise Lost*:

he who would not be frustrate of his hope to write well hereafter in laudable things ought himself to be a true poem, that is, a composition and pattern of the best and honorablest things.[42]

Hall further contends that contemporary poets don't make big claims in their poetry. They don't try to "justify the ways of God to men," says Hall, invoking Milton.[43] As A. E. Housman quipped,

> And malt does more than Milton can
> To justify God's ways to man.[44]

One might take as an emblem of reduced ambitions Donald Justice's sonnet "The Wall," an unassuming digest of *Paradise Lost* ("As for the fruit, it had no taste at all" [9]),[45] or perhaps better Ronald Johnson's 1977 *Radi os*—an "erased" version of Milton's epic, with only a few of the original's words left from each line:[46]

O
                 tree
        into the World,
                     Man

                     the chosen
Rose out of Chaos:
                      song,

42. *An Apology for Smectymnus, CPEP*, 850.

43. Hall, *Breakfast Served Any Time All Day*, 156.

44. A. E. Housman, "LXII. Terence, this is stupid stuff," 1896, in *A Shropshire Lad* (New York: Henry Holt, 1932), LXII.21–22.

45. Donald Justice, "The Wall," 1960, in *Complete Poems* (New York: Knopf, 2009), 13.

46. Ronald Johnson, *Radi os*, 1977 (Chicago: Flood Editions, 2013).

This stripping away of words is clever, and critics such as Derek Mong have said insightful things about what remains.[47] But such a spare project cannot aspire to Miltonic heights (much less Danny Snelson's recent recomposition of Johnson, a Platonic third remove.)[48]

Throughout her career, Elizabeth Bishop was often condescendingly regarded as a "modest," "charming" poet. David Orr proposes that Bishop might have been a Miltonic poet all along, aspiring to an unconventional "greatness" that makes her so beloved of writers whose styles otherwise have little in common: John Ashbery, James Merrill, Marianne Moore, Octavio Paz, Mark Strand.[49] Seamus Heaney confirms that Bishop was brought up to be "reticent, opposed to and incapable of self-aggrandizement," the embodiment of good manners and of the voice that permits its tongue to be governed.[50] But sometimes Bishop allows her tongue to govern rather than be governed, and when that happens, Heaney asserts, she writes poetry of "vision and epiphany," as in the close of "At the Fishhouses."[51] She—who usually "limited herself to a note that would not have disturbed the discreet undersong of conversation between strangers breakfasting at a seaside hotel"[52]—breaks into an epic generalizing voice as she interprets the very fabric of the universe:

> I have seen it *over* and *over*, the *same* sea, the *same*,
> slightly, indifferently swinging *above the stones*,

We get two more solemn repetitions of *above the stones* in successive lines, with reiterations of *your ... your ... your ... tasted ... taste ... knowledge ... flowing ...* before the Miltonic finale:

47. Derek Mong, "Ten New Ways to Read Ronald Johnson's *Radi os*," *Kenyon Review* 37, no. 4 (July/August 2015): 78–96.

48. Danny Snelson, *Radios* (Los Angeles: Make Now Press, 2016).

49. David Orr, "The Great(ness) Game," *The New York Times Sunday Book Review*, February 19, 2009.

50. Seamus Heaney, *The Government of the Tongue: Selected Prose, 1978–87* (New York: Farrar, Straus and Giroux, 1988), 101.

51. Ibid., 102.

52. Ibid.

and since
our *knowledge* is historical, *flowing*, and *flown.*[53]

Heaney's celebration of Bishop's visionary "heave" confirms that some writers look back occasionally (and nostalgically, even covetously) to a voice, an ambition, that they wish were still available to them, despite everything they have been taught.[54] (Heaney himself wrote his very first poem "in pastiche Miltonic blank verse.")[55] In order to attain that voice and ambition, however, the poet must find a context, *other* voices, through which the magnificence will stand out—as Bishop's final voice in "At the Fishhouses" stands out against the more casual voice with which she commences.

"Join voices" (*5.197*)

Milton's capacious style, like Bishop's in "At the Fishhouses," contains several voices, one of his greatest distinctions. (As Ann Baynes Coiro notes, there are over fifty instances of the word "voice" itself in *Paradise Lost.*)[56] The voice cited at the outset of this chapter might be nicknamed Milton's "Mighty Arm": the powerful intonation that makes us feel, as Heaney once said of reading W. B. Yeats's later works, we are "sitting on a bronze horse."[57] James Russell Lowell, anticipating Heaney's equine image, termed this "long swell of his verse under him like a steed that knows his rider."[58] Many readers have likened Milton

53. Elizabeth Bishop, *The Complete Poems: 1927–1979* (New York: Farrar, Straus and Giroux, 1979), 65–66, my italics.

54. Heaney, *The Government of the Tongue*, 105.

55. Mark Medley, "The Griffin Poetry Prize Questionnaire: Seamus Heaney," *National Post*, May 30, 2011.

56. Ann Baynes Coiro, "Sufficient and Free: The Poetry of *Paradise Lost*," in *Milton Now: Alternative Approaches and Contexts*, ed. Catharine Gray and Erin Murphy (New York: Palgrave, 2014), 108n62.

57. Seamus Heaney, "A Soul on the Washing Line," interview, *The Economist*, June 22, 1991: 100.

58. James Russell Lowell, *The Writings of James Russell Lowell: Literary Essays* (Cambridge: Riverside Press, 1890), 90.

to an "organ-voice," blasting all the stops.[59] Not everyone likes this; Ivor Gurney felt it "too colossal. Too Bach-like."[60] This style traverses Heaven and Earth, making fearless judgments. It is granitic, sweeping, bold. It speaks of "Almighty Power" (1.44), of large elemental things: waves, skies, and floods. One can hear it in Milton's invocation of God's universe "won from the void and formless infinite" (3.12), or even in his depiction of Satan's wicked elevation to tyrant:

> High on a throne of royal state, which far
> Outshone the wealth of Ormus and of Ind (2.1–2)

There's moral condemnation here, but also sheer magnitude. We sense it in the line—De Quincey found it "tremendous"[61]—that depicts the angels guarding the forbidden gates of paradise: "With dreadful faces thronged and fiery arms" (12.644). It can fortify and embolden us even as it consigns us all to darkness.

There are other voices. One, Milton took from Protestant plain speaking, what he praised as "the sober, plain, and unaffected style of the Scriptures,"[62] which anticipates Thomas Sprat's 1667 critique of "all the amplifications, digressions, and swellings of style."[63] Its most famous example can be found in the sonnet "On His Blindness": "They also serve who only stand and wait." We hear it in God's defensive statement that Adam and Eve were "Sufficient to have stood, though free to fall" (3.99); it's in the blazing self-laceration of Satan's dismissal of his followers: "they adore me on the throne of Hell" (4.89). We think of Eve's ruefully stark confession to the Son: "The serpent me beguiled

59. Alfred Tennyson, "Milton. *Alcaics,*" in *The Works of Alfred Lord Tennyson*, ed. Karen Hodder (Ware, U.K.: Wordsworth Editions, 1994), 558.

60. *Ivor Gurney: Collected Letters* ed. Robert Kelsey Rought Thornton (Manchester: Carcanet, 1991), 31.

61. Thomas De Quincey, *Confessions of an English Opium-Eater*, 1821, ed. Joel Faflak (Peterborough, Ontario: Broadview Press, 2009), 121.

62. Milton, "Of Reformation," cited in Ida Langdon, *Milton's Theory of Poetry and Fine Art: An Essay, With a Collection of Illustrative Passages from His Works* (New Haven, Conn.: Yale University Press, 1924), 297.

63. Thomas Sprat, *History of the Royal Society*, 1667, ed. Jackson I. Cope and Harold Whitmore (London: Routledge, 1959), 39.

and I did eat" (10.162, hewing closely here to the King James Bible's Genesis 3:13: "The serpent beguiled me, and I did eat"); or her ultimate admission to Adam: "thou to me / Art all things under Heav'n" (12.617–18). This simple style is a huge Miltonic resource; though it is rarely part of his reputation, it ought to be.

A third component of the epic voice could be called "professorial." It strives to expound, to make distinctions, to light up the mysterious, as in these speculations on the origin of light: "Dwelt from eternity, dwelt then in thee, / Bright effluence of bright essence increate" (3.5–6). That is not plain speaking. Or here is God trying to explain how Adam and Eve must be left free to fall:

> I else must change
> Their nature, and revoke the high decree
> Unchangeable, eternal, which ordained
> Their freedom; they themselves ordained their fall. (3.125–28)

Some readers don't like this; Alexander Pope objected that Milton made God speak like "a School-Divine."[64] Yet the manner is a deliberate part of the ecology of styles in *Paradise Lost*. The narrator yearns to get to the bottom of things, and will not spare any readers.

There are still other voices: a sneering, sardonic, low, abusive voice, which was there from the beginning of Milton's career, but which developed no doubt in Milton's years of polemical writing.[65] Sonnet 12 scoffed at those who failed to appreciate his divorce pamphlets as "owls and cuckoos, asses, apes and dogs."[66] Moloch, the most pugnacious warrior of Hell in *Paradise Lost*, speaks as if he were delivering punches: "them let those / Contrive who need, or when they need, not now" (2.52–53). Even God can be coarse:

---

64. Alexander Pope, "First Epistle of the Second Book of Horace Imitated," in *The Poems of Alexander Pope*, ed. John Butt (New Haven, Conn.: Yale University Press, 1963), 102.

65. Annabel Patterson, *Milton's Words* (Oxford: Oxford University Press, 2009).

66. Milton, Sonnet 12, *CPEP*, 149, line 4

I called and drew them thither
My Hell-hounds, to lick up the draff and filth
Which man's polluting sin with taint hath shed
On what was pure, till crammed and gorged, nigh burst
With sucked and glutted offal (10.629–33)

Paradise Lost is not genteel! At the other extreme is a charming, evocative voice. It might be called the spiritualist side, not quite worldly, the one who in "Il Penseroso" sees the "gay motes that people the sunbeams," or the side that imagines himself "dissolved" in "ecstasies" at a church service, or lingering in "archèd walks of twilight groves."[67] This Milton survives in *Paradise Lost*'s evening song of Eve to Adam: "Sweet is the breath of morn, her rising sweet" (4.641–56). This Milton sees the "Etrurian shades / High overarched" that "embow'r" the brooks of Vallombrosa (1.303–4); he envisions God "Dark with excessive bright" (3.380); he conceives the evening mist and the marsh and the "laborer's heel / Homeward returning" (12.631–32). The so-called "pre-Romantic" poets of the eighteenth century were deeply responsive to this side of Milton.

Barbara Lewalski locates a somewhat broader range of voices: "colloquial, dialogic, lyric, hymnic, elegiac, mock-heroic, denunciatory, ironic, oratorical, ornate, plain"; all of these are incorporated, she says, into Milton's "sublime epic high style."[68] She also confirms that *Paradise Lost* encloses many genres or modes, from pastoral to georgic, from tragic to lyric—what Edgar Allan Poe archly characterized as "a series of minor poems."[69] The bigness or greatness, then, of epic isn't only the size of its battles or its rhetorical formulas, but its capacity for *inclusion*—its performance as a place where styles and sensibilities contend. As noted in the first chapter, the surprising bigness of *Lycidas*, and of "The Nativity Ode," and of *Comus*, comes from a clash of

67. Milton, "Il Penseroso," *CPEP*, 51–52, lines 165, 133.
68. Lewalski, *The Life of John Milton*, 461.
69. Edgar Allan Poe, "The Poetic Principle," 1850, in *Essays and Reviews*, ed. G. R. Thompson (New York: Library of America, 1984), 70.

styles—high versus low, sublime versus pastoral, militant versus sensi-tive—that are reconciled by their inclusion. Catalogues run through Milton's work from the beginning to end. Why? Because, as Balachan-dra Rajan has speculated, the "encyclopedic quality," so often present in Milton, is "designed to suggest to us an order from which nothing is excluded."[70] Adam and Eve in Eden, we are told, pray in a "vari-ous style" (5.146), making difference part of their "unanimous" voice (4.736). Even that author of evil and exemplar of difference, Satan, is put to work for God, "His glory to augment" (2.386).

"words unknown" (12.55)

Readers marvel at the sheer range of Milton's vocabulary, his knowledge of etymology, the unpredictability of his idiom—produc-ing "wild, foggy, smoky, wordy books," in Carl Sandburg's praise.[71] Readers notice the liberties Milton takes with parts of speech, his ten-dency to bend the given to his will. What Thomas Corns gracefully re-fers to as "the original pleasure of the text … its freshness, its technical brilliance, its brave innovation and its extreme felicity" owes in large part to Milton's verbal profusion.[72]

Milton's poetry is often called "Latinate." In some respects this is accurate. Milton was utterly fluent, composing Latin poetry as well as serving as the Latin Secretary for the Commonwealth. Milton's fre-quently Latinate words (as well as Latinate syntactical constructions) can make *Paradise Lost* sound regal and lofty, much like Virgil's *Aene-id*. At the same time, because so much of Latin in Milton's time was re-cently imported into English, it had a flavor of experimental "newness" and cosmopolitanism about it that kept Milton from sounding too

70. Balachandra Rajan, *The Lofty Rhyme: A Study of Milton's Major Poetry* (Coral Gables, Fla.: University of Miami Press, 1970), 108.

71. Carl Sandburg, "To the Ghost of John Milton," 1928, repr. in *The Complete Poems of Carl Sandburg*, revised and expanded edition (New York: Houghton Mifflin Harcourt, 2003), 384.

72. Thomas Corns, *Milton's Language* (Oxford: Basil Blackwell, 1990), 8.

venerable.[73] It's hard to think of a great passage in *Paradise Lost* that doesn't contain the flavor of a noticeable Latinate word: *admire, celestial, combustion, constellations, descend, determined, diffused, dismal, eccentric, eminent, equal, erroneous, fallacious, incumbent, malignant, mortal, oblivious, omnific, oppression, perdition, perfidious, pernicious, ponderous, precedence, prevenient, providence, transcendent, vicissitude* all come to mind. But Milton's vocabulary is also firmly grounded in plain Anglo-Saxon: *break, dark, day, death, do, done, God, good, hand, lost, love, mind, man, mother, night, pride, rash, right, soft, woe, works.*[74] Like Spenser, he can sometimes be deliberately archaic, as with *aread* (advise, 4.962) or *frore* (cold, 2.595). And he pressed upon multilingual etymological roots in Greek, Hebrew, French, Italian, Spanish, Dutch, Aramaic, Syriac[75]—leading Johnson (citing Butler's *Hudibras*) to snort that he wrote in a "*Babylonish Dialect*,"[76] and F. R. Leavis to assert that he had "renounced the English language."[77] So to call him "Latinate" makes him sound one-dimensional in his word choice, when he is rather multidimensional, often juxtaposing and overlaying intonations with virtuoso skill. Here are two examples of Milton writing in adjacent registers:

Satan exalted sat, by merit raised
To that bad eminence (2.5–6)

"Eminence" works off "bad"—"bad" shatters "eminence" to pieces. "Exalted" is deflated by the almost ribald "sat" (an echo of *Sat*an). And again, later:

By center or eccentric, hard to tell (3.575)

73. John Broadbent, *"Paradise Lost": Introduction* (Cambridge: Cambridge University Press, 1972), 116.

74. See William Engel, "John Milton's Recourse to Old English: A Case-Study in Renaissance Lexicography," *LATCH: A Journal for the Study of the Literary Artifact in Theory, Culture, or History* 1 (2008): 1–30.

75. John Hale, *Milton's Languages: The Impact of Multilingualism on Style* (Cambridge: Cambridge University Press, 1997).

76. Christine Rees, *Johnson's Milton* (Cambridge: Cambridge University Press, 2010), 127.

77. F. R. Leavis, "Milton's Verse," in *Revaluation: Tradition and Development in English Poetry* (London: Chatto and Windus, 1936), 52.

The scientific part is the Latin; the ignorant shrug of the shoulders is plain Old English. "Hard to tell": a phrase that Milton might have spoken every day of his later life.

For the four-hundredth anniversary of Milton's 1608 birth, many were keen to argue that Milton was "better than Shakespeare."[78] Gavin Alexander, leaning on the *Oxford English Dictionary* (*OED*), claimed that

Milton is responsible for introducing some 630 words to the English language, making him the country's greatest neologist, ahead of Ben Jonson with 558, John Donne with 342 and Shakespeare with 229.[79]

Yet as Alexander readily conceded, the *OED* over-attributes neologisms to major authors, whose work was until recently more readily surveyed. The advent of encoded electronic text editions of early printed books reveals that rather few of the words formerly credited to Milton—for instance, *boasted* (1.510), *effulgence* (3.388), *brimming* (4.336), *jubilant* (7.564), *self-esteem* (8.572), *loquacious* (10.161)— genuinely originated with him. (Though *Pandemonium* did [1.756; 10.424]!) Still important are the new meanings he gives to extant words, such as when he takes "decency" to mean "a charming act" (8.601), or "clang" for the scream of birds (7.422), or "speakable" to mean capable of speech (9.563), or "scowl" as a verb (2.491). Even more noticeably, Milton overturns conventional grammatical function, converting adjectives into nouns, such as when "obscure" comes to mean obscurity itself: e.g., "the palpable obscure" (2.406). Or he turns a verb like "roam" into a noun: Satan "began ... his roam" (4.537–38); or "consult" from a verb into a noun, such as "the great consult began" (1.798). Some of these words he (and we) might have done without, but his "ingrate" as a noun, deriving from the adjective, is an act of genius (3.97). "Azure" for sky is beautiful (1.297). So also is his turning of

78. See Nigel Smith, *Is Milton Better Than Shakespeare?* (Cambridge, Mass.: Harvard University Press, 2008).

79. John Crace, "John Milton—Our Greatest Word-Maker," *The Guardian*, January 28, 2008, https://www.theguardian.com/uk/2008/jan/28/britishidentity.johncrace.

some adjectives into verbs: "may serve to better us and *worse* our foes" (6.440). The point of Milton's lexical and grammatical practice is not how many absolutely new words he invented, but what he does with the existing English stock. As Milton himself said, he sought

the adorning of my native tongue; not to make verbal curiosities the end, that were a toilsome vanity, but to be an interpreter and relater of the best and sagest things among mine own citizens throughout this island in the mother dialect.[80]

It was Adam's duty, not God's, to name the animals, and then when God prescribed a life of solitude for Adam, "Our author" (5.396) proposed a better alternative, and got it. So it is with the language Milton inherited and endeavored to change.

"ambiguous words" (6.568)

The texture in such passages is found also in the inventive punning of the poem. Because of Milton's reputation for nobility of expression, his wordplay goes underappreciated. But Milton was "an exceptionally conscious poet," so if you think there's any chance for a pun, a trip to the dictionary will likely confirm your hunch.[81] His puns retard the reader's progress, such as when Beelzebub sneers at humans as "The puny inhabitants" (2.367) whom the fallen angels ought to displace from Eden. Compared to the gargantuan devils, people are certainly "puny," as in "diminutive." Yet as Patrick Hume pointed out as early as 1695, they are also *puisné*, in the French sense of "born since, created long since us."[82] Some instances strike the reader immediately, such as the motif of punning on tasting in Book 9 of *Paradise Lost*, from the "distaste" of God for Adam and Eve's sin (9) to their "fruitless" quarreling (1188). The sonorous passage in Book 1 that describes Satan, rising from the Lake of Hell, is throughout compromised by language that

80. *The Reason of Church Government, CPEP*, 840.
81. Irene Samuel, "The Development of Milton's Poetics," *PMLA* 92, no. 2 (March 1977): 231.
82. Patrick Hume, *Annotations on Milton's* Paradise Lost (London: Jacob Tonson, 1695), 65.

suggests the comic nature of the act: While Satan's wings have "unusual weight," he somehow still "lights" on land (1.227–28). And once he lands, we read "such resting found the sole / Of unblest feet" (1.237–38), where the connection of "sole" and "soul" is suggested. The undercurrent of bodily functions further debases Satan's supposed sublimity:

Forthwith upright he *rears* from off the pool ... *backward* ... *midst* ... *air* ... *solid* ... *liquid* ... *subterranean* ... *wind* ... *thund'ring* ... *entrails* ... *bottom* ... *stench* ... *smoke* ... (1.221–37, my italics).

Milton, it is good to see, was not too noble for this scatological jest; he justified it in his polemical prose by asserting that you "must speak obscenely" to describe villains.[83] The narrator wants you to be seduced by Satan's grandeur, even as you see that it is hot air. This is the complex mischief of Milton's poem.

Milton's pressure on the multiple intonations of words is found not only in the Hell passages (where deviousness and duplicity are a way of life) but in Paradise as well. When Satan flies for the first time into Eden, the air, we are told, "inspires / Vernal delight" (4.154–55), an inspired turn in which the physical air (*spirare* is the Latin for *breathe*) itself brings poetry (inspiration) to the heart—not the first time that Milton associates something physical with something traditionally seen as unphysical. This attention to the commingling of the literal and spiritual is what Jonathan Richardson and his son partly had in mind in their 1734 edition of *Paradise Lost*:

A reader of Milton must always be upon duty; he is surrounded by sense, it rises in every line, every word is to the purpose; there are no lazy intervals, all has been considered, and demands, and merits observation. Even in the best writers you may sometimes find words and sentences which hang on so loose you blow 'em off; Milton's are all substance and weight; fewer would not have served the turn, and more would have been superfluous.[84]

83. Kent Lehnhof, "Scatology and the Sacred in Milton's *Paradise Lost*." *English Literary Renaissance* 37, no. 3 (2007): 429.

84. Jonathan Richardson and Jonathan Richardson, *Explanatory Notes and Remarks on Milton's "Paradise Lost" with the Life of the Author and a Discourse on the Poem* (London, 1734), cxliv.

The Richardsons call this quality of Milton's poem a Homeric "silent majesty." Epic sumptuousness is not inconsistent with complexity and attentiveness.

"passionate syntax"

Yeats once said he sought a "powerful and passionate syntax."[85] By "syntax," I mean pattern and cadence, the length of clauses and phrases relative to each other, the way a sentence "moves" (slowly, hastily, wanderingly), what Linda Gregerson celebrates as their "sparkling, tonic rigor."[86] Edward Le Comte refers to Milton's "loose and floating" style;[87] Empson, to the "sliding, sideways, broadening movement" of Milton's poetry.[88] Corns rightly observes that *Paradise Lost* was influenced by the periodic prose of that era, of which Milton wrote a great deal.[89] None of these readers complains of this style as a burden, or as an annoyance that must be tolerated. They like its difficulty. In this respect, Tasso's *asprezza* doesn't mean difficulty in the sense of aggravation. It means the reader has to slow down to savor the intricate dish. Take Book 4, where the Milton luxuriates in speculating whether the motion of the sun or of the earth brings on the close of day and fall of darkness, only to curtail such thoughts:

> whether the prime orb,
> Incredible how swift, had thither rolled
> Diurnal, or this less voluble Earth
> By shorter flight to th' east, had left him there
> Arraying with reflected purple and gold
> The clouds that on his western throne attend:
> *Now came still evening on* (4.592–98, my italics)

85. William Butler Yeats, *Essays and Introductions* (London: Macmillan, 1961), 522.
86. Linda Gregerson, "The Frank Enthusiast: An Interview with Linda Gregerson," by Sara Hoover and Michaelean Ferguson, ed. Lee Griffith, *The Pinch* 27, no. 2 (Fall 2007): 142.
87. Edward Le Comte, *A Dictionary of Puns in Milton's English Poetry* (New York: Columbia University Press, 1981), xiii.
88. Empson, *Some Versions,* 162.
89. Corns, *Milton's Language,* 44.

This passage epitomizes Milton's decision about the relative importance of "high" knowledge as opposed to the more mundane kind. From the human point of view, all that matters is the beauty of the advent evening. How affectingly direct that last line is after what has come before it!

Milton's syntax achieves distinction of this contextual sort in assorted ways. The stringing together of syllables that must be articulated slowly can give an effect of temporal extent, such as in "Nine times the space that measures day and night / To mortal men" to describe how long Satan has lain prostrate (1.50–51). When Milton adds strong pauses to the middle of a line, however, the effect can be one of great activity, even though resistance is being described. An example of playing broken lines off whole ones occurs when he describes Satan tempting Eve and his hope to

> thence raise
> At least distempered, discontented thoughts,
> Vain hopes, vain aims, inordinate desires
> Blown up with high conceits engend'ring pride. (4.806–9)

Milton enumerates first the elements of vanity through *caesurae*, and then, in a larger unbroken unit, relates the total product of these vanities, which is pride. By adding many pauses, Milton can also get an effect of tentativeness, such as when Adam and Eve approach the Son after the Fall: "He came, and with him Eve, more loath, though first" (10.109). A hesitant walk. A few lines further, there is an effect of laborious enumeration in Adam and Eve's

> guilt,
> And shame, and perturbation, and despair,
> Anger, and obstinacy, and hate, and guile. (10.112–14)

Here as elsewhere in *Paradise Lost* are "woven close, both matter, form and style."[90]

90. Milton, Sonnet 11, *CPEP*, 147.

"order from disorder sprung" (*3.713*)

Much has been written about Milton's highly artificed word order, taken from the Italian and Latin poets. A telling ingredient of this style is an uncolloquial arrangement. Milton is in love with parallelism and its variations, such as the parallel adjective-noun. Eve has instant knowledge of "nuptial sanctity and marriage rites" (8.487); Satan has "lost happiness and lasting pain" (1.55). Almost every page exhibits this pattern:

> For contemplation he and valour formed,
> For softness she and sweet attractive grace (4.297–98)

The lines conform to each other with those opening prepositional "for" phrases, but there is a difference in the respective weight of "contemplation" and "softness." As Milton's feminist critics have taught us to notice, "contemplation" is more substantial, more favorable than "softness." Though Eve is given two adjectives, they don't weigh as much as Adam's nouns. There is both likeness and difference in these lines, symmetry and asymmetry, as though Milton were trying to get us to snap our fingers in rhythm, but not to be too predictable with sameness. (We will discover later that Adam and Eve are not perfectly balanced opposites.) Sometimes the adjective-noun can be placed imaginatively at the line's beginning and ending, as in the account of Eve recovering with Adam's help from a bad dream: "So prayed they innocent, and to their thoughts / *Firm peace* recovered soon and *wonted calm*" (5.210, my italics). The balance Adam and Eve find is seen in the balanced phrases at the beginning and end of the second line. This is why we know that our experience of *Paradise Lost* is a musical one, even if we can't always say why.

Another pattern Milton loves is *chiasmus* (or *antimetabole*), parallelism with the second element reversed. In Book 7, the poet relates his plight as a social and political outcast in a couplet that is hard to forget because of the A:B::B:A syntax: "though *fall'n* on *evil* days / On *evil* days though *fall'n*" (25–26, my italics). In *Don Juan*, Lord Byron wittily one-upped Milton with a double chiasmus of Milton:Avenger:-Time::Time:Avenger:Miltonic:

> If, fallen in evil days on evil tongues,
>   Milton appeal'd to the Avenger, Time,
> If Time, the Avenger, execrates his wrongs,
>   And makes the word "*Miltonic*" mean "*sublime*."[91]

But chiasmus calls great attention to itself, and so Milton can soften it by writing an approximate chiasmus: "Sonorous metal blowing martial sounds" (1.540). At first, it looks like pure parallelism: "*sonorous metal* blowing *martial sounds*" which is adjective-noun/adjective-noun, ABAB (my italics). But there is also a complicating chiasmus: a degree of parallelism in "metal" and "martial" that links them, just as with "sonorous" and "sounds." So the chiasmus is between *sonorous . . . metal . . . martial . . . sounds* or ABBA. This is parallelism at the level of grammar, chiasmus at the level of sound. It would soon prove tedious to cite many more instances, but it is not at all tedious to listen to them as you read the poem.

Some inversions of word order have become Milton's signature, such as his practice (derived from Latin) of placing adjectives on both sides of the noun they modify: "temperate vapors bland" (5.5) where most writers would say "bland and temperate vapors." When we're told that his blindness keeps him from seeing "human face divine," our "face" is located between two spheres of being, the human and the divine (3.44). A similar pattern (this time derived from Italian) is the adjective-noun-and-adjective: "th' upright heart and pure" (1.18) instead of "the pure and upright heart"; "taut compression is the result."[92] This type of isolated adjective is remarkable in the penultimate line of *Paradise Lost*: Adam and Eve leaving Eden "with wand'ring steps and slow" (12.648). (Compare "with slow and wand'ring steps,"

91. George Gordon Lord Byron, *The Major Works*, ed. Jerome McGann (Oxford: Oxford University Press, 2008), 375.
92. G. K. Subbarayudu, "'High Disdain from Sense of Injured Merit': A Note on Milton's Grand Style," in *Paradise Lost, Book I*, ed. C. Vijayasree (Delhi: Dorling Kindersley, 2006), 92.

which preserves the same meter.) "wandering steps and slow" could stand for the Miltonic voice itself: *I will not sound like everyone else!*

Agari Masahiko finds scores of inversions that make English obey the drama of the situation rather than rules. It's not which grammatical custom they break, but how they function to generate meaning. When Adam confesses "here passion first I felt / Commotion strange" (8.530–31), the inversions—not to mention the lack of transition to the phrase "Commotion strange"—make it appear that sexual drive comes first, is overwhelming. Masahiko notices how, when Eve greets Adam back after his lesson with Michael, "she him received," embracing Adam between the pronoun and the verb (12.609).[93] It's almost cute. "What in me is dark / Illumine" saves the best for last as the enjambed "Illumine" retroactively bursts out of the "dark" (1.22–23). Not all of Milton's inversions work this way, but many do. At the least, he commands you to attend to them. This practice extends into characterization, to underline vulnerabilities. The first time Satan speaks, in Book 1, he interrupts ("but O") what appears to be a prepared speech ("If thou beest he") to express his horror the stark recognition of just how awful the Fall has been (1.84). Then the more orderly, consoling passage, "if he" re-asserts itself, with all of its adjective-noun combinations: *mutual league, united thoughts, equal hope, glorious enterprise, equal ruin* (1.87–91, my italics). It sounds like a prepared speech, made up of talking points. From any other poet, we would have such devices then many times. I don't mean that Milton doesn't have any formulas, for he of course does. But he doesn't wallow in his own extraordinary discoveries and exploit them. Hence, they come as surprises.

"amorous delay" (*4.311*)

Milton's rearrangement of conventional word order is nowhere clearer than in syntactic suspension or postponement: his poetics of "sweet reluctant amorous delay" (4.311). This phrase, cited repeated-

93. Agari Masahiko, *Inversion in Milton's Poetry* (New York: Peter Lang Publishing, 2001).

ly by eighteenth-century poets such as Erasmus Darwin and Anna Seward as one of the most fascinating in the entire poem, enacts Eve's own powers of postponement through the cumulating adjectives, unexplained and unresolved until we arrive at the noun "delay." Milton also suspends *verbs* so as to give them maximum impact. When Satan speaks before the fallen angels, we read "His proud imaginations thus displayed" (2.10). The withheld verb augments the size of the display; Satan's deceptive ostentation can't be ruled out. Another good example can be found in the first description of Eve's hair: "She as a veil down to the slender waist / Her unadornèd golden tresses *wore*" (4.304–5). The length of Eve's hair is indicated as the sentence defers its completion until it reaches Eve's waist. Here again, style serves sense. When Adam and Raphael start talking, Eve is depicted as follows:

> which Eve
> Perceiving where she sat retired in sight,
> With lowliness majestic from her seat,
> And grace that won who saw to wish her stay,
> *Rose* (8.40–44, my italics)

This is exquisite. The three-line long suspension acts like a drumroll, and helps makes humble royalty out of Eve. The strongly accented first syllable of the line, "Rose," participates in the effect. At other times, Milton inverts only the noun-agent of a line. When Satan is squat as a toad at the ear of Eve and is prodded in that position by the angelic guard, we read "So started up in his own shape the fiend" (4.819). First the action, then the order of the words suggests the process of Satan's transformation, until "fiend" unequivocally signals who he is. *Paradise Lost* is a dramatic as well as a narrative poem, and part of that drama is found in its syntax.

Deferral can manifest itself when the sentence runs across the physical ending of the line into the next, without pause. I concur with Geoffrey Hill's contention that Milton was a "supreme master of enjambment." This is, along with his rather elastic yet firm metrical pattern, the feature that has most troubled readers. Samuel Johnson faults Milton for not keeping his lines "distinct," citing with approval a critic who claims that "Blank verse seems to be verse only to the eye," almost prose.[94] Milton knew there would be resistant readers. In his combative preface, "The Verse," he decries rhyme as being unnecessary to heroic poetry (Homer and Virgil didn't rhyme), and he defines "true musical delight" as consisting "only in apt numbers, fit quantity of syllables, and *the sense variously drawn out from one verse into another, not in the jingling sound of like endings*."[95] The "sense variously drawn out" champions a sustained forward motion, chiming back to the praise of music in "L'Allegro":

> with many a winding bout
> Of linkèd sweetness long *drawn out,*
> With wanton heed, and giddy cunning,
> The melting voice through mazes running;
> Untwisting all the chains that tie
> The hidden soul of harmony[96]

(And there's *wanton* and *mazes* again, enticing words we heard in Book 4 of *Paradise Lost*.) Milton is not talking about constant enjambment, that is, occurring in every line, but "variously." He vaunts how his poem recovers "ancient liberty ... from the troublesome and modern bondage of rhyming,"[97] analogous to modern statesmen recovering the liberty of the ancient world, or Protestants recovering the purity of the primitive church. Milton's enjambment gives his poem an element of formal instability. That takes some getting used to, but the instability is offset by stability, just as liberty for Milton is meaningless without law and discipline. We notice in this passage that Milton has juxtaposed enjambment with "apt numbers" and "fit quantity

94. Johnson, *The Lives of the Poets*, 204.
95. *CPEP*, 291; my italics.
96. *CPEP*, 46, lines 139–44, my italics.
97. Milton, "The Verse," *CPEP*, 291.

of syllables." That is, you can have acceptable enjambment only when your meter and syllable count are relatively regular.

Milton often enjambs lines in such a way that the break enhances his emphasis by the gap in the spacing. In his subtle discussion of enjambment in *Paradise Lost*, Archie Burnett notices numerous instances of expressive line endings, such as the depiction of Satan's flight:

> So he with difficulty and labor hard
> Moved on, with difficulty and labor he (2.1021–22)

He asks the reader to imagine the first line with "moved on" at the end; the appearance of "moved on" after the break (bracketed by the laboriously repeated "difficulty and labor") enforces the impression of Satan's upstream battle, "like driving with the brake slightly engaged."[98] In Book 9, after Adam has tried, unsuccessfully, to talk Eve out of leaving his side, the poem reads:

> So spake the patriarch of mankind, but Eve
> Persisted (9.376–78)

What appears to Adam to be Eve's obduracy at this moment is indicated by the appearance of "persisted" after a line break, which usually indicates closure. The syntax itself ... persists. The result is what Donald Davie terms the "eventfulness" of *Paradise Lost*.[99]

Milton did not believe that every line should be enjambed.[100] But he would certainly have agreed in principle with Robert Pinsky, who holds that "the line and syntactical unit are not necessarily the same."[101] The relation between the two elements, the resulting pull or dance, is pleasing and expressive. A poet can make his sentences "per-

---

98. Archie Burnett, "Sense Variously Drawn Out: The Line in *Paradise Lost*," *Literary Imagination: The Review of the Association of Literary Scholars and Critics* 5, no. 1 (2003): 75.

99. Davie, "Syntax and Music," 73.

100. James Whaler estimates that between 60 and 80 percent of the lines are enjambed. *Counterpoint and Symbol: An Inquiry into the Rhythm of Milton's Epic Style* (1952; repr. New York: Haskell House, 1971), 13.

101. Robert Pinsky, *The Sounds of Poetry: A Brief Guide* (New York: Farrar, Straus, and Giroux, 1998), 30.

form," as he "sometimes pauses at a line ending and sometimes streaks or leaps or strains across it."[102] The reader gets the satisfaction of regularity from the syntax that ends at the line, as well as a sense of adventure from the syntax that leaps beyond it—what Michael Longley calls "propulsion."[103] Longley associates it with Milton's poetry, contending that *Paradise Lost* "should be inhaled regularly as an antidote to much contemporary practice," much of which, he implies, is inert.[104] The same principle of poetry is articulated more fully by Heaney when he claims that a poem must be responsive to two motions, one "towards liberation and beatitude ... but countered by an implicit acknowledgment of repression and constraint."[105]

"unattempted yet in prose or rhyme" (*1.16*)

Other mid-seventeenth-century epics rhymed, a practice that tended to invite the line and the syntax to align. Here are the opening lines from an epic on the theme of King David, Abraham Cowley's *Davideis*, first published in 1656. Milton (who admired Cowley) would have known the poem.

> I sing the *Man* who *Judah's scepter* bore
> In that right hand which held the *Crook* before;
> Who from best *Poet*, best of kings did grow,
> The two chief *gifts Heav'n* could on *Man* bestow.
> Much danger first, much toil did he sustain,
> Whilst *Saul* and *Hell* cross'd his strong fate in vain.[106]

Contrast this yet once more to the restless enjambment in Milton's first lines:

102. Ibid., 29, 27.
103. "Interview: Michael Longley and Jody Allen Randolph," *Colby Quarterly* 39, no. 3 (September 2003): 306.
104. Ibid.
105. Seamus Heaney, *The Redress of Poetry* (New York: Farrar, Straus and Giroux, 1995), 33.
106. Abraham Cowley, *Davideis*, in *Poetry and Prose*, ed. L. C. Martin (Oxford: Clarendon Press, 1949), 33.

Of man's first disobedience, and the *fruit*
Of that forbidden tree, whose mortal *taste*
Brought death into the world, and all our woe,
With loss of Eden, till one greater *man*
Restore us, and regain the blissful seat,
Sing heav'nly Muse, that on the secret *top*
Of Oreb, or of Sinai, didst *inspire*
That shepherd, who first taught the chosen seed,
In the beginning how the heavens and *earth*
Rose out of Chaos: or if Sion *hill*
Delight thee more, and Siloa's brook that *flowed*
Fast by the oracle of God, I *thence*
Invoke thy aid to my advent'rous song,
That with no middle flight intends to *soar*
Above th' Aonian mount, while it *pursues*
Things unattempted yet in prose or rhyme. (1.1–16, my italics)

Cowley's rhyming couplets and regular meter parcel things out, step
by step. In Milton, blank verse launches the desire to "soar / Above." It
carries the suggestion of daring and abandon and assertiveness—even
poetic fervor. The narrator (in doubt about his fitness) is trying to
get up a head of steam: rhymes would drag the desired momentum.
But it is not only absence of rhyming couplets that defines *Paradise
Lost*'s verse. Milton's poem derives kinetic power from the syntax that
hurtles over the line ending, as if the poet were impatient to get to
his task.

Milton's verse in *Paradise Lost* can be located somewhere near
the middle of a continuum between continuous prose and more con-
ventional, end-stopped verse. He wanted a sense of containment to
stretch, which is different from the impression that prose wishes to
give. Early readers, attracted to Milton's story but worried about Mil-
ton's radical style, sought to render *Paradise Lost* in a tamed version.
Some added rhyme, such as John Dryden (1674) and John Hopkins
(1699), though Hopkins not without repentance: "when I did it, I
did not so well Perceive the Majesty and Noble air of *Mr. Milton's*

style as now I do; and were it not already done, I must confess I never should attempt it."[107] Here is Dryden "tagging" Milton's verses (from 1.220):

> Is this the Seat our Conqueror has given?
> And this the Climate we must change for heaven?
> These Regions and this Realm my Wars have got;
> This Mournful Empire is the Loser's Lot;
> In Liquid Burnings, or on Dry to dwell,
> Is all the sad Variety of Hell.[108]

Others, such as George Smith Green (1756), didn't tame by rhyming, but by "enclosing" Milton's blank verse—that is, by removing the enjambment, sometimes allowing for twelve-syllable lines. Here is Green's "paraphrase":

> Of Adam's Fall and the forbidden Tree
> Whose fruit brought Sin and Death into the world,
> With Loss of paradise and Immortality,
> To Him and to his Sons—sing, heavenly MUSE!
> THOU—that at first, with mighty Wings outspread,
> Dove-like sat'st brooding o'er the vast Abyss
> And mad'st it pregnant!
> Impart a beam of thy celestial Brightness,
> To purify my Thoughts and sanctify my pen
> That—with no middle Flight intends to soar,
> And treat of Themes yet unessay'd by Man.[109]

Green pauses longer at the close of lines. His sentences are shorter than Milton's. As a result, the version lacks urgency and sweep. Green claims a desire in his "Preface" to get rid of Milton's "roughness," chopping the poem into smaller pieces to make it less difficult, less disori-

107. John Hopkins, *Milton's "Paradise Lost" Imitated in Rhyme, in the Fourth, Sixth and Ninth Books* (London: Ralph Smith, 1699), n.p.

108. John Dryden, *The State of Innocence and the Fall of Man: An Opera* (London, 1678).

109. George Smith Green, *A New Version of the "Paradise Lost": or, Milton Paraphrased*, 1756, reprinted in *The Critical Review, Or, Annals of Literature, 1756–1763*, vols. 1–2, ed. James G. Basker (London: Pickering and Chatto, 2002), 359.

enting, and, by his own admission, less sublime.[110] In this respect, he is not averse to allowing Milton's lines to end with falling stresses (see "BRIGHTness" above, or "immorTALity," or "PREGnant," which have unstressed final syllables), which Milton almost never does. As such, Green transmits Milton's ideas, but little of his music, "the ways it roils, disorients, then reorients."[111]

"the foot of Paradise" (*9.71*)

As J. Allyn Rosser affirms, "You will learn everything there is to learn about meter" by reading all of *Paradise Lost*.[112] For Milton's meter, one needs a few principles, common sense, and some practice. *Paradise Lost* is written in blank verse, the unrhymed iambic pentameter lauded by Thomas Jefferson as "the most precious part of our poetry."[113] This ten-syllable line consists of five "feet," with each foot an unstressed syllable and a stressed syllable: *I HATE to SEE that EVEning SUN go DOWN* (from "The St. Louis Blues"). Milton doesn't always write this regular line; that would be tedious—in fact, he can play with regularity to indicate tedium: "And swims or sinks, or wades, or creeps, or flies" (2.950). Rather he departs, sometimes boldly, from this base pattern, then returns to it. The analogy might be a comedy team: the regular line is the straight man; the variation is the comedian. This is what John Creaser means when he says that Milton's verse is radical *and* regular at the same time.[114]

In metrical verse, one experiences the interplay of the expected rhythm (in this case iambic) and the heard rhythm (the way one ac-

110. Ibid., ii–iv.

111. Daisy Fried, "Sing, God-Awful Muse! On Milton and the Nipple Nazi of Northampton," *Poetry Magazine*, July/August 2009.

112. J. Allyn Rosser, "Caveat Lector," in *Planet on the Table: Poets on the Reading Life*, ed. Sharon Bryan and William Olsen (Louisville, Ky.: Sarabande Books, 2003), 146.

113. Thomas Jefferson, "Thoughts on English Prosody," 1786, in *Writings*, ed. Merrill D. Peterson (New York: Library of America, 1984), 618.

114. John Creaser, "Prosodic Style and Conceptions of Liberty in Milton and Marvell," *Milton Quarterly* 34, no. 1 (2000): 9.

tually reads the stresses in a line). This is not only the strategy of good metered verse, but the pleasure of it: constant departure and return. Read the line naturally, without imposing a heavy beat on it; the regular meter and the variation will take care of that themselves. Milton rarely has more than ten syllables in a line, so be prepared to elide an unstressed vowel. The last line of the poem should sound, not like this, "They HAND in HAND with WAN der ing STEPS and SLOW," but like this: "They HAND in HAND with WAND'ring STEPS and SLOW."[115] He almost never ends a line with an unaccented syllable, and he only rarely offers more than two variations in a single line. These metrical practices—limited variations, rising final stresses—exert a strong force on behalf of regularity, giving Milton the chance to exercise "freedom within form."[116] The norm is iambic pentameter. It is almost always there, even when Milton soft-pedals it.

Here are a few of Milton's most common variations, though the reader may disagree with my scansion.[117] One is heavy stressing at the beginning of a line, such as "SING HEAV'nly MUSE" (1.6). The position of the stress, disturbing the rising iambic meter, conveys great enthusiasm, even desperation. Milton can vary his meter more than once in a line as well. Satan's indignation in not being recognized by two younger angels is rendered thus: "NOT to know ME ARgues your SELF unKNOWN" (4.830). There is a reversed first foot here (NOT to), and then a reversed middle foot (ARgues), before the line recovers its regularity with two rising feet. Even the very first line of the poem plays with meter: "Of MAN'S FIRST DISoBEDience, and the FRUIT," with three consecutive stressed syllables (MAN'S FIRST DIS), and three consecutive unstressed syllables (ience and the) before that final FRUIT, an audacious irregularity (disobedience!) that

115. Milton here saves us the trouble by contracting the syllable himself; see Mindele Treip, *Milton's Punctuation and Changing English Usage, 1582–1676* (London: Methuen, 1970).

116. Eliot, "Milton," 79.

117. Metrists are prone to dissent! But I commend Creaser as preeminent on this subject, and Robert Bridges before him. See Creaser, "Prosodic Style"; and Robert Bridges, *Milton's Prosody* (Oxford: Oxford University Press, 1901, rev. 1921).

perplexed Louis MacNiece.[118] But remember that the iambic meter undergirds the variant line, which one can easily see by imposing the rising meter on the variant. It doesn't sound good or natural, but it works. In a celebrated passage, Satan spots Eve alone in the garden just before the temptation, and the lines evince a regular yet pliable meter (9.421–25). Crucial variants enforce what's happening. The first is "EVE SEParate" (422). The double stress makes Eve stand out, just what Satan desires! *EVE*! *SEP*! She is both *separate* in the sense of "outstanding," and also separated from her husband. In line 423 there is another crucial variant, a surprising falling stress, "WHEN to" as Satan's luck changes dramatically. In line 424, the third foot contains a double stress: "EVE SEP"—again! What was before a wish has now been granted. The last line ends with Eve, so to speak, captured, "VEILED in," which metrically echoes "WHEN to." The last line is wonderfully unbroken and sweeping after what has come before it. What was unresolved, halting in the first four lines, becomes settled in the last. The subtle, internal half rhyme (*veiled, cloud, stood*) enforces the sense of completion.

"in fit strains pronounced" (*5.148*)

This chapter began with a lament that Milton's multifaceted language in *Paradise Lost* appears to be at such odds with contemporary poetry. Yet Milton's epic style needs no excuse, but rather open-mindedness, and a receptivity to "the poet with his many voices."[119] It also, I believe, craves recitation—as Philip Pullman enjoins, you have to "take the lines in [your] mouth and utter them aloud."[120] "The way to defend Milton against all impugners," Hazlitt said, "is to take

118. Louis MacNiece, *Modern Poetry: A Personal Essay* (New York: Haskell House, 1938), 122.

119. Homer, *The Odyssey*, trans. Robert Fitzgerald (New York: Farrar, Straus and Giroux, 1998), 421.

120. Philip Pullman, introduction to *John Milton's "Paradise Lost"* (Oxford: Oxford University Press, 2005), 2.

down the book and read it."[121] By turns, Milton can be delicate, propulsive, intricate, arrogant, and ravishingly beautiful. Just as he urged his own students to heed to *genera dicendi*, or the classical doctrine of suiting words to the occasion, he wrote "perspicuously, elegantly, and according to the fitted style of lofty, mean, or lowly."[122] But appreciating those things requires accepting *Paradise Lost* as a book that makes demands on its readers. It requires a slow, attentive re-reading, not a solitary skim.

Denis Danielson made a recent prose version of *Paradise Lost* because he believes too many readers can't—or won't—get through the poem, as it offers too much "linguistic obscurity."[123] (As Donald Sutherland's burnt-out professor laments in *Animal House*: it "doesn't translate very well into our generation.") What must reach this generation of readers, Danielson determines, is *Paradise Lost*'s great story, especially its theological issues and political controversies; aren't Homer, Virgil, Dante, read today precisely because they exist in modern translation? If Sophie Gee is right in surmising that *Paradise Lost* is "now virtually unreadable" for most,[124] I guess it's better that it be read in paraphrase than not at all, just as some people in the seventeenth and eighteenth centuries thought when they made their versions of the epic, whether in English, German, Italian, or Latin.[125] Danielson's position is realistic; to a degree, it is persuasive. Still, it all comes down to whether or not the reader thinks poetry is intrinsic or extrinsic to *Paradise Lost*. There is nothing that is inherently objectionable about the meaning of Danielson's version of Milton's poem, except that all of the excitement and exhilaration, and much of its subtlety, has been hollowed out:

121. *The Collected Works of William Hazlitt*, 61.

122. "Of Education," *CPEP*, 977.

123. Denis Danielson, ed., *"Paradise Lost": Parallel Prose Edition* (Vancouver: Regent College Publishing, 2008), ix–x.

124. Sophie Gee, "Great Adaptations," *The New York Times*, January 13, 2008, 35.

125. See Angelica Duran, Islam Issa, and Jonathan R. Olson, eds., *Milton in Translation* (Oxford: Oxford University Press, 2017).

Tell me the story, Heavenly Muse: of humankind's first trespass, of forbidden fruit whose lethal taste brought death and sorrow to our world, and drove us out of Eden—until one greater human should redeem us and regain the happy place we lost. You, on the shrouded peak of Horeb or Sinai, inspired that shepherd who first taught God's chosen people how, in the beginning, the heavens and the earth rose out of chaos. Now I ask: Be my inspirer too. Or if Mount Zion pleases you more, with Siloam's waters flowing near the temple of God, then from there I seek your help. For my daring story aims to surpass the ancient muses of Helicon, striving to achieve what no one, in poetry or prose, has ever even attempted.[126]

Danielson makes no poetic claims for his translation (though it's preferable to Joseph Lanzara's or Nancy Willard's paraphrases).[127] His rationale is that it brings readers into the tent.

Would Milton have welcomed such an audience, attuned only to his plot, with no particular care for his poetry? Hadn't he already conceded to such an audience with the prose summaries he prefaced to his poem, scarcely a year after first publishing it? Milton wanted a book that would find "fit audience ... though few" (7.31); "something so written to aftertimes, as they should not willingly let it die."[128] He wanted a book that—considering how much time it took him to prepare for it, and how much delay he endured—would be the companion not of a few days or weeks or months. He wanted a book that would be the companion of a life, one that we should carry with us, learning the poet's song, singing it with him as we go.

126. Danielson, "Paradise Lost": Parallel Prose Edition, 13.
127. See Joseph Lanzara, John Milton's "Paradise Lost" in Plain English: A Simple, Line by Line Paraphrase of the Complicated Masterpiece (Belleville, N.J.: New Arts Library, 2009); and Nancy Willard, The Tale of Paradise Lost (New York: Atheneum, 2004).
128. The Reason of Church Government, CPEP, 840.

WORKS CITED

There are estimated to be at least as many studies of Milton as there are lines in the poem—"much arguing, much writing, many opinions"![1]

For a more comprehensive bibliography, consult Dartmouth University's *Milton Reading Room*, which includes selected criticism, some of which is available online: https://www.dartmouth.edu/~milton/reading_room/bibliography/a-b/text.shtml.

R. G. Siemens earlier surveyed Milton scholarship for *The Cambridge Companion to Milton*, ed. Dennis Danielson (Cambridge University Press, 1999); reproduced at *Early Modern Literary Studies (EMLS)*: https://extra.shu.ac.uk/emls/iemls/postprint/CCM2Biblio.html.

Unless otherwise noted, all references to Milton's works are from *The Complete Poetry and Essential Prose of John Milton*, edited by William Kerrigan, John Rumrich, and Stephen M. Fallon (New York: The Modern Library, 2007) (*CPEP*).

Addison, Joseph. "Addison's Papers on *Paradise Lost*." 1712. Reprinted in *Milton: The Critical Heritage*, edited by John Shawcross, 147–220. London: Routledge and Kegan Paul, 1970.

Allen Randolph, Jody. "Interview: Michael Longley and Jody Allen Randolph." *Colby Quarterly* 39, no. 3 (September 2003): 294–308.

Alvarez, A. "A Talk with Robert Lowell." 1965. Reprinted in *Robert Lowell: Interviews and Memoirs*, edited by Jeffrey Meyers, 99–108. Ann Arbor: University of Michigan Press, 1988.

Amis, Kingsley. "The Hangover." In *Everyday Drinking: The Distilled Kingsley Amis*, 79–89. London: Bloomsbury, 2010.

Amis, Martin. Interview by Sue Lawley. *Desert Island Discs*. BBC Radio 4. December 29, 1996.

Arnold, Matthew. "Milton." In *The Works of Matthew Arnold*, vol 4, edited by Thomas Burnett Smart, 42–50. London: Macmillan, 1903.

1. Milton, *Areopagitica*, in *CPEP* 958.

Auden, Wystan Hugh, and Normal Holmes Pearson. *Poets of the English Language*. Vol. 3, *Milton to Goldsmith*. New York: Viking Press, 1950.

Bell, Millicent. "The Fallacy of the Fall in *Paradise Lost*." *PMLA* 68 (1953): 863–83.

Belsey, Catherine. *John Milton: Language, Gender, Power*. Oxford: Basil Blackwell, 1988.

Bentley, Richard. *Milton's "Paradise Lost." A New Edition*. London: Jacob Tonson, 1732.

Berryman, John. "Wash Far Away." In *The Freedom of the Poet*, 367–83. New York: Farrar, Straus and Giroux, 1976.

Bishop, Elizabeth. *The Complete Poems: 1927–1979*. New York: Farrar, Straus and Giroux, 1979.

Blake, William. *The Marriage of Heaven and Hell*. 1790. Reprinted in *The Poems of William Blake*, edited by W. H. Stevenson, 101–24. London: Longman, 1971.

Boesky, Amy. "The Maternal Shape of Mourning: A Reconsideration of *Lycidas*." *Modern Philology* 95, no. 4 (May 1998): 463–83.

Borges, Jorge Luis. *Borges at Eighty: Conversations*. Edited by Willis Barnsteone. New York: New Directions, 1982.

Boswell, James. *Boswell's Life of Johnson*. Vol. 1. New York: Oxford University Press, 1953.

Bridges, Robert. *Milton's Prosody*. Oxford: Oxford University Press, 1901. Rev. 1921.

Brisman, Leslie. *Milton's Poetry of Choice and Its Romantic Heirs*. Ithaca, N.Y.: Cornell University Press, 1973.

Broadbent, John. Paradise Lost: *Introduction*. Cambridge: Cambridge University Press, 1972.

Bryant, William Cullen. "Calhoun's Diminished Stature." (September 20, 1837.) In *Power for Sanity: Selected Editorials of William Cullen Bryant, 1829–1861*, edited by William Cullen Bryant II, 74. New York: Fordham University Press, 1994.

Bryson, Michael. *The Tyranny of Heaven: Milton's Rejection of God as King*. Newark: University of Delaware Press, 2004.

Buchanan, James. *The First Six Books of "Paradise Lost": Rendered into Grammatical Construction*. Edinburgh, 1773.

Budick, Sanford. *Kant and Milton*. Cambridge, Mass.: Harvard University Press, 2010.

Burnett, Archie. "Sense Variously Drawn Out: The Line in *Paradise Lost*." *Literary Imagination: The Review of the Association of Literary Scholars and Critics* 5, no. 1 (2003): 69–92.

Burns, Robert. Letter to William Nicol, June 18, 1787. In *The Letters of Robert Burns*, 2nd ed., vol. 1, edited by G. Ross Roy. Oxford: Oxford University Press, 1985.

Burrow, Colin. "Shall I Go On?" *London Review of Books* 35, no. 5 (March 7, 2013): 3–8.

Burt, Stephanie. *The Poem Is You: 60 Contemporary American Poems and How to Read Them*. Cambridge: Belknap Press, 2016.

Burt, Stephanie (writing as Stephen Burt). "In Defence of Minor Poets." *Partisan Magazine*, April 5, 2016. http://www.partisanmagazine.com/blog/2016/4/2/h71c3htrsnuiypwtunmmnsuokp5wvx.

Byron, George Gordon Lord. *The Works of Lord Byron with his Letters and Journals and his Life By Thomas Moore*. 14 vols. London: John Murray, 1832.

———. *Lord Byron: The Major Works*. Edited by Jerome McGann. Oxford: Oxford University Press, 2008.

Campbell, Gordon, and Thomas N. Corns. *John Milton: Life, Work, and Thought*. Oxford: Oxford University Press, 2008.

Cavanagh, Michael. "A Meeting of Epic and History: Books XI and XII of *Paradise Lost*." *English Literary History* 38, no. 2 (June 1971): 206–22.

Chatman, Seymour. "Milton's Participial Style." *PMLA* 83, no. 5 (October 1968): 1386–99.

Coiro, Ann Baynes. "Sufficient and Free: The Poetry of *Paradise Lost*." In *Milton Now: Alternative Approaches and Contexts*, edited by Catharine Gray and Erin Murphy, 83–108. New York: Palgrave, 2014.

Cole, Henri. "John Berryman at 100, A Celebration: Panel 2 with April Bernard, Henri Cole, and A. Van Jordan." YouTube video, 47:10. The Poetry Society of America, along with Columbia School of the Arts, Barnard Women Poets, and Heyman Center for the Humanities. Posted by SoF/Heyman, May 7, 2015. https://www.youtube.com/watch?v=saOKq1dPsyg.

Coleridge, Samuel Taylor. *Biographia Literaria*. 1817. Reprinted in *Collected*

Works of Samuel Taylor Coleridge, vol. 7, edited by James Engell and
W. Jackson Bate. London: Routledge, 1983.

———. *Table Talk*. 1835. Reprinted in *The Collected Works of Samuel Taylor
Coleridge*, vol. 14, edited by Carl Woodring. London: Routledge, 1990.

Collier, John. *Milton's "Paradise Lost": Screenplay for Cinema of the Mind*.
New York: Knopf, 1973.

Collins, Billy. "Aristotle." In *Picnic, Lightning*, 101–3. Pittsburgh: University
of Pittsburgh Press, 1998.

Corns, Thomas. *Milton's Language*. Oxford: Basil Blackwell, 1990.

Corso, Gregory. "Some of My Beginning.... and What I Feel Right Now."
In *Poets on Poetry*, edited by Howard Nemerov, 172–81. New York: Basic
Books, 1966.

Cowley, Abraham. *Poetry and Prose*. Edited by L. C. Martin. Oxford: Clar-
endon Press, 1949.

Crace, John. "John Milton—Our Greatest Word-Maker." *The Guardian*,
January 28, 2008. https://www.theguardian.com/uk/2008/jan/28/
britishidentity.johncrace.

Creaser, John. "Prosodic Style and Conceptions of Liberty in Milton and
Marvell." *Milton Quarterly* 34, no. 1 (2000): 1–13.

Cummings, Brian. "Revolutionary English." In *The Literary Culture of the
Reformation: Grammar and Grace*, 421–31. Oxford: Oxford University
Press, 2002.

Curran, Stuart. "God." In *The Oxford Handbook of Milton*, edited by Nich-
olas McDowell and Nigel Smith, 525–33. Oxford: Oxford University
Press, 2009.

Daiches, David. *Milton*. London: Hutchinson University Library, 1957.

Danielson, Dennis. *Milton's Good God: A Study in Literary Theodicy*. Cam-
bridge: Cambridge University Press, 1982.

———, ed. *"Paradise Lost": Parallel Prose Edition*. Vancouver: Regent
College Publishing, 2008.

Darbishire, Helen. *The Early Lives of Milton*. London: Constable, 1932.

Darwin, Charles. *Charles Darwin: His Life Told in an Autobiographical
Chapter, and in a Selected Series of His Published Letters*. Edited by
Francis Darwin. London: John Murray, 1892.

Davie, Donald. "Syntax and Music in *Paradise Lost*." In *The Living Milton:*

Essays by Various Hands, edited by Frank Kermode, 70–84. London: Routledge and Kegan Paul, 1960.

Dawson, Erica. "Interview with Erica Dawson, Featured Poet." By Madison Jones. *Kudzu House*, December 13, 2015. http://kudzuhouse.org/ interview-with-erica-dawson-featured-winter-solstice-poet/.

De Quincey, Thomas. *Confessions of an English Opium-Eater*. 1821. Edited by Joel Faflak. Peterborough, Ontario: Broadview Press, 2009.

———. "Milton." 1839. Reprinted in *Works*, vol. 6. Edinburgh: A. and C. Black, 1862–63.

Dickinson, Emily. *The Letters of Emily Dickinson, 1845–1886*. Edited by Mabel Loomis Todd. Boston: Little, Brown, 1906.

Dobranski, Stephen. *Milton, Authorship, and the Book Trade*. Cambridge: Cambridge University Press, 1999.

Dryden, John. *The State of Innocence and the Fall of Man: An Opera*. London, 1678.

Du Bartas, Guillaume de Salluste. *The Divine Weeks and Works*. 1608. Translated by Josuah Sylvester. Edited by Susan Snyder. Oxford: Clarendon Press, 1979.

Duran, Angelica, Islam Issa, and Jonathan R. Olson, eds. *Milton in Translation*. Oxford: Oxford University Press, 2017.

Dyer, Geoff. "By the Book." *The New York Times Sunday Book Review*, July 2, 2016: 6.

Eliot, George. *The George Eliot Letters*. Vol. 5, *1869–1873*. Edited by Gordon S. Haight. New Haven, Conn.: Yale University Press, 1955.

Eliot, T. S. "Milton." *Proceedings of the British Academy* 33 (1947): 61–79.

Emerson, Ralph Waldo. "Milton." 1838. In *The Conduct of Life: Nature and Other Essays*, 75–91. London: J. M. Dent, 1908.

———. *The Journals and Miscellaneous Notebooks of Ralph Waldo Emerson*. Vol. 4, *1832–1834*. Edited by Alfred R. Ferguson. Cambridge, Mass.: Harvard University Press, 1964.

Empson, William. *Some Versions of Pastoral*. London: Chatto and Windus, 1935.

———. *Milton's God*. London: Chatto and Windus, 1965.

Engel, William. "John Milton's Recourse to Old English: A Case-Study in Renaissance Lexicography." *LATCH: A Journal for the Study of the Literary Artifact in Theory, Culture, or History* 1 (2008): 1–30.

Equiano, Olaudah. *The Interesting Narrative of the Life of Olaudah Equiano.* 1789. Edited by Angelo Costanzo. Peterborough, Ontario: Broadview Press, 2001.

Falconer, C. *Essay on Milton's Imitations of the Ancients with Some on the Paradise Regained.* London, 1741.

Fish, Stanley. *Surprised by Sin: The Reader in "Paradise Lost."* Berkeley: University of California Press, 1971.

———. "The Temptation to Action in Milton's Poetry." *English Literary History* 48, no. 3 (Autumn 1981): 516–31.

Fletcher, Angus. "Standing, Waiting, and Traveling Light: Milton and the Drama of Information." In *Colors of the Mind: Conjectures on Thinking in Literature,* 68–80. Cambridge, Mass.: Harvard University Press, 1991.

Forsyth, Neil. "The English Church." In *Milton in Context,* edited by Stephen B. Dobranski, 292–304. Cambridge: Cambridge University Press, 2010.

Fowler, Alastair, ed. *Spenser's Images of Life.* By C. S. Lewis. Cambridge: Cambridge University Press, 1967.

———. *Milton: "Paradise Lost."* New York: Routledge, 2006.

Franaszek, Andrzej. *Miłosz: A Biography.* Translated by Aleksandra and Michael Parker. Cambridge, Mass.: Harvard University Press, 2017.

Fried, Daisy. "Sing, God-Awful Muse! On Milton and the Nipple Nazi of Northampton." *Poetry Magazine,* July/August 2009.

Frost, Robert. "A Masque of Mercy." In *The Poetry of Robert Frost: The Collected Poems, Complete and Unabridged,* edited by Edward Connery Lathem, 493–524. New York: Henry Holt, 1979.

Froula, Christine. "When Eve Reads Milton: Undoing the Canonical Economy." *Critical Inquiry* 10, no. 2 (December 1983): 321–47.

Gee, Sophie. "Great Adaptations." *The New York Times,* January 13, 2008.

Gilbert, Sandra M., and Susan Gubar. "How Are We Fal'n? Milton's Daughters." In *The Madwoman in the Attic: The Woman Writer and the Nineteenth-Century Literary Imagination,* 187–308. New Haven, Conn.: Yale University Press, 1979.

Ginsberg, Allen. "Basic Poetics." A class taught at the Naropa Institute, April 24, 1980. Audio recording (1:26:13) available at http://archives .naropa.edu/digital/collection/p16621coll1/id/373/. Transcript of

relevant material available at https://allenginsberg.org/2017/10/
monday-october-9/.

Gray, Erik. *Milton and the Victorians*. Ithaca, N.Y.: Cornell University Press,
2009.

Green, George Smith. *A New Version of the "Paradise Lost": or, Milton Para-
phrased*. 1756. Reprinted in *The Critical Review, Or, Annals of Literature,
1756–1763*, vols. 1–2, edited by James G. Basker. London: Pickering and
Chatto, 2002.

Greenblatt, Stephen. "The Lonely Gods." *New York Review of Books* 58, no.
11 (June 23, 2011): 6–10.

Gregerson, Linda. "The Frank Enthusiast: An Interview with Linda
Gregerson." By Sara Hoover and Michaelean Ferguson, edited by Lee
Griffith. *The Pinch* 27, no. 2 (Fall 2007): 138–47.

Gurney, Ivor. *Ivor Gurney: Collected Letters*. Edited by Robert Kelsey
Rought Thornton. Manchester: Carcanet, 1991.

Hair, Donald S. *Fresh Strange Music: Elizabeth Barrett Browning's Lan-
guage*. Kingston, Ontario: McGill-Queen's University Press, 2015.

Hale, John. *Milton's Languages: The Impact of Multilingualism on Style*.
Cambridge: Cambridge University Press, 1997.

Hall, Donald. *Breakfast Served Any Time All Day: Essays on Poetry New and
Selected*. Ann Arbor: University of Michigan Press, 2003.

Hayden, Robert. *Collected Poems*. Edited by Frederick Glaysher. New York:
Liveright Publishing, 1985.

Hazlitt, William. *The Collected Works of William Hazlitt: Lectures on the
English Poets and on the Dramatic Literature of the Age of Elizabeth*. Vol. 5.
Edited by A. R. Waller and Arnold Glover. London: J. M. Dent, 1902.

Heaney, Seamus. *The Government of the Tongue: Selected Prose, 1978–87*.
New York: Farrar, Straus and Giroux, 1988.

———. "A Soul on the Washing Line." Interview. *The Economist*, June 22,
1991.

———. *The Redress of Poetry*. New York: Farrar, Straus and Giroux, 1995.

Hemans, Felicia. *Selected Poems, Letters, Reception Materials*. Edited by
Susan J. Wolfson. Princeton, N.J.: Princeton University Press, 2010.

Herman, Peter. *Destabilizing Milton: "Paradise Lost" and the Poetics of Incer-
titude*. New York: Palgrave Macmillan, 2005.

Hill, Christopher. *Milton and the English Revolution*. London, Penguin, 1977.

Hill, Geoffrey. British Academy Lecture. John Milton Quatercentenary Symposium, December 6, 2008.

Hollington, Michael, and Lawrence Wilkinson, eds. *Paradise Lost, Books XI–XII*. By John Milton. Cambridge: Cambridge University Press, 1976.

Homer. *The Odyssey*. Translated by Robert Fitzgerald. New York: Farrar, Straus and Giroux, 1998.

Hopkins, Gerard Manley. *Gerard Manley Hopkins*. Edited by Catherine Phillips. Oxford: Oxford University Press, 1986.

Hopkins, John. *Milton's "Paradise Lost" Imitated in Rhyme, in the Fourth, Sixth and Ninth Books*. London: Ralph Smith, 1699.

Housman, A. E. "LXII. Terence, this is stupid stuff." 1896. In *A Shropshire Lad*, 41–43. New York: Henry Holt, 1932.

———. *The Name and Nature of Poetry*. Cambridge: Cambridge University Press, 1933.

Hugo, Richard. *The Triggering Town: Lectures and Essays on Poetry and Writing*. New York: W. W. Norton, 1979.

Hume, Patrick. *Annotations on Milton's "Paradise Lost."* London: Jacob Tonson, 1695.

Hunter, G. K. *Paradise Lost*. London: George Allen and Unwin, 1980.

Hurston, Zora Neale. *Dust Tracks on a Road: An Autobiography*. Philadelphia: J. B. Lippincott, 1942.

Ives, Charles. "125. Evening." 1921. Reprinted in *129 Songs*, edited by H. Wiley Hitchcock, 291. Middleton, Wis.: American Musicological Society, 2004.

Jarrell, Randall. "The Obscurity of the Poet." In *Poetry and the Age*, 3–27. New York: Alfred A. Knopf, 1953.

Jefferson, Thomas. "Thoughts on English Prosody." 1786. Reprinted in *Writings*, edited by Merrill D. Peterson, 593–622. New York: Library of America, 1984.

Johnson, Ronald. *Radi os*. 1977. Reprint, Chicago: Flood Editions, 2013.

Johnson, Samuel. *The Lives of the Poets*. 1779. Edited by John Middendorf. New Haven, Conn.: Yale University Press, 2010.

Justice, Donald. "The Wall." 1960. Reprinted in *Collected Poems*, p. 13. New York: Knopf, 2009.

Kastan, David Scott, ed. *John Milton: "Paradise Lost."* Cambridge: Hackett, 2005.

Keats, John. *The Poetical Works and Other Writings of John Keats.* Vol. 5. Edited by Maurice Buxton Forman, Harry Buxton Forman, and John Masefield. New York: Charles Scribner's Sons, 1939.

Keillor, Garrison, ed. *Good Poems.* London: Penguin Books, 2002.

Kooser, Ted. *The Poetry Home Repair Manual: Practical Advice for Beginning Poets.* Lincoln: University of Nebraska Press, 2005.

Kunitz, Stanley. "The Sense of a Life." *New York Times Book Review*, Oct. 16, 1977.

Labriola, Albert C. "'All in All' and 'All in One': Obedience and Disobedience in *Paradise Lost.*" In *"All in All": Unity, Diversity, and the Miltonic Perspective*, edited by Charles W. Durham and Kristin A. Pruitt, 39–47. Selinsgrove, Penn.: Susquehanna University Press, 1999.

Langdon, Ida. *Milton's Theory of Poetry and Fine Art: An Essay, With a Collection of Illustrative Passages from His Works.* New Haven, Conn.: Yale University Press, 1924.

Lanzara, Joseph. *John Milton's "Paradise Lost" in Plain English: A Simple, Line by Line Paraphrase of the Complicated Masterpiece.* Belleville, N.J.: New Arts Library, 2009.

Lauder, William. "An Essay on Milton's Imitations of the Moderns." *Gentleman's Magazine* 17 (1747): 24–286.

Leavis, F. R. "Milton's Verse." In *Revaluation: Tradition and Development in English Poetry*, 42–67. London: Chatto and Windus, 1936.

Le Comte, Edward. *A Dictionary of Puns in Milton's English Poetry.* New York: Columbia University Press, 1981.

Lehnhof, Kent. "Scatology and the Sacred in Milton's *Paradise Lost.*" *English Literary Renaissance* 37, no. 3 (2007): 429–49.

Leonard, John. *Faithful Labourers: A Reception History of "Paradise Lost," 1667–1970.* 2 vols. Oxford: Oxford University Press, 2013.

Leslie, Michael. "The Spiritual Husbandry of John Beale." In *Culture and Cultivation: Writing and the Land*, edited by Michael Leslie and Timothy Raylor, 151–72. Leicester, U.K.: Leicester University Press, 1992.

Lewalski, Barbara K. "Milton on Women—Yet Once More." *Milton Studies* 6 (1974): 3–20.

———. *The Life of John Milton: A Critical Biography.* Oxford: Blackwell, 2000.

Lewis, C. S. *A Preface to "Paradise Lost."* New York: Oxford University Press, 1942.

Lieb, Michael. "S.B.'s '*In Paradisum Amissam*': Sublime Commentary." *Milton Quarterly* 19, no. 3 (October 1985): 71–73, 75–78.

Logan, William. "Milton in the Modern: The Invention of Personality." In *Green Thoughts, Green Shades: Essays by Contemporary Poets on the Early Modern Lyric*, edited by Jonathan Post, 160–75. Berkeley: University of California Press, 2002.

Loewenstein, David. *Milton: "Paradise Lost."* Cambridge: Cambridge University Press, 1993.

Longfellow, Henry Wadsworth. "Milton." In *The Sonnets of Henry Wadsworth Longfellow*, edited by Ferris Greenslet, 56. Boston: Houghton Mifflin, 1907.

Loscocco, Paula. *Phillis Wheatley's Miltonic Poetics.* New York: Palgrave Pivot, 2014.

Lowell, James Russell. *The Writings of James Russell Lowell: Literary Essays.* Cambridge: Riverside Press, 1890.

Lowell, Robert. "Waking Early Sunday Morning." In *Near the Ocean*, 15–24. New York: Farrar, Straus and Giroux, 1967.

Lucas, John. *John Clare.* Plymouth, U.K.: Northcote House, 1994.

Machacek, Gregory. *Milton and Homer: "Written to Aftertimes."* Pittsburgh: Duquesne University Press, 2011.

MacNiece, Louis. *Modern Poetry: A Personal Essay.* New York: Haskell House, 1938.

Malcolm X, with Alex Haley. *The Autobiography of Malcolm X.* New York: Grove Press, 1965.

Martz, Louis. "The Rising Poet, 1645." In *The Lyric and Dramatic Milton: Selected Papers from the English Institute*, edited by Joseph H. Summers, 3–33. New York: Columbia University Press, 1965.

Marvell, Andrew. "On Mr. Milton's *Paradise Lost*." 1674. Reprinted in *The Poems of Andrew Marvell*, rev. ed., edited by Nigel Smith, 180–84. London: Pearson Education, 2007.

Marx, Karl. *Theories of Surplus Value*. 1863. Translated by G. A. Bonner and Emile Burns. London: Lawrence and Wishart, 1951.

Masahiko, Agari. *Inversion in Milton's Poetry*. New York: Peter Lang Publishing, 2001.

Masters, Edgar Lee. *Vachel Lindsay*. New York: Charles Scribner's Sons, 1935.

McCaffrey, Isabel. *"Paradise Lost" as "Myth."* Cambridge, Mass.: Harvard University Press, 1959.

McColley, Diane. *A Gust for Paradise: Milton's Eden and the Visual Arts*. Urbana: University of Illinois Press, 1993.

McMahon, Robert. *The Two Poets of "Paradise Lost."* Baton Rouge: Louisiana State University Press, 1998.

Medley, Mark. "The Griffin Poetry Prize Questionnaire: Seamus Heaney." *National Post*, May 30, 2011.

Mohamed, Feisal G. *Milton and the Post-Secular Present: Ethics, Politics, Terrorism*. Palo Alto, Calif.: Stanford University Press, 2012.

Mong, Derek. "Ten New Ways to Read Ronald Johnson's *Radi os.*" *Kenyon Review* 37, no. 4 (July/August 2015): 78–96.

Moore, Leslie. *Beautiful Sublime: The Making of "Paradise Lost," 1701–1734*. Palo Alto, Calif.: Stanford University Press, 1990.

Moore, Marianne. "Review of Denis Saurat's *Blake and Milton*." 1925. Reprinted in *The Complete Prose of Marianne Moore*, edited by Patricia Willis, 232–33. New York: Viking, 1986.

Muir, John. *A Thousand-Mile Walk to the Gulf*. Edited by William Frederic Badé. Boston: Houghton Mifflin, 1916.

Newton, Thomas, ed. *Paradise Lost*. By John Milton. Vol. 2. London, 1790.

Nicholson, Marjorie Hope. *John Milton: A Reader's Guide to His Poetry*. New York: Farrar, Straus and Giroux, 1963.

Oliver, Mary. *A Poetry Handbook*. San Diego: Harcourt Brace, 1994.

Orr, David. "The Great(ness) Game." *The New York Times Sunday Book Review*, February 19, 2009.

Ostriker, Alicia. "Dancing at the Devil's Party: Some Notes on Politics and Poetry." *Critical Inquiry* 13, no. 3 (Spring, 1987): 579–96.

Parker, William Riley. *Milton: A Biography*. 2 vols. Oxford: Clarendon Press, 1968.

Partner, Jane. "Satanic Vision and Acrostics in *Paradise Lost*." *Essays in Criticism* 57, no. 2 (January 2007): 129–46.

Patterson, Annabel. *Milton's Words*. Oxford: Oxford University Press, 2009.

Pinsky, Robert. *The Sounds of Poetry: A Brief Guide*. New York: Farrar, Straus and Giroux, 1998.

―――. "The American John Milton: The Poet and the Power of Ordinary Speech." *Slate*, August 2008. https://slate.com/culture/2008/08/milton-s-400th-anniversary.html.

Poe, Edgar Allan. "The Poetic Principle." 1850. Reprinted in *Essays and Reviews*, edited by G. R. Thompson, 71–94. New York: Library of America, 1984.

Poole, William. *Milton and the Making of "Paradise Lost."* Cambridge, Mass.: Harvard University Press, 2017.

Pope, Alexander. "First Epistle of the Second Book of Horace Imitated." In *The Poems of Alexander Pope*, edited by John Butt, 634–49. New Haven, Conn.: Yale University Press, 1963.

Pound, Ezra. "The Renaissance: I—The Palette." *Poetry* 5, no. 5 (February 1915): 227–34.

Prince, F. T. *The Italian Element in Milton's Verse*. Oxford: Oxford University Press, 1954.

―――, ed. *Milton's "Paradise Lost" Books I and II*. Oxford: Oxford University Press, 1962.

Pullman, Philip. Introduction to *John Milton's "Paradise Lost,"* 1–10. Oxford: Oxford University Press, 2005.

Quint, David. *Inside "Paradise Lost": Reading the Designs of Milton's Epic*. Princeton, N.J.: Princeton University Press, 2014.

Raine, Kathleen. "Dylan Thomas." *New Statesman and Nation* 50, no. 6 (November 14, 1953): 594.

Rajan, Balachandra. *The Lofty Rhyme: A Study of Milton's Major Poetry*. Coral Gables, Fla.: University of Miami Press, 1970.

Read, Sophie. "Rhetoric and Rethinking in Bentley's *Paradise Lost*." *The Cambridge Quarterly* 41, no. 2 (June 2012): 209–28.

Rees, Christine. *Johnson's Milton*. Cambridge: Cambridge University Press, 2010.

Richardson, Jonathan, and Jonathan Richardson. *Explanatory Notes and*

Remarks on Milton's "Paradise Lost" with the Life of the Author and a Discourse on the Poem. London, 1734.

Ricks, Christopher. *Milton's Grand Style*. Oxford: Clarendon Press, 1963.

Rogers, John. "ENGL 220: Milton. Lecture 20—*Paradise Lost*, Books XI–XII." Open Yale Courses video, 45:43. Recorded Fall 2007. https://oyc.yale.edu/english/engl-220/lecture-20.

Rosser, J. Allyn. "Caveat Lector." In *Planet on the Table: Poets on the Reading Life*, edited by Sharon Bryan and William Olsen, 133–47. Louisville, Ky.: Sarabande Books, 2003.

Rumrich, John. *Milton Unbound*. Cambridge: Cambridge University Press, 1996.

Samuel, Irene. "The Development of Milton's Poetics." *PMLA* 92, no. 2 (March 1977): 231–40.

Sandburg, Carl. "To the Ghost of John Milton." 1928. Reprinted in *The Complete Poems of Carl Sandburg*, rev. ed., 384. New York: Houghton Mifflin Harcourt, 2003.

Schwartz, Regina. *Remembering and Repeating: Biblical Creation in "Paradise Lost."* Cambridge: Cambridge University Press, 1988.

Shakespeare, William. *The Chronicle History of Henry the Fifth*. London, 1600.

Shelley, Mary. *Frankenstein, or, The Modern Prometheus*. London: Lackington, Hughes, Harding, Mavor and Jones, 1818.

Sheridan, Thomas. *Lectures on the Art of Reading, in Two Parts, Containing Part I: The Art of Reading Prose. Part II: The Art of Reading Verse*. London, 1775.

Shore, Daniel. "Milton's Depictives and the History of Style." In *Cyberformalism: Histories of Linguistic Forms in the Digital Archive*, 154–89. Baltimore, Md.: Johns Hopkins University Press, 2014.

Sidney, Sir Philip. *An Apologie for Poetrie*. London, 1595.

Smith, Nigel. *Is Milton Better Than Shakespeare?* Cambridge, Mass.: Harvard University Press, 2008.

Smith, Zadie. "Zadie Smith's Holiday Picks." *The Guardian*, June 21, 2001.

Snelson, Danny. *Radios*. Los Angeles: Make Now Press, 2016.

Snyder, Gary. "Milton by Firelight." 1959. Reprinted in *Riprap and Cold Mountain Poems*, 9–10. Berkeley, Calif.: Counterpoint, 2009.

Song, Eric B. *Dominion Undeserved: Milton and the Perils of Creation*. Ithaca, N.Y.: Cornell University Press, 2013.

Spence, Joseph. *Observations, Anecdotes, and Characters of Books and Men.* 1820. Edited by J. M. Osborn. Oxford: Oxford University Press, 1966.

Spenser, Edmund. *The Faerie Queene.* London: 1596.

Sprat, Thomas. *History of the Royal Society.* 1667. Edited by Jackson I. Cope and Harold Whitmore. London: Routledge, 1959.

Stallings, A. E. "Presto Manifesto!" *Poetry Magazine* 193, no. 5 (February 2009): 450.

Stein, Arnold. *Answerable Style: Essays on "Paradise Lost."* Minneapolis: University of Minnesota Press, 1953.

Steiner, George. *The Death of Tragedy.* New York: Hill and Wang, 1961.

Stevens, Wallace. "Like Decorations in a Nigger Cemetery." In *Collected Poetry and Prose,* 121–28. New York: Library of America, 1997.

Subbarayudu, G. K. "'High Disdain from Sense of Injured Merit': A Note on Milton's Grand Style." In *"Paradise Lost," Book I,* edited by C. Vijayasree, 80–93. Delhi: Dorling Kindersley, 2006.

Summers, Joseph. *The Muse's Method.* London: Chatto and Windus, 1962.

Swift, Jonathan. *Milton Restor'd, and Bentley Depos'd.* London: E. Curll, 1732.

Tate, Allen. Letter to Donald Davidson, May 14, 1926. In *The Literary Correspondence of Donald Davidson and Allen Tate,* edited by John Tyree Fain and Thomas Daniel Young, 166. Athens, Ga.: University of Georgia Press, 1974.

Tennyson, Alfred. "Milton. *Alcaics.*" In *The Works of Alfred Lord Tennyson,* edited by Karen Hodder, 558. Ware, U.K.: Wordsworth Editions, 1994.

Teskey, Gordon. *The Poetry of John Milton.* Cambridge, Mass.: Harvard University Press, 2015.

Traubel, Horace. *With Walt Whitman in Camden.* Vol. 3. New York: Mitchell Kennerley, 1914.

Treip, Mindele. *Milton's Punctuation and Changing English Usage, 1582–1676.* London: Methuen, 1970.

Turner, James G. *One Flesh: Paradisal Marriage and Sexual Relations in the Age of Milton.* Oxford: Clarendon, 1987.

Vendler, Helen. *Coming of Age as a Poet: Milton, Keats, Eliot, Plath.* Cambridge, Mass.: Harvard University Press, 2003.

Waddington, Raymond B. *Looking into Providences: Designs and Trials in "Paradise Lost."* Toronto: University of Toronto Press, 2012.

Waldock, A. J. A. *"Paradise Lost" and Its Critics.* Cambridge: Cambridge University Press, 1966.

Watkins, W. B. C. "Creation." In *Milton: A Collection of Critical Essays,* edited by Louis Martz, 121–47. Englewood Cliffs, N.J.: Prentice-Hall, 1966.

Wesley, John. "To the Reader." In *An Extract from Milton's "Paradise Lost." With Notes.* London: 1763.

Whaler, James. *Counterpoint and Symbol: An Inquiry into the Rhythm of Milton's Epic Style.* 1952. Reprint, New York: Haskell House, 1971.

Wilbur, Richard. "An Interview with Richard Wilbur." By David Curry. 1962. Reprinted in *Conversations with Richard Wilbur,* edited by William Butts, 3–16. Jackson: University Press of Mississippi, 1990.

Wilburn, Reginald A. *Preaching the Gospel of Black Revolt: Appropriating Milton in Early African American Literature.* Pittsburgh, Penn.: Duquesne University Press, 2014.

Willard, Nancy. *The Tale of Paradise Lost.* New York: Atheneum, 2004.

Williams, Charles. "An Introduction to Milton's Poems." 1940. Reprinted in *Milton Criticism: Selections from Four Centuries,* edited by James Thorpe, 252–67. London: Routledge and Kegan Paul, 1951.

Wiman, Christian. "Milton in Guatemala." 1998. Reprinted in *Ambition and Survival: Becoming a Poet,* 10–23. Port Townsend, Wash.: Copper Canyon Press, 2007.

Wittreich, Joseph. *Feminist Milton.* Ithaca, N.Y.: Cornell University Press, 1987.

———. "'Inspired with Contradiction': Mapping Gender Discourses in *Paradise Lost.*" In *Literary Milton Text, Pretext, Context,* edited by Diane T. Benet and Michael Lieb, 133–61. Pittsburgh, Penn.: Duquesne University Press, 1994.

Wollstonecraft, Mary. *A Vindication of the Rights of Women.* 1792. Reprint, New York: W. W. Norton, 1967.

Woolf, Virginia. *The Diary of Virginia Woolf.* Vol. 1, *1915–1919.* Edited by Annie Oliver Bell. San Diego: Mariner Books, 1979.

Wordsworth, William. "Preface of 1815." In *The Prose Works of William Wordsworth,* vol. 3, edited by W. J. B. Owen and Jane Worthington Smyser, 23–39. Oxford: Oxford University Press, 1973.

Yeats, William Butler. *Essays and Introductions.* London: Macmillan, 1961.

INDEX